"Don't GIFT-WRAP the GARBAGE"

Down-to-Earth Daily Meditations for Women

"Don't GIFT-WRAP the GARBAGE"

Karen Stroup

ave maria press   Notre Dame, Indiana

---

www.avemariapress.com

International Standard Book Number: 0-87793-968-3

Cover and text design by Brian C. Conley

Cover Photo: Photodisc

Printed and bound in the United States of America.

Library of Congress Cataloging-in-Publication Data
Stroup, Karen.
"Don't gift-wrap the garbage" : down-to-earth daily meditations for women / Karen Stroup.
    p. cm.
ISBN 0-87793-968-3 (pbk.)
    1. Women--Religious life. 2. Spiritual life--Meditations. I. Title.
BV4844 .S77 2002
242'.643--dc21

                                                2002006556
                                                CIP

To the children of relatives and friends
who have allowed me to love them
as if they were my own:

Malia Ann Heyd
Caroline Leigh Heyd
Duncan Gordon Arnfield
Natalie Elise Dodd
Gregory Sumner Schneider

Acknowledgments

I could not have written a single word about God without the kindness, love, and support of many people. It is largely through them that I have come to know the God who walks beside me in the most mundane aspects of life. To these people I owe more thanks than it is possible to give.

Without the people in my literary world, this book would never have been born. My agent, Linda Roghaar, not only represented this project with great passion and professionalism, but also held my nervous author hand on many occasions. The folks at Ave Maria Press, especially Bob Hamma and Julie Hahnenberg, took a chance on a Protestant preacher lady and shepherded the manuscript through its many stages with tact and skill. Sr. Mary Ann Heyd, OP, graciously joined me by reflecting and writing about two special days: the Assumption and the Immaculate

Conception. I am grateful for her contributions. Paul Leggett provided invaluable help in tracking down appropriate scripture passages for each meditation and encouragement when I felt overwhelmed. Many thanks to them all.

Some groups have been so formative in my faith life that I could not have become a person who could write a book like this without them. Primary among them are the people of the congregations I have had the honor to pastor: Eastwood Christian Church in Nashville, Tennessee; Central Christian Church in Springfield, Tennessee; Cropper Christian Church in Pleasureville, Kentucky; and First Christian Church in Winchester, Kentucky. Other communities of faith have fed me while asking nothing in return: Chapel of the Cross in Chapel Hill, North Carolina; Church of the Holy Cross in Dunn Loring, Virginia; the sisters and regulars of St. Agnes' House in Lexington, Kentucky; the worshiping community of Lexington Theological Seminary; the Cathedral of the Incarnation in Nashville, Tennessee; and the Monday Morning Wellness Group at Gilda's Club, Nashville.

I have been blessed with many spiritual teachers, not only those in official capacities but also wise people of faith who have shaped my Christian journey as mentors and guides: Ruel W. Tyson, Jr.; Hank Kenney, S.J.; Rev. Loren Broadus; Rev. Dr. Peter Morgan; Rev. Dr. Anthony L. Dunnavant; Rev. Dr.

Lanny C. Lawler; Ruth Brockett; Marie Wiggins; Rev. Dr. Liston O. Mills; Fr. Mark Beckman; Dr. Philip Chanin; and Jackie Ivie. Soul friends have shared the path to God and made the journey joyful: Rev. Jackie Summers, Rev. Michael Duncan, Sherry Schindler, Dr. Volney P. Gay, Greg Rumburg, Amy Reeves, Ami Faenza, Ann Darden, Sid Burton, and Jim Womack.

My family gave and continues to give me a Christian home in which to grow and mature, and for that I am eternally grateful. They wish to remain anonymous, but the fact that they are represented by initials says nothing about the magnitude of my love for them: my parents, G. and B.; my sister L. and her husband J.; my sister D. and her husband J.

Finally and most important are the people who have stayed awake with me in my Gethsemanes and rejoiced with me in front of my empty tombs: Dave Krinsky, Harry Tueting, Sharyn Dowd, Paul Leggett, Rev. Laura Rey, Carol Sumner, Heather Wibbels, Tim Ellsworth, and Kevin and Debbie Dodd. You all have taught me about grace, the most important lesson for me to learn—but the most difficult. I thank you deeply for your friendship.

Introduction

Life is, on balance, a whole lot more about washing dishes than it is about courageous acts of heroism, more about grocery shopping than the great ideas of history. Or at least my life is.

My spiritual life is the same way. Always has been. Since childhood, I've impatiently waited for a visit from an angel, a voice from the sky, or a vision of God. So far, though, there's been only silence.

No, not silence—that's not fair. But my experiences of God have come in the most ordinary aspects of my life: going to school and work, being in love, having my heart broken, going to dinner parties, yawning my way through meetings.

And to be fair, there was indeed a time when my life was full of "consolations," as the mystics called them, or emotional experiences of God's presence. There were no outward signs or blinding raptures, but quite often I did have a spine-tingling sense that God was near and once in a while was flooded with a deep sense of peace. My first spiritual director, Fr. Hank Kenney, SJ, taught me that these were, indeed, consolations. I finally believed him when I experienced their opposite: desolation, the bleak, utter absence of any sense of God. Luckily, consolation outweighed desolation a hundredfold.

For a while, anyway. The length of my "mystical" period—subdued as it was—was brief. For three or four years my prayer life was a cycle of consolation, desolation, and the most common spiritual state, dryness. After those few years, dryness was not a passing phase; I realized I had been trained and equipped for life in the desert.

Teresa of Avila reported a period of dryness that lasted seventeen years. I distinctly remember telling a friend, many years ago, that I could never go on that long without consolation. That's when I learned that God has a wicked sense of humor and to never say "never" where God is concerned. I'm up to nine or ten years of dryness as I write, and have accepted, for the most part, that this is the way God has chosen to relate to me.

I hope that doesn't sound too sad. It is disappointing, of course. As a child I didn't know there was a name to be put to what I longed for, but long for it I did. I wanted the spirituality of the few, the proud, the saints. Instead, I have been given a spiritual life that is common as clay.

But I have to admit that this unremarkable spirituality has sustained me through some very difficult times. When I was diagnosed with breast cancer at the age of thirty-six, one of the ways I tried to make things "all right" was by believing that God would finally begin visiting me with the raptures that, by then, I knew the mystics frequently had when they were ill. That didn't happen. But my dry-as-a-bone spiritual life got me through initial diagnosis, treatment, the news that my cancer had metastasized and that I was terminal, the loss of love, loss of a career, and the loss of the option of motherhood.

On the day I was diagnosed, I sat in the exam room desperately telegraphing God: "I cannot do this. I am incapable of it. I simply do not have what it takes to get through cancer, treatment, and maybe even death." Apparently I was wrong. It was an utter surprise to me, but I discovered that through my common, ordinary spiritual life, God had created in me more strength, courage, and hope than I could ever have imagined.

These days I still learn from the writings of the great mystics, but I know that is not my path. Mine runs through the ordinary: walking the dog, eating pizza with friends, ironing clothes, reading books to my nieces and nephew. It is this very domestic spirituality that guides me to God.

I am no spiritual master, and as much as I once wanted to be, I'm satisfied to be one of the millions with whom God chooses to relate through the simplest aspects of day-to-day life. We ordinary believers love God and want to be good Christians even though our names will never appear on any list of spiritual giants. My spirituality is simple, plain, and concrete, and I can write about it only because I know God has created a whole lot more of us than Teresa of Avilas. A word of caution: Budding spiritual masters should look elsewhere for spiritual reflection. My pedestrian thoughts will only make you impatient.

So I am a common woman with a common spirituality. I have been given the opportunity to share my view of God's world only because I have picked up some credentials during my journey. I am an ordained pastor in the Christian Church (Disciples of Christ) and have had the honor of serving several congregations in that capacity. I have a Ph.D. in religion and psychology, and some training as a spiritual director. I have taught college and divinity students, led retreats, written articles about God, and preached through the entire lectionary.

That's my resume, the experiences that have given me enough credibility as a spiritual person to be given the opportunity to write this book. But quite honestly, my best preparation for this work has been day-to-day life. Any authority I have comes from getting through life the same way you do: one day at a time. Once again—I'm not the spiritual guru sitting on a mountaintop offering wisdom to a gathered crowd. Instead, I'm one of the crowd, sharing the notes I've jotted down as I've followed the great masters.

I'm offering these scribblings specifically to women, my sisters in the faith, because I think the way our lives often go tends to lead us on the path of the ordinary and day-to-day. Of course there are women politicians, executives, entrepreneurs, scholars, and saints—I'm not saying that being female makes us ordinary. Quite the opposite, in fact. I'm saying that even Sandra Day O'Connor probably knows how to get red wine stains out of the carpet, and that these common, feminine experiences can teach us much about God.

What You Should Know About People

My friends and family have taught me the most important and lasting lessons about God that I have learned. I couldn't write about my day-to-day life without mentioning them, and so I have. Sadly, the violence that permeates today's culture means that some of those folks want to remain anonymous. So here's the system: If a name has quotation marks around it the first time it appears in a meditation—"Gary"—then you know you won't find a person named Gary in my life who has done or said the things you read in the meditation. Such a person exists and has done or said these things, but I've changed identifying characteristics so much that the best detective couldn't find "Gary." On the other hand, if a name doesn't have quotation marks around it—Sharyn Dowd—then that's someone you could meet and talk to if you and everyone I love came to the same party.

A Word About Language

I am a feminist. My definition of that word is "someone who believes that God loves women just as much as God loves men." That feminism has led me to grapple with some issues about the way we use the English language. For centuries, we have used the word "he" as the third person pronoun and "man" for the human race, assuming that these words included women as well as men. There is a movement afoot, called inclusive language, which suggests that these words no longer necessarily include women. If they did, it would be possible to say, "Your mother is a fine man." Where I come from, them's fightin' words.

So I make a point of using words that are more inclusive: humankind, human beings, people. Since this book is written for women, I feel free to use "she" as the third person pronoun. Any men who accidentally pick it up should be assured that this pronoun includes you too. And despite the fact that it drives English teachers (and one friend) absolutely crazy, I have followed the growing convention of using "they," "them," and "their" to talk about people in the third person singular.

Then there's the more difficult language issue: God. God does not have a body, and bodies are what give us our gender. Therefore, God is not male or female. God is not a man, and God is not a woman. To constantly use "he" and "him" to talk about God suggests, at an unreflective level, that God is male. In fact, God has qualities that are stereotypically assigned to women as well as those stereotypically assigned to men.

At this point in my own spiritual life, I say "she" and "her" when I talk about God. But since I've not always been at this point, since I may well change in the future, and since most people are not at this point, I have only occasionally used feminine pronouns to speak about God in this book. I don't want simple language to get in the way of the most important thing: relationship with God. So I've mostly neutralized my language about God. If you, the reader, think of God as a "he," then you can easily read this book that way. You can do the same thing if God is "she" to you right now. Please understand that I am not trying to make a radical statement here. I am simply approaching this issue as a pastor. I know that there are a goodly number of women for whom male language about God is painful; it makes sense, then, to simply neutralize the language so everybody can fill in the blanks with whatever they're accustomed to.

ME, MYSELF, AND I

I use the word "I" a lot in these meditations. That's not because I believe I'm the center of the universe or that I believe my experience is normative. Quite the contrary: It goes against everything I was taught in homiletics to speak in the first person singular. Neither are preachers to use "you." Any pronoun but "we" suggests the one preaching is holding herself aloof from the generalized statements she's making.

I've approached this work differently. I am well aware that many women have experiences dramatically unlike mine, and I don't want to give the impression that those differences are not legitimate. I use "we" only when I'm fairly confident that ninety-five percent of my readers would agree with what I'm saying. The rest of the time I use "I," hoping that you will be able to echo that "I" for yourself. If you cannot, then perhaps my experience can teach you something—if only the wrong way to do things.

It's also very likely that some of my interpretations of our common religious life will upset you. You may have come to conclusions directly opposite to my own. That's okay. The purpose of these meditations is not to give "the answers"—because I have none—but to provide fodder for thought. If a meditation helps you clarify your thought on a particular matter, and that thought is diametrically opposed to my own, then I think I've done my job right. I believe our faith has enough room in it for a wide range of beliefs on important matters, and I also believe that God is the final authority on everything.

A Special Guest

As a Protestant pastor who grew up Protestant, I've never been exposed to spirituality that's deeply connected to Mary, the mother of Jesus. It doesn't make sense, then, for me to write about Marian holy days; those meditations would have no integrity.

So I am happy to welcome, as a guest author, Sr. Mary Ann Heyd, OP. Sr. Mary Ann is a Sinsinawa Dominican who made her final profession on August 5, 1952. Since then she has earned her B.A. from Edgewood College and MRE from St. Meinrad College. She taught in Catholic schools for many years, and for the past eleven, has served in pastoral ministry, currently at St. Mary Church in Kenosha, Wisconsin. Sr. Mary Ann's nephew is married to my sister, and that's how this felicitous relationship began. I welcome Sr. Mary Ann and thank her for joining me in this project. Her name appears on the meditations she has written.

Using This Book

How to Use the Calendar

One of the great joys of writing meditations for every day of the year is the opportunity to reflect on holidays, holy days, and holy people: Independence Day, Christmas Day, and St. Francis of Assisi, for example. It doesn't matter what year you are using this book of meditations; these days will fall on the same dates.

But there are other special days that are what the church calls "movable." As everybody knows, Easter is on a different date each year. The problem then becomes how to write about movable feasts and fasts without making the book useless after a particular year has passed. There may be a better way to manage this than the one I've chosen, but it's the best I could think of.

I have simply assigned a date to each movable occasion. Mother's Day, for example, is dated May 10*. Like each meditation that talks about a movable observance, the date is marked with an asterisk. As you use this book, you will be aware of special days like Mother's Day coming up. If it comes after May 10*, then skip the Mother's Day meditation and just follow in sequence until Mother's Day actually arrives. Then go back to May 10*. After that, you can return to reading the meditations that match your calendar. If Mother's Day comes before May 10*, jump ahead and read it, and then the next day, go back to the meditation following the last one you read. When you come to Mother's Day again, skip ahead to the one following it.

Lent and Easter are more difficult, because they cover several weeks. My suggestion is that you do the same thing that you would with Mother's Day—jump ahead or go back, depending on the actual date of Ash Wednesday, the first day of Lent. But because this period is so long, you may want to take a pencil, cross out the existing dates, and write in the actual calendar days on the meditations. Continue changing dates through the meditation for "Sunday After Easter." Here is the date of Ash Wednesday for whatever year you are using this book:

March 5, 2003	February 6, 2008
March 25, 2004	February 25, 2009
February 9, 2005	February 17, 2010
March 1, 2006	March 9, 2011
February 21, 2007	February 22, 2012

TWO SPECIAL SEASONS

The vast majority of the meditations in this book begin with something very concrete from everyday life. As I've said, that's pretty much who I am and how my life with God works.

But even someone as concrete as I must occasionally step back and meditate on things that are important but may not necessarily appear in my own life on a day-to-day basis. Examples would be war, divorce, or prejudice. It's difficult to think about these things without some abstraction. That's why I have devoted the period of Lent to such topics. You will find that the Lenten meditations have a different "feel" to them than the others . . . and that feel is not necessarily pleasant. But Lent is a good time for discipline—the discipline of thinking abstractly, and the discipline of facing difficult issues.

I've also done something a little different with the season of Advent. Those meditations are, in fact, rather concrete, but they are concerned with the experience of pregnancy. I go further into my reasons for writing about aspects of pregnancy, and for gathering them in the Advent season, in the meditation for December 1. But I do want to say a word to women who—like me—don't have children or have adopted them and so can't relate to the experience of pregnancy.

I have found that meditations about pregnancy "work" for me, a non-mother, in a couple of ways. First, it's an experience that most of my family and friends have been through, and I feel a part of it through them—though my participation is definitely vicarious. It's also true that God gives all women the opportunity to be generative. Sometimes that generativity means children; sometimes it means birthing books, works of art, community organizations, and a whole host of other things that must grow inside of us for a time before they can be born. For this second kind of women—again, including me—the meditations on pregnancy will have to work as analogies . . . but I think they do.

I realize that some women deeply grieve the fact that they've never borne a child, and that these meditations might be painful for them. Many of them were difficult to write. But in this matter as in everything else, I have come to understand that the answer is not to avoid the pain, but to feel it and take it to God. These Advent meditations may be bittersweet for you and me, but in so being they may bring us closer to God. I hope that is the case for you. It has been for me.

January 1
A Young Girl

One of my fondest memories as a congregational pastor is the Christmas play we put on one year. I wrote and directed it and tried to portray what Christmas might have been like had it happened in the twentieth century. The wise men, for example, were professors from the area divinity school, and the inn that had no room was the local hotel. In keeping with tradition, I cast a man in his forties as Joseph and a sixteen-year-old girl as Mary. Seeing that familiar story translated into modern times really helped me understand some things in a way I never had before.

Because the play was set in modern times, the Mary character was a normal teenage girl. I gave her a best friend named Prisca (who appears in Paul's letters as the leader of one of the earliest congregations), and they met in the local diner to talk about being in love and getting married. They ooh'ed and aah'ed over Mary's engagement ring as only very young women can.

The girl who played Mary was a beautiful young woman. She memorized all her lines perfectly and kept the other actors going. And she lost herself in the part to such an extent that at every single rehearsal, the other cast members would fall silent when she spoke her modernized version of the Magnificat.

As the director, I saw the actress—and more important, Mary—through middle-aged eyes. I realized that what Mary *didn't* know about life, love, and marriage could fill the Grand Canyon. I realized she didn't understand how beautiful she was, how breathtakingly fresh, unspoiled, and brave.

And so I learned once again how very wise is our God. To have sent Gabriel to an older woman, one who knew something of the world's ways, could have been a disaster. She'd have had enough experience to be able to imagine just a little of what was ahead, and if she'd been sane, she would have said no. But God sent Gabriel to Mary. She responded in a way only a young person can—with a bit of fear, yes, but with utter sincerity, faith, and purity of intention. That Christmas, I learned a lot about God's wisdom.

But [Mary] was much perplexed by [Gabriel's] words and pondered what sort of greeting this might be.
(Luke 1:29)

January 2
Clearance Sales

One of the biggest shopping days of the year is January 2. It's on that day the stores start clearing out their winter merchandise and putting up displays of "cruise wear," which as far as I can tell is summer clothing for people rich enough to fly to warm countries. In any case, by the time February rolls around and it's really, really cold, you can't find a pair of mittens to save your life. The most dedicated shopper can look and look, but the best coat she's going to find is one that has a ripped lining and is languishing on the seventy-five percent off rack.

I have to laugh at Americans, myself included, when I think about all this. It seems to be against our nature to live in today. When we're children, we can't *wait* to be teenagers; when we're teenagers, we lust for adulthood; twenty-somethings yearn for their thirties, when they think they'll get respect at work; thirty-somethings long for their forties, when they expect the reward of money at work; and everybody forty-something and over wants to be young again.

That's a shame. We live best, and we're happiest, when we allow ourselves to *live in the moment*. There's nothing quite like that feeling of competing in a sport, creating a work of art, even figuring out a business plan—that feeling of complete and utter absorption. Too rarely, we find ourselves forgetting that time is passing. Everything we think and feel and are is wrapped up in that particular moment.

Jesus told us not to be worried about tomorrow. We should allow today's worries to be enough for today. He's right, of course; as far as I know, worrying has never changed one single thing. It's a call to trust in God, really. To live in the moment means we trust that God will provide for us in the future—provide not only food and shelter and money, but also love, friendship, and happiness.

"Therefore I tell you, do not worry about your life, what you will eat or what you will drink, or about your body, what you will wear." (Matthew 6:25)

JANUARY 3
Resolutions

So how many of your resolutions have you broken already?

We Americans have a national disease: we really and truly believe we can fix ourselves. We think we can pull ourselves up by our bootstraps. We're certain we can apply ourselves and take the steps necessary to meet our goals. From our perspective, it's always better to be able to do this alone, but if it's absolutely necessary, it's acceptable to ask for a little help from a professional.

The grand joke here, of course, is that Americans don't have a very accurate view of human nature. What's even wilder is that many of us don't have a *Christian* picture of human nature. Our faith tells us that although we are, indeed, made in the image of God, we have also fallen from that image. We can't control *anything* completely, not even ourselves. We are limited and sinful creatures, and expecting to be able to perfect ourselves is a tremendous overestimation of the power we hold.

Yes, of course, there are some things we can change about ourselves. The urge to better ourselves is evidence, in itself, that we are made in the image of God. We do, indeed, *want* to grow and change for the good, and sometimes we make progress.

But we don't need to carry the unreasonably heavy burden of trying to make ourselves perfect. The only one who can do that is God. So I'm all for resolutions. And I'm also for a particular response when we break them: not guilt, not self-punishment, but a rueful laugh at human nature, and gratitude that our perfection is ultimately in the hands of God.

I do not understand my own actions. For I do not do what I want, but I do the very thing I hate.
(Romans 7:15)

January 4
Women's Magazines

Yuck! The January women's magazines. These magazines are evil.

The evil in women's magazines is that they give us visual image after visual image of what we're supposed to look like. Here in the United States, the ideal is something like this: tall (though not *too* tall) and leggy. Very thin, except in one particular place. *There*, be as big as possible. Blond with a face beautiful enough to launch a thousand ships.

The evil in this gets us in two ways. The first is how it comes after our daughters, nieces, and grand-daughters. In their youth, their bodies are close enough to the iconic ideal that they too often develop anorexia and bulimia in an attempt to cross the line to perfection. Most American girls grow up believing they aren't pretty enough.

It's also nearly impossible for a woman to age gracefully in this culture. The ideals we get are six-teen-year-old models and stunning, willowy actresses against whom we measure ourselves. What makes it worse is that some very few middle-aged women continue to look sensational. Not "sensational-for-her-age," but just plain old sensational. Take Cher and Madonna, for example. Both are middle-aged. If they can do it, why can't we?

Into the midst of all this agony comes a word of freedom: God doesn't care one teeny tiny bit what we look like. Really. Put Cher and a model from *Cosmo* next to a street woman and a sixty-year-old gardener, and what God is going to see is four beautiful souls. Period.

The final question is this: To whom are we going to give the authority to determine what we should look like? Some money-driven women's magazine editor? Fashion models? Actors and actresses? Or God?

Let your adornment be the inner self with the lasting beauty of a gentle and quiet spirit, which is very precious in God's sight. (1 Peter 3:4)

JANUARY 5
Storing Christmas Decorations

I hate taking down Christmas decorations. The house just doesn't look the same; it seems empty, somehow. I guess it makes sense that putting away the same decorations year after year would leave me with the same feeling year after year.

Only thing is, Christmases aren't the same year after year. Each has its own special flavor, one we can't always appreciate until a few days have gone by. Sometimes it's pretty ordinary—maybe loud and raucous and filled with family, bunches of people who love us. Some Christmases are quite different. The most striking for me, I suppose, was the one when my father was in Vietnam. The most impressive presence in our Christmas celebration that year was my father's absence.

Maybe that's why it's so sad to take down Christmas decorations. They're evocative of the holy day that has recently passed, but they quite naturally dredge up memories of earlier Christmases too. And maybe we idealize our childhood Christmases a little. Or maybe a partner or spouse was in our lives for several Christmases and is no more. It can be rather melancholy.

What saves it for me is packing away the crèche, which I save until last. I've never thought about it before, but I think I understand now why I leave the baby Jesus in the manger for the very, very last. When I pick up that baby Jesus and carefully wrap him and tuck him into the box, I look forward to the grown Jesus who will speak to me in the coming weeks after the Epiphany and who will rise on Easter, not so terribly many days away. If I keep my eyes on Christ, then the sadness of leaving Christmas behind becomes the joy of anticipation.

This is the one of whom the prophet Isaiah spoke when he said, "The voice of one crying out in the wilderness:

'Prepare the way of the Lord, make his paths straight.'" (Matthew 3:3)

JANUARY 6*
The Epiphany

(Observed the Sunday after January 1)

I spent a very happy sojourn in the Episcopal Church during my twenties. I will always be grateful to that denomination for introducing me to things that simply didn't exist in the one I grew up in and to which I finally returned: the liturgical year, a focus on spirituality, respect for tradition. So in my first year among the gentle Anglicans, I was introduced to this holiday called Epiphany, something I'd never heard of. The big, long official name of this holy day in the Episcopal Church is "The Epiphany, or the Manifestation of Christ to the Gentiles." It took me a while to figure out that "the gentiles," represented by the three wise men, actually meant "everybody who isn't a Jew." And so now, my heart skips a beat every Epiphany.

It's pretty clear from reading scripture that we gentiles weren't part of the original plan. We get to read about Peter and Paul arguing the issue of whether it was okay to welcome a gentile into the church, and whether such gentiles first had to become Jews. Even Jesus seemed reluctant at first! In Mark and Matthew, at least, he is portrayed as intending to minister only to the Jews at first.

It's one of the strangest puzzles in all of human history. We who are now Christians owe a debt of thanks to the early Jewish Christians who decided we were welcome at the banquet table. And yet the long stretch of the church's history can be read as a cycle of persecuting the Jews, ignoring the Jews, persecuting the Jews, and so on.

So I thank God each year for those wise men from the East; it had to be a long and difficult journey for them, and I can't help but wonder what kind of reception they got when they reached Jewish lands. Most Jews of the time thought gentiles were ritually unclean and generally nasty people. So I also thank God for the openness Jewish Mary and Joseph showed those travelers.

When they saw that the star had stopped, they were overwhelmed with joy. On entering the house, they saw the child with Mary his mother; and they knelt down and paid him homage.
(Matthew 2:10-11)

JANUARY 7
Girlfriends

I had a fight with one of my best friends the other day. Well, not a fight, exactly. More like a fuss. But both of us huffed off, and neither of us has yet called the other to apologize. I don't worry about whether that will happen—it always does eventually.

Most of us gotta have girlfriends. We need them to see chick flicks with and to shop with, to give us honest opinions on new haircuts, to honestly tell us whether those green capri pants make us look fat. More seriously, we need girlfriends so we have a place to go when it hurts to be a woman. Those occasions range from the relatively minor, like having menstrual cramps, to the most profound, like being pregnant and not wanting to be. The men in our lives can love us, support us, and care for us during these times, and it's wonderful when they do. But no man can understand some things that every woman does.

I thank God for my girlfriends. While it's the source of a lot of tension *and* delight, God for some reason has divided the human race into male and female. The men in our lives are important, absolutely. But God has also given us the gift of others who know what it's like to be us without thinking.

I do believe I'll pause right this minute to call my friend and apologize. And I'll also tell her that having this fuss has reminded me that her friendship is a profound gift from God.

Some friends play at friendship but a true friend sticks closer than one's nearest kin.
(Proverbs 18:24)

January 8
Wrinkles

Unlike most women I know, I like wrinkles. Maybe it's because I'm not yet wrinkled too badly and some day I'll have to eat my words. But I do have deep crow's-feet and laugh lines. I've never bought any product to take away wrinkles because I want them there. They signify that someone has been here.

I've heard it said that in old age, people get the faces they deserve. Surely one of the things that means is that if you've been a grumpy person for seventy years, then you're going to develop wrinkles that make you look grumpy all the time. I've seen this result, and I'll bet you have too. My crow's-feet and laugh lines mean my face is beginning to reflect who I am. Look at a bunch of teenagers and you'll see what I mean. Not a single wrinkle on them; how can we know their temperaments, their personality traits?

My wrinkles also show that God's been here. A human being has to live a certain length of time to get wrinkles, and so every time I look at my crow's-feet I realize that God has kept me here, in this life, for a good long while. Not everyone is so lucky; some people tragically die before they're old enough for wrinkles.

So I don't think I'll ever get a facelift or an acid peel. It would be like marring the work of a great painter, and I don't know any artist who is greater than God.

The righteous flourish like the palm tree, and grow like a cedar in Lebanon. They are planted in the house of the Lord; they flourish in the courts of our God. In old age they still produce fruit; they are always green and full of sap. (Psalm 92:12-14)

JANUARY 9
Meetings

I don't know anyone who likes meetings. Obviously *somebody* does, or there wouldn't be so many. I'm certain I'm not alone in my feelings because I've probably seen a zillion cartoons that make fun of meetings. Maybe hating meetings is one of those things that comes with being human, like opposable thumbs.

I try to console myself when I have to go to meetings by remembering that even God has meetings. There are several intriguing Bible passages that suggest this. At the beginning of the book of Job, God is having a meeting when Satan shows up and makes the little bet that will lead to so much misery for poor Job.

Then, in Genesis, God proposes to create people "in our own image." I've always found that plural fascinating. Of course biblical scholars have some very persuasive interpretations of that statement. Maybe the "our" was the Trinity. Maybe the "our" was God and the angels. I suspect it was something else: a meeting. Everybody knows that anything created by committee is a disastrous failure. So maybe that's the reason we human beings have so many annoying faults, like getting sick, fighting wars, and dying.

I'm kidding, of course. What these passages and the teaching of the church tell us is that it is the very nature of God to be communal. God is never alone. I love the doctrine of the Trinity because it reminds me of this fact, and it means we, made in God's image, are also meant to live in community. I may sometimes *feel* abandoned or lonely, but the fact that I am made in God's image means that can't be so.

No doubt divine meetings don't have the features of human meetings that drive us all crazy. Until we get to that perfect world, though, we can allow meetings, however bad they are, to remind us that we are not alone.

One day the heavenly beings came to present themselves before the Lord, and Satan also came among them.
(Job 1:6)

January 10*
Baptism of the Lord

(Observed the Sunday after Epiphany Sunday)

One of the worst stories I've ever heard about growing up in the church universal came from a young woman whose father was a Church of Christ minister. She had listened to him preach hellfire and brimstone Sunday after Sunday and was terrified of hell. At the age of eight she asked to be baptized and waited in utter terror for that day to arrive. She was so afraid because her church believed that if you got in a car accident on the way to your baptism, you still went to hell.

Jesus' baptism tells me this is extremely bad theology. Jesus didn't *need* to be baptized; he was the one person in all eternity who had no sin. John the Baptist recognized this fact and protested the idea that *he* should baptize the son of God. But Jesus insisted because he wanted to show everyone who followed him the entrance to the kingdom of God. In being baptized when it wasn't necessary, Jesus went against the letter of the law, if not the spirit. Just so, God isn't constrained by any human rules. The church, thank heavens, has given us the doctrine of "baptism by desire." So if my parishioner had, indeed, gotten killed on the way to her baptism, God would most definitely have considered her a Christian.

I'm not saying there's no need to be baptized; I'm saying that Jesus' decision to be baptized shows us that God's goodness isn't necessarily logical or consistent. I wish I could whisper that truth to every single unbaptized child who lives in terror.

John would have prevented him, saying, "I need to be baptized by you, and do you come to me?"
(Matthew 3:14)

JANUARY 11
Snow and Cocoa

A friend went to England and brought me back a canister of Cadbury's cocoa mix—very different from the wimpy stuff we get in the good old U.S.A. My tongue celebrates the arrival of each sip. No incompletely puffed dehydrated marshmallows. No grainy residue on the side of the cup. Now, *this* is cocoa.

It amazes me that the cheapest store-brand mix and the most expensive specialty powder all start with the same ingredient: cocoa. It comes from the cacao plant in Central and South America.

When I sit looking out the window at snow, warm and cuddly in a blanket, sipping on a wonderful cup of cocoa, I think of the person processing the cocoa beans. I imagine her opening the pods and picking out the beans to dry. Her hand may have touched a cocoa bean that was ground and ended up in my can of cocoa. She and I are separated not only by miles, but hemispheres, language, culture, class, weather. Were we to meet we probably couldn't even talk to each other. But when she picked that bean, some of the atoms or molecules on her hands came off on the bean, stayed there through the processing, and went down my throat with the last sip. In a very real way, I am connected to that woman whose life I can barely imagine. She is part of me.

The church teaches us that all Christians are part of the body of Christ, therefore connected. That's true, but it's an awfully abstract image. Much better, I think, my vision of molecules from the bean picker's body introducing themselves to molecules of mine.

And yours. It's hard to know how far we'd have to go to trace it, but in some way, it is possible that an atom that was once a part of your body is now a part of mine. Spiritually, as Christians, we are part of each other. Physically, we could be too. We are connected.

And you thought we hadn't even met.

> *Sing praises to God, sing praises;*
> *For God is the king of all the earth;*
> *sing praises with a psalm.*
> *God is king over the nations.*
> *(Psalm 47:6a, 7-8a)*

JANUARY 12
Dogs

My dog Buzz is a Shih Tzu, so even though I keep his hair cut short (hence the name), it still takes a lot of time to care for him. He's a very picky eater, and sometimes I spend more time making his dinner than I do mine.

But then there's the other side of Buzz. He springs into my lap, presses himself against my chest, and rests his head on my shoulder. As I pet him, I know all is right with the world.

Dogs don't care what we look like. We can be fresh out of bed with our hair sticking straight up, or really slicked up for a special evening out on the town. Doesn't matter to a dog. We can feel slender and fit and attractive, or fat and flabby and disgusting. Dogs don't care. They love us no matter what.

That's why I believe dog love is the closest we get in this life to knowing what God's love is like. There's absolutely no ambivalence in the way a dog loves. It's startling to realize that God adores us just as deeply as do our dogs. More, in fact, because unlike our dogs, God is very aware of our faults. Dogs are able somehow to give us unconditional love, and it's awfully nice to be reminded that God is as close to us as Buzz is when he leans on my chest. God doesn't care what we look like or how we feel about ourselves—the love is free, unconditional, calming, and warm.

I know it's a cliché, but God spelled backward. . . .

He was in the wilderness forty days, tempted by Satan;
and he was with the wild beasts.
(Mark 1:13)

January 13
Encountering Weirdos

It's been a few years ago, but I had a very strange experience at the grocery store. I was power shopping, running up one aisle and down the next, throwing things into the cart. There was a woman behind me doing the same thing. She kept up with me, but she stayed far enough behind that I couldn't get a good look at her without turning around and pointedly staring—which would have been rude, and which my mother-trained psyche would never allow.

The reason I *wanted* to see my fellow shopper was that she was talking on and on, in a rather loud voice, about what a terrible time she was having finding the right dress for a party. And what made *that* weird was the fact that she was alone.

In other words, I was shopping in close proximity to a real nutcase. Not only was she talking to someone who didn't exist, but she was talking about something as silly as a party dress. Usually people *that* crazy talk about God and prophecy, or about politics and the deep, dark conspiracies that truly run the world. Figures that *my* psychotic person would be shallow enough to obsess about clothes.

Then when I was checking out, I looked over at the next lane and saw the same woman. She was talking on a cell phone. I had to laugh at myself. I'd decided what she was like on the basis of very little evidence and was about as far off from reality as you can get. From an objective perspective, *I* was the one who was most off kilter.

Now, it's true that this was several years ago, and only a few people had cell phones. Certainly I'd never before heard anyone talking on the telephone at the same time they were shopping. Today, of course, it's common as clay. But this was a good lesson for me. It's one thing to learn it, remember it, and even believe it; it's quite another to experience it: judge not.

"Do not judge, so that you may not be judged."
(Matthew 7:1)

JANUARY 14
Busy, Busy

"Soccer moms" became an important demographic in a recent election, and I know the women they mean. Many of my friends are soccer moms. They are bright, well-educated women, most with stimulating careers. They love their children tremendously and want to give them every possible opportunity they didn't have when they were growing up.

I discovered the downside to that desire when I pastored in Springfield, Tennessee. I ran the youth group, and if we tried to plan any activity at a time other than early Sunday evening, it was just about impossible. Somebody had ball practice: football, soccer, softball. Somebody had music lessons: guitar, piano, cello. Someone had cheerleading practice or rehearsal for show choir. These children, ranging in age from five to seventeen, seemed to have every single moment of their lives jam-packed with activities. The extracurricular stuff filled their weeknights, their Saturday mornings, and sometimes even their Sundays.

I also know the mothers of these kids. They're completely worn out. They come home from work and slap together some kind of dinner, then chauffeur the kids to practice. They are exhausted and wish for a measure of peace they just can't seem to find.

But peace never comes out of staying busy. When we fill up our lives with have-tos and ought-tos and shoulds, then we leave very little time to listen to what God is saying to us.

Here's another way to look at it. Once when I was pastoring another church and working myself to exhaustion, someone taped a photocopied ad to my office door. The text was what was important: "Even God took a day off." Can't we?

For the sun rises with its scorching heat and withers the field; its flower falls, and its beauty perishes. It is the same way with the rich; in the midst of a busy life, they will wither away. (James 1:11)

January 15*
Martin Luther King, Jr.

(Observed third Monday of January)

I like the Episcopalians for lots of reasons. One is that among the many sculptures of saints in their National Cathedral, there is one of the Rev. Dr. Martin Luther King, Jr. Now, King will never be officially declared a "saint." The denomination he belonged to doesn't believe in canonization, and there's too much information about his failings for him to be a candidate anyway.

Like King, I grew up without the concept of saints. I discovered them only as an adult, and immediately fell in love with the idea of honoring ordinary people who could so clearly walk the path of Jesus. But the funny thing is that today we've largely lost the idea of saints as ordinary people. Even when she was still alive, Mother Teresa was treated as if she were a different kind of human being than the rest of us.

That's why I like to learn from the example of people who will never be canonized but were still outstanding followers of Christ. King fits in that category. Sure, he was controversial—he remains so to this day. But that's all to the good; knowing the way he's perceived today gives me a better idea of how controversial Jesus was in his day. We twenty-first-century

Christians tell ourselves that if we'd lived in the first century and heard Jesus preaching, we'd have immediately dropped everything to follow him; it's more realistic that many of us would have found him as offensive as some did King. After all, King was simply out to change the country; Jesus was out to change eternity.

If a man hasn't discovered something that he will die for, he isn't fit to live. (Martin Luther King, Jr.)

JANUARY 16
Losing Things

Recently I had one of those "horrible things that happen to everybody" *finally* happen to me. I've been using computers since the mid-seventies, when they were crude indeed, and I'd never had the tiniest problem. But I guess my number came up on the Great Karma Wheel of Life and my hard drive crashed. I was devastated by what I'd lost: the manuscript of my dissertation, two versions of a murder mystery I haven't been able to sell, every paper I wrote in graduate school, all the sermons I've ever preached, and the first three chapters of my *new* novel. And, of course, I hadn't been making backups of my files.

We all know it feels awful to lose things, but we rarely stop to ask ourselves why. Part of our distress, of course, is the actual loss of whatever it was. If we've lost a pair of gloves, we're irritated about having to buy another. But I think the distress of lost property, however valuable financially or sentimentally, is that it reinforces our deep-down fear that we could lose something we can't live without: God's love.

Human relationships have taught us that it is, indeed, possible to lose someone's love. Most everyone's been jilted, and fights with friends or relatives can leave us without love we really counted on. Losing love feels awful.

The good news is that we don't have to worry about losing God's love. That's what Jesus Christ is all about. Jesus tells us that we can't absent-mindedly lose God's love as we can an umbrella, because God has sent Jesus chasing after us, yelling and hollering, "Hey, hey you! You lost something!" We can't even lose God's love by sinning, and that's because of the cross.

So even though a lot got lost when my hard drive went to Computer Heaven, when I put it in perspective, it's not so bad. I may not have a computer file, but I definitely have God's love.

For I am convinced that neither death, nor life . . .
will be able to separate us from the love of God in
Christ Jesus our Lord. (Romans 8:38-39)

JANUARY 17
Names

Through some brilliant academic research (consisting of reading *What Shall We Name the Baby?* in the supermarket checkout line), I've discovered that my first name, Karen, means "pure." My middle name, Leigh, is the old spelling for a lea, or a meadow. And Stroup is a name with origins in Alsace-Lorraine (so I've been told) that means "one with the tousled hair." All put together, that means "The goody-goody with bed head who lives in a meadow."

The Bible tells us names are important. God made Adam and named him "dust from the ground." A revealing name—quite descriptive. When Moses encounters God in the burning bush and asks God's name, all he gets is, more or less, "I am me." Pretty mysterious.

But the secrecy stops when the God we Christians know as Yahweh sent Jesus to live a human life. Jesus' name in the language of the time would have been pronounced "Yeshua." The name means "he will save." Any citizen of the civilized world of that time who heard or read about Jesus knew, immediately upon hearing his name, who he was and what he was going to do.

While God's ways are often mysterious to us, the basic and most important thing about God is right out in front, with no secrecy at all. Jesus, the son of God, came to save us.

God said to Moses, "I am who I am." (Exodus 3:14)

JANUARY 18
Beautiful Women

If you're a woman of a certain age, you remember very well an advertising campaign that had as its slogan, "Don't hate me because I'm beautiful." These words were put into the mouths of some of the most beautiful women in the world, and if I'm honest, I have to admit I did hate them just a little bit.

How could I not? Every study I've ever read about physical attractiveness has shown it to be an advantage in every situation imaginable. Given two equally attractive candidates, test subjects who were asked to conduct interviews with them hired the one who was most qualified according to the fake resume the actors brought with them. But when faced with one plain genius and one beauty who could barely spell, those same test subjects offered the position to the beautiful woman.

It can be depressing to be an average-looking woman. Or "pleasant-looking." Or to have a "kindly face." Or a face that "shows character." We've learned over the years that women more beautiful than us are always going to do better.

Thank God it doesn't work that way in God's world. When I try to imagine heaven, I can never decide whether everyone will be beautiful there, or whether our cultural stereotypes of beauty will be burned away. But on one issue there is no doubt: all the truisms with which I've consoled myself over the years are, in fact, true. True beauty *does* come from within. Beauty has more to do with who one *is* than with what one looks like. It helps, as I move through a world that constantly reminds me that I'm not beautiful according to its standards, that God doesn't agree.

Charm is deceitful, and beauty is vain, but a woman who fears the Lord is to be praised.
(Proverbs 31:30)

JANUARY 19
Cleaning

When I was growing up, my father was in the Army and some of his assignments included a lot of travel. The day before he was due back from his trips, my mother went into a cleaning frenzy. It must be genetic, because both of my sisters and I clean like crazy before family comes to visit. If there's a housekeeping gene, though, I think it exists in a whole lot of women. My friends do the same thing I do. Company coming? Clean. I sometimes have to remind myself that people are more important than a clean house.

So my mother discovered when my father returned from a year in Vietnam. In the weeks before he returned, the house got the most thorough cleaning it ever had. Everything shone. There wasn't a speck of dust anywhere.

We jubilantly greeted my father at the airport and drove him home. Since he'd come straight from Vietnam, Dad naturally wanted a shower. We allowed him this desire, of course, but sat impatiently waiting for him to finish. Finally Mom went back to check on him, and we girls heard her yelling—and Mom never yelled.

What had happened was this: Having come from rather primitive living conditions, including open, communal showers, my father hadn't remembered to pull the shower curtain when he took his shower. He had so enjoyed the warm water that he was completely oblivious to the mess he was making. What my mother found when she went into her formerly immaculate bathroom was an inch of water.

She didn't yell for long. Of course the most important thing was that her husband was home, not that the bathroom looked nice. Even her cleaning was, at its deepest level, about a person and not a house. I wish I could remember that when I get the cleaning bug.

"What God has made clean, you must not call profane." (Acts 10:15)

JANUARY 20
Getting Gifts

I love getting gifts. I don't give a hoot about how much it cost or where it came from; what I want is evidence that someone knows who I am and what I like. There are a couple of people in my life who always seem to know *exactly* what I'd like. One is a girlfriend and the other, believe it or not, a guy friend who's in his thirties, unmarried, and *not* gay.

God, as usual, throws a wrench into all this human custom. Very often, God gives us gifts we think we don't want. We're not as reticent about expressing our disappointment to God as we would be to friends. A very common prayer in response to a gift is, "Why are you doing this to me?"

I was at a retreat when the nun who was leading it told us she had begged God, over years and years, for the gift of patience. She finally got her present in the form of a classroom full of second-graders.

Everyone laughed. We'd all had the experience of getting what we'd asked from God in a form we didn't expect. The funny thing is that unlike human gift-givers, God always knows the right present to give. Sometimes it takes me years to acknowledge that fact, but it's nevertheless true. So if I realize God has sent me a gift and I think it's the wrong one, I'd do well to think again.

For by grace you have been saved through faith, and this is not your own doing; it is the gift of God.
(Ephesians 2:8)

JANUARY 21
Gift-Wrapping the Garbage

Loren Broadus is a remarkable man. He was one of my professors when I was in seminary, and the most unassuming man on the faculty. He didn't teach "important" classes like Bible or theology; instead, he taught the practical courses, which didn't get much respect from faculty or students.

Loren has written innumerable books, all of them theologically based but completely accessible. He writes so that any Christian can understand what he's saying. That's a skill most professors (and many clergy) don't have. Loren's books always deal with very practical matters: ethics, suffering, life balance, procrastination.

Loren always offers very practical advice, often in memorable sayings, such as "Don't gift-wrap the garbage." (He graciously gave his permission to use his maxim as the title of this book.) Of course I don't literally gift-wrap the garbage. The image of wrapping garbage in pretty paper and putting bows on top is ridiculous. Yet very often this is exactly what I do. Not gift-wrapping the garbage means I don't spend time and energy on things that aren't important. I don't give anything more time than it deserves. I'm not bogged down with guilt and anxiety for trying to be perfect when it's neither possible nor required.

I expect you'll agree with me when I say that now, many years out of seminary, I realize Loren was probably the smartest professor there.

"Do not give what is holy to dogs; and do not throw your pearls before swine." (Matthew 7:6)

JANUARY 22
Paying the Bills

It really doesn't take much skill to pay bills. Once you've learned how to write a check, and stuff, seal, and stamp an envelope, you've got it down. So why are there so many gadgets out there that promise to make paying the bills easy?

Part of the reason paying bills is so hard is that there's almost never enough money. Whether the bill payer gets $20K or $100K a year, it somehow fails to comfortably cover all the debts. So we worry. There are a very few people in the world who don't have to worry about paying the bills. These super-rich folks probably don't write their own checks. I assume they have accountants to do that. They can have just about anything they want and don't have to worry about affording it. But even the super-rich worry. They may not worry about making the rent, but they do worry about *losing* their money.

Apparently there's no way to win. Money equals worry. Unless, of course, I take my Christian faith seriously. According to the gospels, Jesus talked about money more than any other subject. I think he knew the power it has in my life, as well as the justice issues that are always there when money's in the picture. Jesus promised that God would make sure I have everything I need. Not everything I *want*, mind you, but need.

Can I believe? It's harder for me to believe this promise than stories of Christ's miracles and his resurrection. It is truly a spiritual discipline to approach paying the bills with a prayerful attitude. Perhaps each time I ready myself to pay bills, I should start by reading the story of the fish with the coin inside.

"Go to the sea and cast a hook; take the first fish that comes up; and when you open its mouth, you will find a coin; take that and give it to them for you and me."
(Matthew 17:27)

JANUARY 23
Thank-You Notes

My mother taught me to always write a thank-you note for any gift, invitation, or kindness. I have to admit that though I try, I can and do forget to write thank-you notes. It amazes me how ungrateful I can be.

Each and every day I wake up in a comfortable bed, take a luxurious shower, walk the sweet Shih Tzu who fills me with joy, and head into the kitchen for coffee and toast. Eighty-five percent of the people on this planet would trade lives with me in a heartbeat. All too often I find my prayers are filled with requests and are oriented toward the future—the different future I would like. Too rarely do I thank God for what I have and for the present moment. I suspect that's largely because in God's household, I am a spoiled brat with a huge feeling of entitlement. I tend to take what I have for granted.

The best cure I've discovered for this is going to church with poor people. Some friends went to Haiti on a week-long mission trip. Despite the crushing poverty the Haitians lived in, they said they pitied the *Americans,* because our level of faith is apparently not high enough to make us sing and dance and shout praise to God—with all the advantages we have.

A good lesson, I think. Perhaps if I get better at thanking God for all the many gifts in my life, I'll get better at thanking people who give me presents too.

Bless the Lord, O my soul, and all that is within me, bless his holy name. Bless the Lord, O my soul, and do not forget all his benefits. (Psalm 103:1-2)

JANUARY 24
My Female Body

One of the gifts of the feminist movement is careful historical scholarship that shows a disturbing theme in Western culture, especially *Christian* culture: devaluing and demonizing the female body. Sadly, many church fathers and great saints (including St. Augustine and St. Thomas Aquinas) have taken the view that woman is nothing more than "a misbegotten male."

That attitude still exists today, though it's rarely spoken aloud. The evidence runs from the sublime to the ridiculous. Pre-teen boys have been known to make jokes about menstruation, dip tampons in ketchup, leave them on the sidewalk, and watch the reactions of people who walk by. At the other extreme, tens of thousands of young girls are subjected to the practice of genital mutilation, in which the clitoris is removed and the lips of the vagina sewn shut. While it is a practice that originated in Africa, there are American doctors who will perform this surgery even today. They say, "If I don't do it, someone else will, and at least I can be sure she doesn't die from infection."

Perhaps worst of all, we women often hate our own bodies. We talk about menstruation as "being on the rag." We punish ourselves with diets and extreme exercises to try to make our bodies match our culture's ideal. We even wear shoes that hurt.

This is not what God has in mind for women! Our bodies are fearfully and wonderfully made. They do what God does—create new life and nourish it. Then there's this: scientists say there is no biological need for female orgasms. Yet we've got 'em. And when God chose to become a human being, it was accomplished through and in the body of a woman.

It will probably be a long time before modern women can learn to love our bodies as much as God does. Thankfully, the church is finally beginning to help us by teaching about the positive aspects of sexuality. I look forward to the day that *all* of God's children perceive their bodies as the gift they are. I think God does too.

I commend to you our sister Phoebe, a deacon of the church at Cenchreae, so that you may welcome her in the Lord as is fitting for the saints, and help her in whatever she may require from you, for she has been a benefactor of many and of myself as well.
(Romans 16:1-2)

JANUARY 25
The Conversion of St. Paul

If God has a Stubbornness Scale that goes from one to ten, with ten being the highest, then Saul of Tarsus would have scored a fifteen. Before his conversion *and* after, he was absolutely, positively, always certain he was correct. Thank goodness God knew a way to get him over to the right side.

Paul was as zealous an apostle of Christ as he had been a persecutor of his followers. But that switch wouldn't have happened had Paul not had his conversion experience on the road to Damascus. God had to knock the man off his feet and blind him to get him to listen.

It's good to know that God can and will go to such extremes to persuade us to follow Jesus. I don't know about you, but I can be awfully stubborn sometimes, even when I'm wrong. Maybe *especially* when I'm wrong. I've never had an experience as dramatic as Paul's—maybe that's because I haven't been *that* wrong yet. It's good to know, though, that if God wants me, and wants me to follow a particular path, God knows just how dramatic that request has to be in order for me to say yes.

Suddenly a light from heaven flashed around him.
[Saul] fell to the ground and heard a voice saying to

him, "Saul, Saul, why do you persecute me?"
(Acts 9:3-4)

January 26
Moving

I hate moving. Let me be clear about this: I *hate* moving. I grew up as an Army brat, and every two or three years my family would pack up and head off. Even after I got out on my own, I still moved around a lot. In my forty-four years of life, I have lived in thirty-two different abodes. That averages out to one every year and a quarter. Now you see why I hate moving.

I guess most Americans like moving more than I do, because we do it a lot. From the start, this nation of immigrants has invited movement. If things didn't work out where you were, you could just pick up and move a couple hundred miles away. These days it seems as if everyone has adopted the lifestyle I grew up with. People move for careers without thinking twice. Seems like no one stays put any more. I guess Carole King felt my bewilderment long before I could articulate it.

What makes all this bearable for me is one little line in the New Testament. Jesus says to his disciples,

"In my father's house there are many mansions." He said he's going on ahead to get things ready for us.

I like that idea. Apparently *all* the "dwelling places," the homes we will live in in the afterlife, fit into God's "house." That means nobody has to go away any more. And if there are different *kinds* of mansions, then maybe we get the ones that suit us best.

This is the way I choose to interpret these few verses. Who knows whether I'm right or not. But it does seem to me that heaven must certainly be a place where you never again have to say good-bye.

"Do not let your hearts be troubled. Believe in God, believe also in me. In my Father's house there are many dwelling places." (John 14:1-2)

JANUARY 27
Dinner Parties

A woman's first dinner party is a kind of rite of passage these days. Unlike our ancestors, we don't have coming-of-age ceremonies in which we're sent off into the bushes to be separated from the tribe while we learn from the teaching elders the mysterious secrets of being adults.

Having folks to dinner is part of what makes us human. I've never heard of any chimpanzee colony inviting its counterpart down the river for a special meal of Bananas Foster. From earliest times, human beings have shared their food.

It's clear in the Bible that hospitality is an extremely important ethic. It may seem strange to us that three strangers could saunter up to Abraham's ranch and he'd invite them in for dinner, but that's the way it worked back then. The reason was very practical: given the harsh conditions in the Middle East, someone refused hospitality could quite literally die.

It's difficult to get across just how important the ethos of hospitality was to our forebears in the faith. Contrary to the common assumptions, Sodom and Gomorrah were destroyed because they failed to provide hospitality. When the body of the law was formed, the Jews found it important to include rules about treating non-Jews well. That might not sound like much, but it's really quite astonishing. It's as if our Constitution had a section on how to treat tourists.

We may not think a thing about the Bible while we're waiting for just the right moment to take the soufflé out of the oven, but we've all had the feeling that comes at the end of a successful dinner party. Everyone's finished eating, pushed back from the table, and is glowing from good food, good wine, and good company. This is the time for the host to rejoice; *this* is the real reward of hospitality.

Do not neglect to show hospitality to strangers, for by doing that some have entertained angels without knowing it. (Hebrews 13:2)

JANUARY 28
Waiting

It was a very bad day at the doctor's office today. I had a minor but nagging eye infection and an early afternoon appointment. I arrived ten minutes early, as required by The Neurotic's Handbook to Life, but didn't get into an exam room for two hours. Then it took another forty-five minutes to see the doctor.

There are innumerable reasons I hate to wait: missing time at work, school, or play. I don't like being bored. But I believe there's also a very profound reason that waiting makes me so frustrated, angry, and tearful: it reminds me I'm not in control of my life. And human beings don't like the feeling of being out of control.

When we are forced to wait at the doctor's office or the airport or for a cab on a rainy day, we get a little dose of a scary proposition: underneath all this order is a whole lot of chaos. After all, if we were in charge, the doctor would see us right away, planes would always run on time, and cabs would stop the first time we signal.

As scary as it may feel to get a hint of the fact that I'm not in control, it's also quite freeing. Once I realize it's not my own efforts that make my life orderly, then I can unload the incredibly heavy burden of responsibility for the well-being of the entire universe and the anxiety that comes along with that burden. In other words, I can be a human being and let God be God.

All will be well, and all will be well, and all manner of things will be well. (Julian of Norwich)

JANUARY 29
Phone Calls

Depending on who you are and what you're doing, phone calls are a blessing or a curse. Folks who work in offices and need long periods of concentration have been known to let loose with a few choice words every time the phone rings.

On the other hand, there are people whose work depends on phone calls. For them, a phone that sits quiet for hours on end is a bad sign. And at home we all enjoy having the chance to catch up with friends and relatives when they surprise us with a call.

That's about the furthest I could push the meaning of phone calls until I watched a movie called *Leap of Faith*. Steve Martin is a con man who poses as a traveling evangelist; by the end of the movie, he actually comes to believe. But one of the best parts of the movie is the choir: it's big, it's black, it rocks. It's where I discovered the ecstasy of gospel music. But more to the point, the choir in this movie sang a song I'd never heard before. The words go, "Jesus is on the main line, tell him what you want."

At first that might seem silly or even disrespectful. But actually it's a pretty good description of the kind of relationship Jesus offers us. Jesus is *always* on the other end of the line—our prayers—and is *always* ready to hear what we want and need. It's not a very sophisticated way to think about it all, but it's a day-to-day image that might convince me more than the highest flights of theology: Any time I want, I can pick up the phone and hear, on the other end, "This is Jesus. Good to hear from you. What's up?"

"And remember, I am with you always, to the end of the age." (Matthew 28:20)

JANUARY 30
The Newspaper

You will not believe what I just saw in a catalog. It looks like those sun shields for cars that start out as round, silvery circles but fold out to cover the whole width of the windshield. In fact, they've used the same technology for this gadget. But what this folds out to is different: a tent. Not a tent to camp in—it's a small one to put on your breakfast table to hold up the newspaper while you eat. It's a two-sided tent, of course, so while you're reading the business section, your better half can be on the other side reading the world news.

But you know how big most newspapers are when they're opened up. Pretty big. How many times have we seen a father in an old television show or a commercial stereotyped as hiding behind his newspaper?

So what this new invention does is allow two people to read the newspaper, hands free, while they eat their oatmeal and drink their coffee. But I can't stand the idea of that big tent in between those people. We spend little enough time with our loved ones as it is; the last thing we need is a gadget that hides them from view while we break bread together.

And it's so ironic that this doodad is made for the newspaper. The paper is one important way to stay connected to the world. Since the rest of humanity is, in God's view, our brothers and sisters, then I really ought to make an effort to find out what's going on in their lives. The newspaper is kind of like a daily family newsletter. But I shouldn't force myself into an either/or situation. I can read the paper and find out about what my distant kin are up to, and I can *also* have a conversation with my close kin across the breakfast table.

This is one product I won't ever want. Shame on them!

"I have other sheep that do not belong to this fold. I must bring them also, and they will listen to my voice. So there will be one flock, one shepherd."
(John 10:16)

JANUARY 31
Cleaning the Toilet

Cleaning the toilet? I know—it's disgusting. Cleaning the toilet is nasty. What's it doing in a book of meditations?

Well, for one thing, these meditations are written for women who live real lives, people who not only go to church on Sunday and make retreats in stunning natural settings, but people who also sweat, sneeze, and excrete. And given the fact that all people excrete, I *hope* someone is cleaning the toilet on a regular basis.

Some readers may find it offensive that I remind them that Jesus Christ, the son of God, used the bathroom. There's really no reason to, um, rub your noses in it, is there?

Yes, there is. Even way back in the first century there were people called gnostics who believed that Jesus hadn't been a real human being. He looked like one, sounded like one, and felt like one, but he couldn't have had a real human body, according to these folks. Otherwise he would have had to do all the disgusting things that human beings do, and surely God would never stoop that low.

But that's just exactly the point. God *did* stoop that low. Jesus was a real, honest, genuine, one hundred percent human being. If we turn our faces away from the earthy aspects of his humanity, then we're missing the entire point of the incarnation. Jesus became what we are so that we might become what he is. St. Athanasius said that, by the way, not me.

And the Word became flesh and lived among us.
(John 1:14)

FEBRUARY 1
Earrings

My parents were pretty strict, so I wasn't allowed to get my ears pierced until I was sixteen. That probably sounds wildly unbelievable in this day of body piercing and tattoos, but things really do change that fast. Anyway, I've gone through periods of wearing lots of different earrings, wearing the same pair almost all the time, and not wearing any. Sometimes I've gone so long that the holes in my ears have started to close. But sooner or later I go back to earrings.

Earrings, of course, are not a world-shaking issue. But what amazes me is that apparently women have worn them since the beginning of the human race. Did Eve wear earrings? Can't say, but all the evidence from the earliest civilizations shows that women wore earrings thousands and thousands of years ago.

I like that because it makes me feel a connection to those sisters of the soul. It's extremely difficult to make the people in the New Testament come alive, and the women in the Old Testament seem almost beyond reach. But when I think of the women in Exodus giving their earrings for the construction of the tabernacle of the Lord, then I realize they cannot have been so entirely different from me.

It's nice to have a connection to the women who lived so long ago and helped begin the faith that led to my own. And that connection joyfully reminds me that the lessons they learned thousands of years ago apply today too.

So they came, both men and women; all who were of a willing heart brought brooches and earrings and signet rings and pendants, all sorts of gold objects, everyone bringing an offering of gold to the Lord.
(Exodus 35:22)

February 2
Presentation of the Lord

For some reason I don't really understand, I tend to get along really well with little old ladies. Maybe it's because I loved my mother's mother so much and felt so much love from her. But whether they're saintly or crotchety, for some reason I've found that elderly women will usually give me an ear.

I certainly give one to them. I think of the elderly prophet Anna, who was eighty-four when she told everybody at the temple that the baby brought by this couple Joseph and Mary to be presented to God was the Messiah. The woman knew what she was talking about, and I've found that so do a lot of other old ladies.

Of course it's possible to live to be one hundred and still be a fool, but it seems to be the case that simply being around this earth for decades upon decades provides people with some wisdom. There's a reason the early churches counted on the leadership of their "elders," the older members among them. Again, that's not to say that an elderly person can't be wrong about religion or anything else; sure they can. But we probably need to borrow a custom from the Asian cultures and give more respect and attention to our elders. If we don't, we're missing a lot of wisdom.

At that moment she came, and began to praise God and to speak about the child to all who were looking for the redemption of Jerusalem. (Luke 2:38)

FEBRUARY 3
Middle-Age Spread

I didn't believe it when I was nineteen. Everything I read told me that our metabolisms change when we hit our forties, but I didn't really think that applied to me. As far as I was concerned, the women who were my mother's age and had become broad in the beam did so simply because they didn't take care of themselves. They ate the wrong food or they didn't exercise enough.

Then I hit *my* forties. It really is true. I can eat the same amount and type of food—or even less; continue the same level of exercise—or increase it; and still the pounds pile on. Needless to say, this is a horrible fate according to our culture, and even the "common sense" medical knowledge of today.

Dr. Suzette Elgin, author of the family of *The Gentle Art of Verbal Self-Defense* books, and, until recently, publisher of "The Language in Health Care Newsletter," has for several years run a small but determined campaign to inform us that all the alarmist studies showing how dangerous even a few extra pounds can be are flawed, and are more than outweighed by studies showing that while it is dangerous to be extremely obese or extremely thin, people (especially women) with ten, twenty, even thirty extra pounds on their bodies do better, physically, than their skinny counterparts. I don't have to tell you that *this* aspect of medical research on weight doesn't get much attention; there is too much money to be made from weight management programs.

This gives me some peace. It's always been difficult to understand why God would create the female body in such a way that after the child-bearing years have passed, it would naturally move in a direction that is dangerous. Dr. Elgin's voice crying in the wilderness suggests this isn't the case at all. It may very well be that it is natural for women in their forties and up to gain weight—and not only natural, but healthy.

I'm putting away my diet books. I'm going to allow God to shape my body. Who better than the one who made it?

I praise you, for I am fearfully and wonderfully made.
(Psalm 139:14)

February 4
Performance Reviews

Most folks in our country have had some experience of being graded. That happens in school, of course, and it also happens in the working world. Most companies big enough to have a human resources department have some kind of performance review for each employee every six or twelve months. They might be given a bonus if they score high or put on notice to improve if they score low. Performance reviews are really just report cards for grownups.

Even if we work in a place that doesn't give formal performance reviews, we know we're always being graded. It's an awful feeling to know your work is constantly being judged.

Fact is, though, that God doesn't give out report cards. God doesn't measure our performance. There are two reasons for that. First, God knows we're all sinful creatures, and while we may not have committed one of the "big" sins, we are all, at base, capable of them. That potential comes along with our birth certificates. So like Adam and Eve, we all flunk the God test. But then there's the second reason God doesn't grade us: The report cards are already in. The work of Jesus Christ has turned us all into A students.

There is therefore now no condemnation for those who are in Christ Jesus. (Romans 8:1)

FEBRUARY 5
Rush Hour

When I lived in northern Virginia back in the '70s, I was twelve miles from my office, close to the D.C. border. On normal days, it took an hour and a quarter to get to work. On snow days, it could take three or four hours. And one day, when the nation's farmers brought their tractors to the capitol and formed a blockade on the major highway in the area, it took me six and a half hours to get to work. It's not that bad in Nashville, but I'm sure it's worse now in northern Virginia, and my California friends have told me horror stories I have to believe.

I know of only one cure for rush hour, at least until the urban planners figure it out: expectations. When I get into the car during rush hour now, I simply *expect* it's going to take me longer to get where I'm going than I want it to, and I *expect* to have at least one fellow driver do something fairly idiotic.

Once I accept the fact that I'm going to be in the car, on the bike, or on foot longer than I want to be, then I can let go of the aggravation and stress these delays cause. Then, magically, what had been a nightmare turns into a gift: time. And it's time when my mind isn't usually taxed. What an opportunity to have a chat with God.

Modern life is so rushed and noisy that it's difficult to find time to listen for that still, small voice. While I don't recommend ecstatic mystical visions on the interstate, I do suggest that this time that usually makes us so anxious can turn into a spiritual gift.

But the Lord was not in the wind: and after the wind an earthquake; but the Lord was not in the earthquake: And after the earthquake a fire: but the Lord was not in the fire: and after the fire a still small voice. (1 Kings 19:11-12, KJV)

FEBRUARY 6
Lunch

"Hey, let's have lunch sometime!"

I don't know whether I was unusually naïve or whether it's a lesson most people need to learn, but when I was a twenty-something in the business world, I took these offers at face value. I would actually call these people up, suggest a time and place to meet, and feel disappointment when they weren't available. After two or three tries, I realized they were *never* going to be available.

What that phrase really means is something like this: "It's a surprise to see you. I'd almost forgotten you existed. If I weren't so busy, it might be nice to take some time to get together and chat, but I'll never have enough time for that. Know I wish you well, but don't expect anything of me."

That might sound like a rather cynical interpretation of a business world nicety, but I think it's an honest one. I confess I've used it myself. While I might like these people and don't want to hurt their feelings, I'm also realistic enough to realize that friendships take time and energy, and I can only maintain so many of them.

The nice thing is that God *never* says, "Let's have lunch sometime." God is always there, always available. God *always* wants to spend time with me, any hour of the day, any day of the year. God is always there, ready to deepen our relationship. In fact, when I *do* schedule a "lunch" with God, and then end up involved in something else and forget our date, God waits patiently with no anger, no judgment. God *always* invites intimacy, *always* makes time for me, and *always* forgives me when I drop the ball.

O Lord, God of my salvation, when, at night, I cry out in your presence, let my prayer come before you; incline your ear to my cry. (Psalm 88:1-2)

FEBRUARY 7
Filling the Tank

I remember when people never filled their own gas tanks. Really. I remember pulling up to the pump, exchanging pleasantries with the attendant, saying yes or no to an oil check, waiting patiently while he returned with my change or charge card receipt, and then tootling along my merry way.

It's not like that anymore. That's not news. I've seen people in thousand-dollar business suits and multi-thousand-dollar evening gowns filling their tanks. You've got to be pretty rich to afford someone to get your car filled with gas for you.

Each time I stand at the pump, squeezing the handle while I watch my car sink lower and lower with the weight of the gas (I have a *very* small car), I like to remind myself that when I run out of gas, God will fill me up.

We all get depleted once in a while. Plain and simple, we are limited creatures; we don't have an endless supply of energy, good will, and love. The symptoms of an empty soul tank are clear: tiredness, depression, impatience, meanness, laziness, and anger. There are more; each soul has its own particular way to register when its tank is getting low.

It's as important to pay attention to those signals as it is the gas gauge. The worst that can happen if I don't get gas is that I'll get stranded. Allowing my soul to get empty can have devastating effects.

So I know where to get my soul filled back up again. And hey—God doesn't even *offer* self-service.

He who descended is the same one who ascended far above all the heavens, so that he might fill all things.
(Ephesians 4:10)

February 8
Groceries

Long, long ago, before Robin Williams was a megastar, he appeared in a movie called *Moscow on the Hudson*. He played an immigrant from the (then) U.S.S.R. who was trying to get established in the United States.

In one of the funniest scenes, he goes to the supermarket. In Russia, he'd had to stand in long lines for each individual piece of food. The supplies often ran out before he got to the front of the line. And the food, when he could get it, was very poor quality.

Even if you've never seen the movie, you can imagine what it would be like for someone who's lived in a world like that to enter an American supermarket for the first time. We have aisles and aisles of every kind of food imaginable, and if the store runs out of something, there's usually a competing brand available. At the very worst, we might have to wait until the next day for the produce or meat truck to arrive.

I don't much like grocery shopping, and I tend to do it late at night when there aren't many people around. I speed up and down the aisles I've memorized, more or less throwing things into the cart. But while I'm doing this, I *do* have a little ritual that has served me well. Each time I throw something in the cart, I thank God for it. "Thank you, God, for kiwi." "Thanks for making chickens." "Thanks for twenty different kinds of jam."

Of course it can get a little silly sometimes. "Thank you, God, for corn dogs" just somehow doesn't sound profound. But you get the idea. We live in amazing abundance. It does us good to recognize it on a regular basis.

> *For to those who have, more will be given.*
> *(Matthew 13:12)*

FEBRUARY 9
The Moon

This is really embarrassing to admit, but until I took astronomy in college, I hadn't figured out that the moon has a regular cycle. I knew that sometimes there were beautiful full moons, and I knew that sometimes I could, strangely enough, see the moon during the day. But I never figured out that there was any order to it all. Thank God ancient astronomers were more observant than I.

The moon has a twenty-eight-day cycle. It begins as a new moon, completely dark, then "waxes," or grows, until it's full. Then it gets smaller, or "wanes," until it's dark again.

I find this regularity soothing. It reminds me that God made the moon and set it to rotate around the earth. More than that, it reminds me that there is order in the universe. That's a very good thing to know. It's not all chaos. Someone, somewhere, *is* in charge and keeps things going the way they're supposed to go.

There are physicists who would argue with me and say there is no order in the universe. The secret, they would like to say, is that it *is* all chaos. But I read enough Stephen J. Hawking to know that in a quantum universe, all that "chaos" just might make sense. What I mean is that one day physicists will come to believe this. Since I know who made it all, I already do.

You have made the moon to mark the seasons; the sun knows its time for setting. (Psalm 104:19)

FEBRUARY 10
Taking Pills

I have a friend, "Mike," who's an AIDS patient. He's had the virus for almost ten years now, and after a few scary episodes early on, he's stayed well for years. That's due to the cocktail of drugs HIV patients take.

If you've never seen the ingredients of the cocktail, you'd be astounded. There are pills to be taken at particular times of the day—*exactly* that time of day—pills to be taken on an empty stomach, pills to be taken with food, pills that have to be taken close together or far apart. Every HIV-positive person I know has a mega-watch to alert them several times a day to take those pills.

There are plenty of folks who depend on modern medicine to keep them alive and well. Most of us stay generally healthy and feel overwhelmed when we get the flu or a sinus infection and have to deal with decongestants *and* antibiotics. I asked Mike once if he resented all the medication he had to take, whether it bothered him to have to stay constantly attuned to the time of day and the contents of his stomach. His reply surprised me, but confirmed my suspicion that his long trial has created in him a spiritual depth he hadn't had twenty years ago. Mike said this: "Each time I take my pills, I raise the water glass in a toast: 'Here's to you, Great Physician. Thanks for keeping me well.'"

"Those who are well have no need of a physician, but those who are sick; I have come to call not the righteous but sinners." (Mark 2:17)

February 11
Breakfast

I'm not a big breakfast eater. Rumor has it there are people in this world who can get out of bed and, within minutes thereof, put food down their throats. I suspect they're aliens.

My friends have pegged me as a "slow waker," and I admit it's true. It takes me a couple of hours before I'm even interested in eating. What that means in practical terms is that I become ravenously hungry in the mid-to-late morning. At that point, if I can find breakfast food, I count myself lucky. An hour later, I'll eat anything.

My strange rhythms do, though, give me a real sense of breakfast as "breaking the fast." One of my favorite gospel stories is when the resurrected Jesus appears to his disciples on the beach and offers them breakfast. I wish the Greek suggested the idea of "breaking the fast," because then I could think of the episode as one of the disciples breaking their fast from seeing Jesus. But the Greek just means a morning meal. Nevertheless, breakfast, to me, is a time to remind myself that as much as my body cries out for food, my soul is longing even more for my Lord.

Jesus said to them, "Come and have breakfast." Now none of the disciples dared to ask him, "Who are

you?" because they knew it was the Lord.
(John 21:12)

FEBRUARY 12
Saying "No" to Children

I don't have children; that's not because I didn't want them, but I waited to have them, and cancer took away my reproductive ability. It has been a joy to befriend the children in my congregations, and I think it's been mutual.

I also have two nieces and a nephew, and I dote on them. I really and truly didn't know, until they were born, that I could love another human being so much. God has been generous in putting children in my life.

Since I'm not a parent, though, I rarely have the task of discipline. That's kind of cheating in the parenting world; I get to be the cool grownup who doesn't say "no." But I've been around enough children to know that very often their wills have to be thwarted to keep them safe. Once on a walk, I saw my niece try again and again to jump from the sidewalk into the street; each time, my sister reigned her in. The little girl cried and screamed and told her mommy she was "mean," but my sister knew what was best for her.

When I want something very, very badly and don't get it—that's everything ranging from the silly, like curly hair, to the serious, like a particular job—I get mad at God. I want what I want, and I figure I know what's best for me. So I'm honest in my prayer and tell God about my anger, but it never fails: very soon, I miraculously end up in a situation where I see a parent say "no" to a child. Of course, God is exponentially wiser than any parent. God has told me "no" on many occasions, and while I grumble for a while, the parenting drama I inevitably run across gradually leads me to peace with that denial.

Endure trials for the sake of discipline. God is treating you as children; for what child is there whom a parent does not discipline? (Hebrews 12:7)

February 13
Showers

I don't usually think twice about taking a shower. It's such a part of my daily routine that it doesn't bring new insights. But after a week of camping where the only showers available were rain showers, I was pretty grimy and stinky. That first shower back home was a revelation.

Something of the same thing happened to Seth, the angel in the movie *City of Angels,* who becomes human. On his second day of mortality, he has a shower. It's clear how many joys it brings him.

Think about it. Just about every single person in the United States today has the option of a warm, gentle, cleansing shower. If I've hurt myself somehow or just played too hard, a hot shower can bring blessed relief to painful muscles. If I'm in a situation that makes me hot, sticky, and miserable, a cool shower can lower my body temperature enough so that I end up not only clean but also cool for a little while. Think of all the products for use in the shower: shampoo, conditioner, soaps ranging from the most basic to very exotic, loofah sponges. Almost everything I use in the shower has a beautiful fragrance to it, a smell that people just a couple hundred years ago would have found only in the most expensive perfumes.

It's good to look at something as ordinary as a shower with fresh eyes every now and then. When I do, I get just a hint of how blessed I am, how lavished with gifts. So from time to time when I take a shower, I try to use all my senses to experience it. I just pay attention to what I'm doing. Chances are I'll find a reason to praise God from something as simple as my daily cleaning.

*I will make them and the region around my hill a
blessing; and I will send down the showers in their season; they shall be showers of blessing.*
(Ezekiel 34:26)

FEBRUARY 14
Valentine's Day

Valentine's Day has lost its roots in the church,
but that's okay. It's become as commercialized as
Christmas, but that's okay too. While people can take
advantage of the heart-shaped boxes of candy, the
bouquets of flowers, and the dinner specials, they
don't have to. What's important on Valentine's Day is
that two people who love each other make a point of
saying so.

True intimacy—and I don't just mean sex—
comes from two kinds of interactions between a couple. The most common is day-to-day intimacy. It
doesn't look very special at first glance; it's nothing
more, really, than living together, sharing the events
of the day, hearing about the latest development in
the office soap opera, and giving foot rubs when it's
been a tough day. This day-to-day intimacy is really
the most important. A couple that doesn't have this
doesn't really have an intimate relationship.

But it's also important to pause and make a special point of saying "I love you" in a way that isn't ordinary and day-to-day. It stops people from feeling that they're taken for granted. The gesture that says "I love you" doesn't have to be extravagant. Diamonds are always nice, of course, but what matters most is that the men who love us communicate in some way that they're glad we're in their lives.

Funny that it works that way with God too. The bulk of our relationship with God is made up of tiny interactions that happen several times a day. But then we also take one special day a week to go to church and make an overt gesture of saying to God, "I love you."

Divine love, human love—they're both wonderful. And they both need to be acknowledged on special occasions.

And if I have prophetic powers, and understand all mysteries and all knowledge, and if I have all faith, so as to remove mountains, but do not have love, I am nothing. (1 Corinthians 13:2)

FEBRUARY 15
Swimming

I'm not much of an athlete. I hated Phys Ed when I was a child because it told me, again and again, that I was a failure. I *did* get swimming lessons, though, and even though I still hate exercise, I know being a good steward of my body means giving it a workout on a regular basis.

So I swim. Unfortunately, I waver in my faithfulness; when I'm doing well, I swim a mile five days a week. When I'm not doing well . . . .

If I allow myself to get away from the pool for a while, I lose the discipline of it. More and more often I tell myself I don't have the time. Finally one day I'll realize it's been months since I've been to swim and that I'm going to have to start at square one building up my stamina. It's not a nice prospect and makes me want to return even less.

Here's what gets me to the pool for the first couple weeks of a new cycle of discipline: I imagine the water as God's love. I like best to swim in an Olympic-sized pool, and when I have access to one, I tell myself that God's love for me exceeds all that water. Before I start my laps, I take a breath and duck down under the water. There I am completely enveloped not only by water, but by God's love. The love is always there. Swimming just makes it tangible.

After a couple of weeks, I don't have to trick myself into going to the pool; being good to my body is self-reinforcing. The more I do it, the better I feel and the more I want to do it. But when I've gotten lazy and out of the rhythm, I make a sort of watery novena. For this many days, I pledge to God, I will go wallow in all that love.

God is love, and those who abide in love abide in God, and God abides in them. (1 John 4:16)

FEBRUARY 16
Arguments

I hate arguing with people, even though I've never gotten into a physical battle. I just loathe the way it feels to have anger making my blood burn and acid churning in my stomach. I'm the kind of person who thrives on peace and will do almost anything—sometimes too much—to keep it.

There are times and places, though, when it's important to fight. That's true for everyone, although exactly what those times and places are differs from person to person. One of mine is fighting for someone who is in unnecessary physical pain. As a minister I've made more hospital visits than I care to remember. One of the questions I always ask is, "Are you having pain?" All too often, the answer is "yes," and invariably I discover that while the patient or a family member has notified the nurses, pain relief hasn't arrived.

So I go to the nurse's station and argue. I start quietly but firmly and state exactly what I want: Mr. Smith in room 4209 needs pain relief NOW. There are always objections—the shifts are changing and he'll be seen to soon, the doctor hasn't ordered it, he already had a shot. And so I argue. I try not to be ugly or insulting, but I definitely show my anger.

It's shocked some of my parishioners over the years to see their minister so angry. For some reason they expect all pastors to be mild-mannered. But despite what the hymns say, Jesus Christ was not meek or mild. He had arguments with people when something was wrong. It can't have been fun to fight with the Pharisees all the time. Maybe his stomach churned too.

I hate arguing and the way it makes me feel. I'm slow to resort to it and I always feel sick afterward. But I think sometimes my Lord requires it of me.

Be angry but do not sin; do not let the sun go down on your anger. (Ephesians 4:26)

FEBRUARY 17
Building a Fire

I love fireplaces. One wonderful year I had a fireplace in my bedroom, so I could go to sleep warmed by its glow and soothed by the dancing shadows on the walls.

Folks who are good at making fires will tell you it's not about big flames. A fire like that looks great, of course, and it's very dramatic. But it will burn out quickly. Much more sensible is one that flames a bit but settles into the depths of the wood and makes the embers glow. That kind of fire will keep you warm a whole lot longer than one that flares briefly and then dies.

That's why I'm always a little skeptical of people who have a reputation for being "really spiritual." When someone tells me about such a person, I ask for the evidence. If it's big and showy, like "Well, she prays *three hours* every single day!" then I suspect we're dealing with a flamer. After all, how do people *know* she prays three hours a day? Either she's told them or she does it in public.

There *are* deeply spiritual people in every congregation, but they tend to be more like glowing embers than dancing flames. They rarely talk about their own spiritual prowess and turn much of their attention to others. There are, in fact, people who pray three hours each day, but they tend to be the least flamboyant folks around.

I have been blessed by knowing some true saints, and I have learned much from them. I recommend this apprenticeship to everyone. My only suggestion is to look for glowing embers, not flames.

"I came to bring fire to the earth, and how I wish it were already kindled!" (Luke 12:49)

FEBRUARY 18
Oops

Have you ever gotten a soft drink can that's empty? I don't mean one made for some sort of special promotion; I mean one that comes in a twelve-pack or case and somehow, mysteriously, didn't get filled. The can's perfect and the pop-top is still sealed. It's a strangely discomforting experience.

Manufacturing and processing have become so sophisticated these days that it's an event to discover an error. Sometimes those bloopers are funny, like an empty soda can. Other times they're not so funny, like a malfunctioning car seat that puts a baby in danger.

The fact is that only God is perfect. I can't expect perfection from myself, other people, or the world around me. The quality of goods I've become used to has a tendency to make me forget that fact. The world's an imperfect place, that's all there is to it. Creation is as fallen as the human race. While I tend to be pretty good at spotting the imperfections in other people, I really need to keep my eyes peeled for the mistakes in my world and myself.

I keep my sealed empty soda can on top of my computer because I sit there almost every day. It's a visual reminder to expect perfection only from the one place I can get it.

For all of us make many mistakes. (James 3:2)

February 19
Quilts

It's hard to remember back to the time when quilts weren't fashionable, but such a time did exist. Quilts were for poor folks who couldn't afford nice bedspreads and comforters. Now they're a staple of the bedding section in every department store, and some sell for hundreds of dollars.

But I have only one quilt—or piece of a quilt. It's a pillow, really, and only one side of it is quilted. The stitches are uneven and the pieces don't come together in perfect corners. But my grandmother made it for me, and I wouldn't trade it for the most expensive quilt in the world. I don't have to tell you why.

The things I most treasure in this life are the ones that were made *for me*, with me in particular as the intended recipient. I have a nice collection of children's drawings carefully pasted in scrapbooks.

These unique objects remind me that my entire life is a custom-made gift from God. Nobody else in all of eternity has been given the same life as mine. Since God is God, the unique life I'm working my way through is the one that is perfect for me. God is in the process of quilting my life together. I'm middle-aged and I still can't see what the pattern is going to be; but given the seamstress and the love with which my life is being made, I wouldn't trade it for any other.

Because if this plan or this undertaking is of human origin, it will fail; but if it is of God, you will not be able to overthrow them. (Acts 5:38-39)

FEBRUARY 20
Glasses

I was inconsolable when I had to get glasses in the fifth grade. What bothered me was not the fact that I had bad eyesight, but that I would look ugly. I hated my glasses every day I wore them and was ecstatic when my parents finally bought me contact lenses. Back in those days, contacts were pretty primitive, and the process of adjusting to them was torturous. But I went through it because I wanted to look good.

Right on schedule, when I turned forty, I discovered that publishers had conspired in a demonic pact to use progressively smaller type fonts. By my forty-first birthday, I had a pair of reading glasses. When I put them on in the pulpit for the first time, my parishioners laughed at me.

Actually, they laughed *with* me. I could laugh at the vanity that made me reluctant to wear my half-eyes, and all the good-natured teasing was a hoot. What happened in between the last day I wore glasses as a teenager and first day I wore them as a middle-aged woman, is that I grew up. I figured out that if there was anything to be upset about, it was my bad vision. I also figured out I was awfully lucky to be living in a time when the cure for my poor vision was easily available. Finally, I figured out that it's more important to be able to see than to look good.

God works on me continually. If I allow it, I will become wiser, more peaceful, and more comfortable with myself. While I may not welcome the changes in my body, I can certainly be open to the ones in my soul.

I believe that I shall see the goodness of the Lord in the land of the living. (Psalm 27:13)

FEBRUARY 21*
President's Day

(Observed third Monday of February)

I've been known to turn purple when people start going on and on about how our "founding fathers" wanted the United States to be a Christian country. The myths of the founding of this country have overtaken the facts in all too many instances. The fact is that most of those founding fathers, Washington and Jefferson among them, were Deists. That means they believed that while God had indeed created the universe, he'd also left it behind right after that, just as a watchmaker builds a watch and then lets it go. Jefferson even published his own version of the New Testament with all the offensive passages edited out—"offensive" being anything that suggested God continued to act in human history.

It's a good thing for us to remember the men who gave so much to found this country. While it's far from perfect, I can't imagine wanting to live anywhere else. But it's a disservice to remember our forebears not for who they really were, but some perfect cardboard myth. Presidents of the United States, like leaders of every other nation on earth past and present, are fallible. They may be very wise, like Washington and Lincoln, but they can still be wrong. The only one who is always right is God, and scripture has always recognized this fact. I do believe George Washington and Abraham Lincoln would have said the same.

Let us have faith that right makes might, and in that faith let us to the end dare to do our duty as we understand it. (Abraham Lincoln)

FEBRUARY 22
Alcoholics

I have a friend who's an alcoholic. He admits he has a problem but won't do anything about it. He's lost his job and his family because of his disease, and he's also lost several of his friends.

Not me. I admit it's hard to be friends with "Michael." When he's drunk, he can be truly obnoxious and totally unreliable. But when he's sober, he's a wonderful man. He's one of the smartest people I know, he can make me laugh so hard my stomach aches, and he has the ability to say just the right thing at the right time.

Having an alcoholic in my life has helped me understand that old church idea—hate the sin but love the sinner. I didn't really get that until Michael, but now I do. I hate his disease and the things it makes him do; I hate the sin that keeps him from acknowledging he's in trouble and seeking help. I absolutely do hate all that. But him I love. Michael will have a place in my heart forever. There may come a day when his alcoholism gets so bad that he's hurtful to me, and then I'll have to stop seeing him. But even then, I'll still love him.

Let love be genuine; hate what is evil, hold fast to what is good. (Romans 12:9)

FEBRUARY 23
Duct Tape

My friend Carol Sumner is a true Renaissance woman. She's incredibly smart and flies around the country fixing people's e-mail systems. She's not just a tech-head, though. She did everything but the dissertation for a doctorate in church history before she found her calling in cyberspace. More than that, she can do anything around the house.

I have seen Carol lay a hardwood floor, tile a bathroom, and build kitchen cabinets. She loves to get power tools for her birthday, and most "handy" men who know her worship the ground she walks on.

Me, I use duct tape. When in high school I took the Armed Forces Battery of Aptitude Tests, on the mechanical exam I scored a 2 (out of 100). I knew that a hammer and a nail went together. After that, I was lost.

I've used duct tape to hold the screens in my antiquated bathroom window that wasn't built to have screens. I've used duct tape to attach a plant hanger to my balcony railing so I can hang my wind chime from it. I've also used duct tape to fix a torn hem at the last minute, hold together my futon frame, and cover the rip in my car's upholstery.

The delightful thing about God is that we are all loved whether we're geniuses or idiots, master craftswomen or all thumbs. I know God gives every person at least one gift, and I think it's important to develop it. But I also know that while my friend Carol is *worthy* of admiration and I am not, God still loves me as much as her. That cheers me, and it also frees me to appreciate her talents rather than be envious of them.

Whatever is true, whatever is honorable, whatever is just, whatever is pure, whatever is pleasing, whatever is commendable, if there is any excellence and if there is anything worthy of praise, think about these things.
(Philippians 4:8)

FEBRUARY 24
Bracelets

When I was a sweet young thing, I took pride in my slenderness. Looking back on it now, I see that I was probably borderline anorexic. But at the time, I loved the fact that I wore a size four ring and that I could squeeze my whole hand through bracelets that were meant to be opened and wrapped around the wrist, then closed.

Today I am a normal woman and my ring size is 6. I can't get my hands through bracelets any more, and that brings me to my point. I have to wear bracelets the way most women wear them now, and that brings with it the frustration of bracelet closures. There are many kinds, but most of them are pretty difficult to put on by yourself. Since I'm unmarried, I often find that I can't wear a piece of jewelry because I can't get it on.

Each time I try to put on a bracelet and fail, I'm reminded that even in this mundane matter, I can't go it alone. I like to think of myself as an independent woman, and I suppose I am. But none of us can do without God. Whether I'm conscious of it or not, whether I like the idea or not, the plain fact is that I get through my days only because God is there moving things around with invisible hands. If God stopped intervening in my life, nothing would work—not just jewelry, but everything from cell division to global economics. It's just pride that makes me think every now and then that I'm doing all this myself. Luckily, there are little humiliations like bracelets to remind me of the truth.

If two lie together, they keep warm; but how can one keep warm alone? (Ecclesiastes 4:11)

FEBRUARY 25
Falling

Many years ago—I mean in the dark ages, when there were only three TV networks—there was a commercial that was unintentionally hilarious. The product being advertised was a gadget that an ill or elderly person could wear around their neck and use to contact somebody if there was an emergency. One of the visuals was an elderly woman flat on her back on the kitchen floor, talking into this gadget: "I've fallen and I can't get up!"

I don't know why we thought it was so funny. Maybe because it was so clear the woman was in no real distress. But I remember late night hosts and Saturday Night Live doing their versions. It was one of those phrases that enter the culture for a while, like "Where's the beef?"

The truly funny thing is that this phrase quite accurately describes the human condition. We've fallen (from innocence) and we can't get up (by ourselves). It's only through the work of Christ that we are picked up from the floor, dusted off, and sent on our way once again.

Actually falling is no fun, but most of the time, thanks be to God, we aren't seriously hurt. Most times the only thing badly bruised is our pride. If we've grown enough to be able to laugh at ourselves, then we can chuckle and say, "I've fallen and I can't get up!"

For there is no distinction, since all have sinned and fall short of the glory of God. (Romans 3:22-23)

FEBRUARY 26
Book Clubs

I've always loved to read, and I belong to a lot of book clubs. Most of them work the same way. They seduce you with the introductory offer: ten books (or five or twenty) for two dollars (or five or twenty). Then you agree to buy a few more books in the next several years. About every three weeks, the club sends you a catalog, and if you like, you can pick out a book, fill in the number on the order card, and mail it in. A couple of weeks later, voila, there's your book.

There is a catch, though. Each catalog describes a featured book. You're not *required* to buy this book, but you have to do something to *not* buy it. In a manner completely opposite to the way most mail order works, you've agreed to pay for books automatically sent to you every three weeks unless you return the card saying not to send them. The clubs hope, of course, that many of their members will forget to send in their cards and will be obligated to buy the books. I've never had it happen, but I'm a very organized person. I have a friend who is incredibly artistic but disorganized, and she's ended up with a whole lot of books she didn't really want.

It's a clever way to make money, but it's also a good metaphor for grace. We human beings, especially we Americans, believe deep in our hearts that we have to earn each and every good thing in our lives. We certainly believe we have to earn heaven. But through Jesus Christ, God has brought remarkable grace into the world. It's as if God has a direct channel to each one of us. Through this channel comes a constant silent call from God: come to me, come to me, come to me. Accompanying that invitation is a gift: love, love, love. And we have to do something to *not* get that love. Grace works in such a way that we must make a conscious decision to turn away from

God. Otherwise, the love keeps coming along with the invitation. Apparently we don't understand grace very well. It's a good thing God has so many ways to teach us about it.

> *For all of you share in God's grace with me.*
> *(Philippians 1:7)*

FEBRUARY 27
Popcorn

A kernel of popcorn is remarkably unimpressive. It's tiny, hard as a rock, and if you put it in your mouth, it doesn't have much flavor. But add some heat and it puffs up to ten times its original size.

I think the small graces God plants among us are a lot like popcorn. God can put just a little grace in a parish in the form of a new member whose brother is schizophrenic and on the streets, and in a few years it will become the city's leading congregation in helping the homeless. God can slide a kernel-sized piece of grace in an unwed mother's life in the form of an elderly neighbor who likes to babysit. In a few years she can be happy, healthy, raising good kids who have a mother who has a job she likes and a father who adores them.

God's grace is mighty powerful. Just a little bit makes a lot.

"If you have faith the size of a mustard seed, you will say to this mountain, 'Move from here to there' and it will move; and nothing will be impossible for you."
(Matthew 17:20-21)

FEBRUARY 28
24/7

I just *love* the fact that the grocery store a mile away from me is open all the time. I'm a night owl, so many times I've gone to the store at 1 a.m. to do my weekly grocery shopping. True, the deli and fish counters aren't staffed, but there are also very few customers, and I can get my shopping done in half an hour. I like the big discount store late at night too.

I could easily go the other way on this tendency toward 24/7 availability. It's possible to see it as a symptom of an ailing American culture where we are so materialistic that we can't even wait until the next day to buy what we want.

But I choose the more positive view. People are different; some, like me, are night owls. Some work second or third shift, and others are early risers (I mean like 4 a.m. early risers). The fact is that God is available 24/7. We don't have to wait for Sunday worship to have a chat with the almighty. I like the idea that when I'm standing in front of the dairy case at 11:30 p.m., someone in this city is probably on her knees in prayer and finding comfort and peace from God.

He is able for all time to save those who approach God through him, since he always lives to make intercession for them. (Hebrews 7:25)

MARCH 1*
Ash Wednesday

I grew up in a denomination that had no concept of the church year and no tradition of seasons. I didn't even hear the word "Lent" until my mid-twenties, when I sojourned in the Episcopal Church. The first Ash Wednesday I ever observed was one of the most remarkable days of my entire life.

I went to the 7 a.m. service and got my ashes. Having someone say to me "Remember that you are dust, and to dust you shall return" made shivers run down my spine. Being touched by the priest as he marked me with ashes was also unsettling. This church wasn't a touchy-feely group, so that was probably the first time he'd ever touched me—and it was not to shake my hand or hug me, but to put this mark of death on my forehead.

I was a college student at the time, so I went about my day, forgetting the ashes until I glanced at a mirror. Each time I thought, "Hey I've got something on my forehead . . . oh yeah, those are ashes and I'm going to die." My church upbringing had taught me nothing about sacramental power, and I was wiped out by a *visible, tangible* sign of God working inside me.

All went well until I was headed for the city bus after my last class. Again, I'd forgotten about my ashes. A young student, probably a freshman, dropped his books, pointed at me, and started yelling, "The Whore of Babylon! Woe to the Whore of Babylon!" After my theological education, I realized he was probably a member of a fundamentalist church that hated Catholics.

But at the moment, I was completely immersed in the experience of being pointed out and ridiculed because of my faith. It felt horrible and good all at the same time. Horrible because . . . well, because being called any kind of whore is upsetting. Being picked out of a crowd is upsetting. And being hated is upsetting. But it was good because for the first time in my life, I understood just a teeny tiny bit of what it was like to be one of the church's martyrs. I didn't go through anything even *close* to what they did, but even though it was a mild version, I had the experience of being *set apart* because of my faith.

What hits me these days on Ash Wednesday is seeing the ashes on other people's foreheads. It reminds me of the fragility of human life, and I treasure each person I see, even the strangers. But it was a very good thing for this "free church" young woman to have her first experience of being "other" simply by being a Christian.

Have mercy on me, O God, according to your steadfast love; according to your abundant mercy blot out my transgressions. (Psalm 51:1)

MARCH 2
Beginnings

It is Mark alone of the three synoptic gospel writers who tells us that Jesus was "driven" into the wilderness by the Holy Spirit. Matthew says the Spirit "led" him, and Luke tells us that Jesus went "full of the Holy Spirit." Those are minor differences, all things considered, but I prefer Mark's version. It is my experience that starting something new is something I usually have to be pushed into.

Beginnings are always difficult, always a little bit treacherous. We never know what's ahead. Beginnings necessarily mean change, and we can comfortably take only so much newness.

Being a human being, Jesus had to have a little of that reticence too. After all, he'd had a simple but safe life in Nazareth for thirty years. What human being would ever *want* to leave all that in order to go into the wilderness? He knew he'd be hungry, thirsty, tempted, and lonely. He knew this was the beginning of his public ministry. If Jesus had even the first clue about how it would all end up—and I think he did— he surely couldn't have been excited and anxious to head into the desert. So it was the Holy Spirit who drove him there, or led him, or filled him so much that he had to go.

The Holy Spirit drives us too. God is always pressing us to go beyond what's familiar and comfortable. Sometimes that pressing becomes so intense that we have to answer with a drastic change—a vocation, a marriage, a new home. The important thing to remember is that this leading of the Holy Spirit will *always* be to our good, even if we can see some scary things ahead when we look down this new path. Whatever or wherever the Holy Spirit is driving us to right now will, in the end, be good for us. Lent is a good time to allow the Spirit to put us at a beginning, whether that's by leading, filling, or driving.

And the Spirit immediately drove him out into the wilderness. (Mark 1:12)

MARCH 3
Time Doesn't Fly

It's trite but true: time is elastic. When we're children, it moves along at a rate we can't see with our young eyes. It always seems that the thing we're waiting for—the end of school, a birthday, Christmas, whatever—is on its way at a snail's pace, and the slowest snail at that.

Adults, on the other hand, usually agree that the older you get, the faster time passes. So many of us would like to slow time down when things are good—our children's earliest years, the first exciting job after college, retirement.

But even adults know that "time flies when you're having fun" means it stalls when you're not. A year may pass in a flash for an adult, but a meeting may feel as if it will never end, or an incision will feel as if it will never heal.

Jesus wasn't having fun out in the wilderness, that's for sure. Forty days doesn't seem so very long to most of us. It's six weeks, more or less, and I'll bet I've said to myself many times, "Hey, I can take anything for six weeks!"

But not the wilderness. Those hot days had to be interminable and the cold nights must have seemed to last forever. Our Lord may have been in the wilderness for forty days and forty nights, but I'm certain it seemed like eternity.

For everything there is a season, and a time for every matter under heaven. (Ecclesiastes 3:1)

March 4
Hunger

It is wonderful to be able to say that life in the United States is such that very few of us have ever had to go hungry without a choice. That's as things should be, and I wish that state on every human being this planet holds.

But always being well-fed cuts us off from one of the experiences our Lord had. For forty days he didn't eat. I've known people who've conducted forty-day fasts; it *can* be done, even though it's awful and it is physically damaging. Our own experience with fasts can give us a glimpse of what it's like to be hungry, but it's only a glimpse.

There was a three-week period in my life when I went hungry unintentionally. It was the start of a new college semester. I'd gone back to school early with no money from my parents, and my student loan wouldn't be in for three weeks. I subsisted on peanut butter sandwiches, bananas, and water. There were probably places I could have gone for food, but at the time I was either too young, confused, ashamed, or clueless to do so.

Being hungry for an extended time, without choice, is a hellish experience. Everything else drops away. It's impossible to care about anything else but our own bodies and the stomach inside that's shrinking and sending us pain to tell us something's wrong.

Jesus went through this terror for forty days, and he did it in a cruel environment. Today we fast by "giving something up" for Lent, and even that has become watered down—we give up not all TV but our favorite program, not all sweets but just chocolate. It's gotten to the point that some people enter Lent with the hope that they'll lose weight.

Of course we can approach Lent that way. We can still accompany our Lord during his nightmarish trial by spiritual reading, saying the rosary, following the Stations of the Cross. But I think we'll know better what it was like to be Jesus if we allow ourselves—for maybe just one day—to become truly hungry.

"Woe to you who are full now, for you will be hungry."
(Luke 6:25)

MARCH 5
Forty Days and Forty Nights

In the church today, we observe Lent for forty days, plus six Sundays that are not a part of Lent because Sunday, the day of the resurrection, is always a feast day. Most of us are aware that Lent lasts forty days because that's how long Jesus was in the wilderness.

But that's not all. "Forty" is a period that punctuates the entire history of the human race. Noah and his family endured rain that lasted forty days and forty nights. After that, the flood stayed for forty days. The Israelites were in the wilderness, eating manna and wandering unhappily, for forty years. Moses spent forty days and nights with God on top of Mt. Sinai. King David reigned over Israel for forty years. Many of the kings, judges, and other faithful people of the Hebrew Bible were given forty years of reign, rule, peace, or some other such reward.

When we travel the Lenten path behind Jesus for forty days and nights, we walk not only in his footsteps but also those of our ancestors in the faith, back almost to the beginning. Through our forty-day observance, we join with God's faithful through thousands of years, and are accompanied—though we cannot see them—by a great cloud of witnesses.

Jesus, full of the Holy Spirit, returned from the Jordan and was led by the Spirit in the wilderness, where for forty days he was tempted by the devil. (Luke 4:1-2)

MARCH 6
Fear

Everybody is afraid of something. Some of us, like me, have phobias (mine is snakes). But there is plenty that is real to be afraid of: illness, war, tornadoes, and of course the biggest of all American fears: speaking in public.

Jesus apparently wasn't afraid to preach when he entered the wilderness—he'd had no trouble teaching the elders in the temple when he was twelve. But because he was a human being, he did fear death. He feared death as we all do, he had to fear death during his forty days in the wilderness, and he feared death the night before he was crucified. He feared death so much that Luke tells us he was sweating blood.

Nobody can get through life without fear. Some people get close—they align themselves so closely with what God intends for them that they fear very little. But if even the son of God was afraid, then so must all of us be.

Just because we follow Christ doesn't mean we won't ever be afraid. We all fear something. Even wise soldiers say that courage doesn't mean lack of fear; it means being afraid and doing it anyway. Following Jesus, though, means that when we are afraid, we have the comfort of knowing that God knows exactly what we're going through, and that, in the end, there will be no more fear.

And [Jesus] said to them, "I'm so scared I think I could die; stay here and keep awake."
(Mark 14:34, author's translation)

MARCH 7
Loneliness

Sometimes people accuse me of being able to see right through them. I have no such power, I really don't. All I have is a good knowledge of human nature. I've learned that through academic study, paying attention to my own reactions, and watching those of other people. One of the things I know, something people think I get through some esoteric power, is that everyone is lonely, at least once in a while.

Some people will deny that. They'll say their lives are full of family and friends and they never want for company. But even folks like these have the wee hours of some nights when for some reason they can't sleep, and the loneliness comes roaring in on them.

Jesus knew what it was like to be lonely. Of course he was lonely in the wilderness, but I imagine he was lonely much of the time. I mean, who could truly understand what his life was like? The gospel writers often report that Jesus went off by himself to pray. He needed to talk to God, the only one who knew him completely, because he was among people who knew him not at all. Even the people who we know were Jesus' closest friends somehow failed him in the end. It's very poignant when he asks his disciples to keep watch while he prays in Gethsemane. The man was facing his own death and his friends couldn't be bothered to stay awake and worry for him.

St. Augustine said there is a God-shaped hole inside all of us. Nothing else will fill it. The thing is that we *will* sometimes be lonely in this life; maturity means accepting that and allowing ourselves to feel the pain of it when it arrives. Trying to stave it off never works and cuts us off from ourselves, our loved ones, and God.

There will be a time when we are lonely no more. I think that will be one of the best things about heaven. But in the meantime, we are called to accept this unhappy aspect of fallen human existence and to talk about it not only with each other, but with Jesus, who understands because he went through it.

*Turn to me and be gracious to me, for I am lonely
and afflicted. (Psalm 25:16)*

MARCH 8
Guilt

I once thought guilt was the one thing about being human that Jesus didn't share with us. He never sinned, so he never had anything to be guilty about.

But there are two kinds of guilt: appropriate and inappropriate. The first, appropriate guilt, comes on us when we do something we know is wrong. Our conscience tells us it's wrong, and quite often there are negative consequences that follow. Jesus never felt that kind of guilt.

But then there's inappropriate guilt. It dogs folks who've been taught certain things are wrong when they're not. It's not wrong, for instance, to love someone of another race. But if you were raised by prejudiced people, you may well feel guilt when that happens. Jesus was taught by the smartest religious authorities of his time. They told him some things were wrong that he later taught were not, like healing on the Sabbath or eating with sinners. His public ministry challenged the accepted religious wisdom of his time, and we live freer lives because he did. But it's difficult to imagine that the first time Jesus broke those "rules," he didn't feel some guilt, even though it was most definitely inappropriate guilt.

The most important thing about guilt is to suffer it for the right things. Figuring out what those things are takes a lifetime, and the only one who ever got it all right was Jesus.

> *Everyone who commits sin is guilty of lawlessness.*
> *(1 John 3:4)*

MARCH 9
The Crucifix

One of the odd differences between Catholics and Protestants is that Catholics have the crucifix as their central symbol, while Protestants use the cross—a crucifix without the body of Jesus on it. I suppose much hay could be made of the theological implications of this choice, but that's best left for another day.

Whichever symbol we choose, by doing so we align ourselves with a person who died a shameful, horrible, ugly death. It's hard to know what those first Christians who venerated a cross were feeling. A friend finally got it across to me this way: wearing a crucifix around our necks is much akin to wearing a silver or gold representation of a man in an electric chair. That idea probably sounds tasteless. And it is—it's horrible. But when Christians adopted the crucifix, that's more or less the equivalent of what they were doing.

It's one of those ironies typical of God, though. No matter what the instrument of death had been—cross, hangman's noose, electric chair, firing squad—God would have changed its meaning entirely by raising Jesus from the dead. The symbol of death then becomes not tasteless but something that evokes God's tremendous power, our thankfulness for the resurrection, and yes—our sorrow for the death of the Son of God.

Those who passed by derided him. (Mark 15:29)

MARCH 10
Illness

One of the tired old stereotypes in our culture is that while women are sick more often than men (evidence of our "weakness"), when men finally *do* become ill, they turn into babies. "Honey, can you get me some soup? Honey, could you bring me the phone? Honey, could you hold the tissue for me while I blow my nose?"

There's a nugget of truth in that stereotype, although it applies equally to women and men. Sooner or later, we all get sick, and it can be really scary. We like to think we have control over our bodies. Evidence? The multi-billion dollar diet industry, plastic surgery, and pumping iron. But when we get sick, all that illusion is stripped away. We realize, at a deep and difficult level, that we are not only *not* in control of our bodies, but that we are in fact quite fragile in many ways. We want to believe everything's under control, but getting sick gives us a peek at the chaos that stirs just beneath the surface of our lives.

The good news is that someone *is* in control—God. It is through God's minute-to-minute action in our lives that we continue to live and breathe. Our lives and health are in the hands of God, not in our own. Accepting that fact can bring with it remarkable freedom. We don't have to be God. That's quite a load off.

Our American culture tells us that if we live right, eat right, exercise right, and meditate/pray/whatever right, we won't get sick. Unfortunately, that's not the case. Everyone gets sick, and the last thing a sick person needs is to feel responsible for her illness.

The prayer of faith will save the sick. (James 5:15)

MARCH 11
Chronic Illness and Disability

If a cold gives us just a glimpse of the chaos under what we think is the firm footing of our world, then a chronic illness rips off the cover and shoves our faces into the reality of our vulnerability. There's a reason so many saints recount serious illness in their lives; chronic illness can be a masterful teacher of the soul.

One of the wisest people I know is a woman named Martha Glennan. Martha was a superior athlete when she was diagnosed with a degenerative bone disease that eventually put her in a wheelchair and robbed her of the use of both legs and most of both arms. Martha understands the best way to relate to God during bad times is honesty. She yells at God when she's angry at a setback in her illness. Martha also thanks God daily for things most of us don't give a second thought: the ability to write, mobility enough to get out of the house and into the sun, and the love of a caring church community.

Long illness or disability can be a time for sudden revelations, like the one given to St. Ignatius. While healing from a battle injury, he discovered God meant him not to be a soldier but a priest. Disability and illness can also teach less dramatic lessons over the long haul. Most of them have to do with an attitude of gratefulness and a deep knowledge that we breathe our next breath only because of God's continuing power of love.

"Which is easier, to say to the paralytic, 'Your sins are forgiven,' or to say, 'Stand up and take your mat and walk'?" (Mark 2:9)

MARCH 12
The Zen of Meetings

Wait—wasn't there an earlier meditation on meetings? I can explain. I truly believe meetings can be a rich source of Christian spirituality. We are made in the image of God. Despite what theologians and biblical scholars say, nobody really knows exactly what that means. But you have to admit it's a great pedigree.

Unfortunately, when I'm in a meeting, I tend to focus on the other side of human nature: sinfulness. Getting stuck in a meeting can make me crabby and prone to remember first and foremost the things I most dislike about every other person in the room.

There's another way to do meetings. I work to develop in myself the discipline of seeing the image of God in the other people in the room. I'll choose someone who's sitting fairly close, and begin by examining his or her face with many small glances.

(Clearly this exercise must be done discreetly, or your subject will start feeling paranoid. So no staring.) In my examination I note every enlarged pore, every mole, every wrinkle. Of course I also notice beautiful eyes and plump lips. I pay attention to the shape of the face, the way the jaw line moves from the ear to the chin. I get a good look at the hair and can usually tell if it's been colored, permed, implanted, or glued on. I also go over what I know about the person's life: married, single and happy about it, single and depressed, whether there are children, and on and on.

Then I remind myself that looking at this person, really *seeing* him or her, necessarily tells me something about God. Even if the person I'm examining is the one in the room I like the least, I absolutely must admit there's something about God to be learned there because this man or woman is made in God's image. If the person's a friend, that's pretty easy to believe; seeing Heather tells me that God is warm and compassionate. If it's an enemy, it's harder. But there's got to be *something* there, because even the folks we like the least have the same maker we do.

> *Then God said, "Let us make humankind in our image, according to our likeness." (Genesis 1:26)*

MARCH 13
Terminal Illness

I am terminally ill. I have metastatic breast cancer, and it is *always* fatal. Nobody ever recovers, and there is no cure. On the other hand, I was pronounced "terminal" in 1995, and I'm still here. My doctor found a combination of drugs that doesn't get rid of the cancer, but keeps it from growing. I have a respite between the diagnosis of a terminal illness and the end stages of the dying process; nobody knows how long that respite will last.

Since my diagnosis, I have received my Ph.D., pastored a church, taught part-time in pastoral care and anthropology, co-written a book, and most important, watched my nieces and nephew grow. People often ask me how I can go on doing these ordinary things when I know I'm going to die soon.

My answer is always the same: What's the alternative? I realized not long after my first cancer diagnosis, even before I found out I was terminal, that the alternative to living my life was sitting around doing nothing, waiting to die. The major problem with that approach is that it's boring.

But I must admit there *are* differences in my life pre- and post-diagnosis. I think about death every single day. I relish each new season with the knowledge that it might be my last. It's easier to love people and easier to forgive them. All this happens because of my constant awareness that death might be just around the corner; in comparison to death, for instance, what's a squabble with someone?

Living this way doesn't make me a hero or saint. What it *does* do is demand that I throw myself completely on the mercy of God. Each day I get out of bed is gravy, a miraculous gift that I cannot explain except that for some reason, God loves me and wants me here on this earth for the moment.

What too many people miss is the fact that we are *all* terminally ill. I don't mean that flippantly; I mean that while I will probably die from cancer six months or two years from now, it's also possible that I could get killed in a car wreck today or a tornado tomorrow. Each of us faces death and it is the extent to which we accept the reality of our own mortality that determines how much of the humdrum is stripped away from our everyday world. If we all believed, every morning, that we were to die that night, I think we would live our days quite differently.

But of course we're afraid of death. We'd be fools not to be. The unknown is always scary, and none of us looks forward to the process of becoming dead. That fear makes many of us deny our mortality. The paradox is that it is precisely *because* life is so short that it is so sweet.

My heart is in anguish within me, the terrors of death
have fallen upon me. (Psalm 55:4)

MARCH 14
Death

There is a theological movement afoot these days that wants to make death a "natural" part of life. Sallie McFague, a well-known theologian, is one of those people. Friends tell me that in class she said, "It's enough for me to know that my body will be returned to the earth and provide food for worms."

I can't get there. I really consider myself to be eco-friendly, but I don't want the worms to have my body. I'm on the side of all the church fathers and mothers who saw death as the ultimate evil, the last, certain proof of our fallenness. I think death is a bad thing, and I don't want it to happen to me.

Woody Allen says, "It's not that I'm afraid to die. I just don't want to be there when it happens." I'm with Woody on this one. And I do believe Jesus would be too. After all, he spent hours in a garden the night before he was going to die, begging God to save him. Jesus Christ, the one perfect human being who ever lived, who was also perfectly God, was afraid to die. God doesn't like death, either. God likes life. Because we are limited and fallen creatures, we all must die. But God likes death so little and loves life so much, that God became a human being and died in order to open a birth canal for all of us to follow. God resurrected Jesus and now, life has the last laugh over death. After earthly death, we have faith that we will have eternal life with God. Life becomes not something with a beginning and an end, but beginning, end, and new beginning. This is the rhythm that guides us into eternity.

Thank God for the new beginning part. But that still doesn't mean we have to like the way we get there.

For the wages of sin is death. (Romans 6:23)

March 15
Grief

It's hard to be a pastor and do funerals. After being in a parish a couple of years, I come to truly love the people in it. When they die, I'm the one who presides at the funeral, reassures everyone that their loved one is alive and with God, and says comforting words at the graveside. And then, I go home and do my own crying.

Everybody grieves. It's a part of living. We're in a strange time right now, when people can live to be twenty or even thirty before they experience the death of someone they love. It didn't used to be that way; death happened all the time, and everyone was familiar with it from first consciousness.

We rejoice in eternal life, yes. We're glad our loved one is with God and now will never again suffer pain or sadness or loneliness. But still, it hurts to lose someone. There's a yawning hole left in our hearts when someone we love dies, and big holes in your heart are bound to hurt. Those holes do heal some, but they never entirely close up. That won't happen until we make the journey to the other side. It hurts to grieve. But it's the price that life exacts for loving.

Jesus began to weep. (John 11:35)

MARCH 16
Abandonment

Being a pastor rips away rose-colored glasses, if you happen to be the sort of person who wears them. It doesn't take long in the parish to see horrible things happen to good people. One of those horrors is abandonment. I can't count the number of times I've been with someone who is bewildered and grief-stricken because a person they trusted walked away.

And to make it worse, abandonment usually happens at the worst times. There's no *good* time to be abandoned, but it's worse when you've just been diagnosed with cancer, discovered you're pregnant, or are trying to live through the limitless pain of a child's death.

Jesus knew what it was like to be abandoned. First Judas, then Peter, then all the rest of them. In his hour of greatest need, Jesus' friends abandoned him. We run-of-the-mill humans are usually luckier than Jesus; most often, we're not abandoned by *everyone.* Most of the time, we can turn to the loved ones who are left to help heal the pain of being abandoned. But there are some folks who walk in the footsteps of Jesus and are left completely alone.

We Christians needn't worry about being completely abandoned because even if things are so bad that we are left hanging on our own figurative crosses, despondent and solitary, we will *always* have company on that cross. Complete abandonment simply doesn't happen anymore.

He came and found them sleeping; and he said to Peter, "Simon, are you asleep? Could you not keep awake one hour?" (Mark 14:37)

MARCH 17
St. Patrick

Much like Christmas and Easter, our American culture has just about overtaken the holy day that remembers Patrick, the saint who converted Ireland to Christianity. Parades, "Kiss me, I'm Irish" buttons, and green beer are fine, but they don't begin to help us understand the greatness of this man.

Patrick evangelized the Irish despite the fact that when he was a teenager, they had captured and enslaved him. After his escape and education in Roman civilization, he went back to Ireland. As an article in *St. Anthony Messenger* reminds us, "no one in 400 years had taken the gospel outside the Roman Empire." Yet Patrick did, and to people he had every right to hate.

The Irish of the fifth century fit anybody's definition of "barbarian": they warred constantly, held slaves, and made human sacrifices. But Patrick took a remarkable step: he combined the barbarians of Ireland with the word and love of God. As a result he started Celtic Christianity.

Before Celtic Christianity, the church's theology had been written entirely by Greek-influenced Romans. While there's nothing wrong with that, the fact that they were all Romans meant that the church had a particular flavor—it was focused very much on the sinfulness of humanity and creation. That theology, written by some of our most beloved church fathers, also scorned women, calling us evil, temptresses, and second-class people.

But Patrick restored balance to the church. Celtic Christianity celebrates creation, recognizes how good it is. Patrick also spoke well of Irish women, calling them strong and courageous. It would take centuries for the church to follow Patrick's view of women, but it did embrace the aspects of Celtic Christianity that made being a Christian a *good* thing, not something that was filled with gloom and doom.

So I wear green on St. Patrick's Day. My name may not sound Celtic, but just one generation back, I'm a Campbell. I drink a green beer or two, and enjoy parades. When I drink my green beer, I raise it in a toast to St. Patrick, the one who did far more than chase the snakes out of Ireland.

This day I call to me: God's strength to direct me,
God's power to sustain me, God's wisdom to guide me.
(St. Patrick)

MARCH 18
Divorce

God meant marriages to be for life. A man and a woman enter into a three-way partnership: wife, husband, and God. When we divorce, we rip apart two people whom God has interwoven to such an extent that it's as if they are one person. Since God was part of that interwoven piece, when it splits apart, we feel as if our ties to the divine are interrupted as well. It feels awful.

Divorce *is* horrible, but it *is not* the end of happiness, and it does not remove us from God's love. Sometimes we human beings, sinners that we are, break promises we've made to God; but God chose to be in a covenant relationship with us: even if we don't keep our side of the bargain, *God still keeps the promises made to us.* That's the new covenant, the new "testament"—the Latin word for covenant.

So when we sin and sin big, it hurts. It hurts for a reason, and we are often only reaping what we have sown. But in a love so big we almost can't imagine it, God continues to love us, to save us, and to put good things into our lives. Divorce is a terrible thing, and given the statistics on failed marriages these days, it could probably be prevented much of the time. But when it does occur, we still have hope.

God sighs, picks up the mess we've made, and fashions it into some new good. Of course, it's always better to keep the vows of marriage; that's where our greatest happiness lies. But even when we don't, God gives us another kind of happiness.

"'For this reason a man shall leave behind his father and mother and be joined to his wife, and the two shall become one flesh.' So they are no longer two, but one flesh." (Mark 10:7-8)

MARCH 19
St. Joseph

I try to put myself into St. Joseph's shoes, and when I do, I am struck by the overwhelming sacrifices he made. He doesn't get much attention in the Bible, so his sacrifices aren't right up front the way Jesus' or Mary's are. Nevertheless, sacrifice he did.

Imagine Joseph as a typical resident of first-century Palestine. He contracted with Mary's parents to marry her and looked forward to a nice long life of bouncing babies on his knees. He probably imagined what it would be like to put his carpentry tools into his son's hands for the first time. He probably assumed one of the many sons he hoped to have would take over the family business. Then, of course, there was the joy of grandchildren. He and Mary weren't likely to be wealthy, but they could have a good life nonetheless.

And then everything blew up in his face. Joseph learned that he was a player in the biggest drama the universe has ever seen. His fiancée was already pregnant, and he was expected to marry her anyway and take care of her and the baby. More than that, Joseph was visited by an angel who explained all this. Quite remarkable.

Remarkable, but not the life he had in mind. To accept his place in this marvelous thing God was doing, Joseph would have to make sacrifices. St. Joseph was one of those men who looks at a situation, quickly figures out the right thing to do, and then does it. Men like that are pretty rare, whether it's the first century or the twenty-first. Joseph did the right thing, even though it meant the end of the life he'd envisioned for himself.

There are many men in our lives who make this quiet kind of sacrifice. I think of my father. He was a drama and music major in college, which he paid for by enlisting in ROTC. By the time he'd graduated and served his obligatory years, there was a baby girl in his life. He figured you couldn't give consistent support to a wife and child as a musician or actor, so he re-upped and spent over twenty years in the Army. He gave up his dreams to do the right thing.

Thank God for men like St. Joseph. Although their sacrifices are quiet and unobtrusive, they change the very fabric of reality.

> *When Joseph awoke from sleep, he did as the angel of the Lord commanded him. (Matthew 1:24a)*

MARCH 20
The Death of Parents

The most unfortunate aspect of human nature is that we sin. Sometimes parents sin, and the results are devastating. Talk to anyone who was emotionally, physically, or sexually abused by a parent. She'll tell you how destructive it was. Children who grow up in this kind of family need a great deal of healing, and I always encourage them to pursue it through activity in their community of faith and through therapy.

But here's another thing about human nature. Our parents are our parents. They may have been terrible people and abused us so badly that we are still healing from it decades later. They may have abandoned us completely. But it seems to be the case that the death of a parent, whether good or bad, greatly loved or vigorously despised, has a huge effect on the children, whether they are young or grown with children of their own.

Having a parent die can be an ambivalent experience. On the one hand, we are freed from the things they did that drove us crazy and sometimes hurt us very badly. But on the other, we are left without whatever good they brought into our lives, and we are left without a parent. It is a terrible thing to be a motherless or fatherless child, even if you're sixty years old. The death of parents simply affects us in ways other deaths never can.

Unfortunately, coming to peace with the death of a bad parent isn't easy; coming to peace with the death of a good parent is devastating. During these times, we need to remember that our God understands what being a parent is like, and Jesus understands what being a child is like. While his father wasn't abusive, you must admit he was quite demanding. Grief is always difficult; when we grieve the death of a parent, we need to seek the shelter of Jesus' arms.

But we do not want you to be uninformed, brothers and sisters, about those who have died, so that you may not grieve as others do who have no hope.
(1 Thessalonians 4:13)

MARCH 21*
Spring Equinox

I love the fact that the spring equinox falls in the middle of Lent. It's the most somber time of the year, but this day reminds me that even in the most horrid events, there is the seed of something beautiful and new.

By now the daffodils and tulips have usually made their appearance, and the trees are starting to bud. The birds that had migrated south start returning. There's an occasional day when it's warm enough to go without a jacket, and the warm sun beating down on a de-coated shoulder is a wonderful feeling. The ground is thawing, and it's time to start thinking about what to plant for the year's garden. Maybe it's time to start some seedlings indoors so they'll be ready for planting right after the last frost. Animals of all varieties are pitching woo, and there will soon be babies all over the place. The human heart seems stirred to love too.

It would be nice if every day of the year was like the spring equinox, so full of promise and good dreams. But life is a combination of the good and the bad. As I said, right now we're in the middle of Lent, mulling over distressing subjects like fear, death, and terrorism. But this is the way God works. Even in Lent, Sundays are feast days. Even in Lent the planet creaks on its axis and turns in such a way that it allows hope to fall from the sky. Life is never all good—not until we reach the kingdom, anyway. But the equinox reminds us that life is never all bad, either.

> *In the light of a king's face there is life, and his favor*
> *is like the clouds that bring the spring rain.*
> *(Proverbs 16:15)*

MARCH 22
Prejudice

I live in the South, and while there are many things I love about it, I groan every time some group goes public to push the Confederate battle flag. No matter how much these folks say it's about "tradition" and not prejudice, it's simply too intertwined with the horrible evil of slavery to separate the two. Flying the Confederate flag as a part of one's "tradition" is much like a non-Jewish German flying the swastika.

The thing to remember is that we are all prejudiced. We were all raised in a culture that told us, implicitly and directly, that some people are inferior. That may be black people, Native Americans, women, Jews, the poor, or just about anyone who's not a wealthy WASP. And it's just about impossible to erase every trace of things we took in along with our mother's milk. We can educate ourselves, yes, and that we should do; we can also condemn prejudice. But if we're honest, we also have to admit we do have our prejudices, no matter how tiny or how deeply buried. Refusing to acknowledge these prejudices only makes us more likely to act on them, which is quite the opposite of what we want.

Jesus, of course, was the least prejudiced person who ever lived. He visited, ate with, and taught even the major "untouchables" of his time, the gentiles. What would Jesus do? The question has become almost trite, but when we are making up our minds about whether something is prejudiced or not, we need to ask it.

Now the woman was a Gentile, of Syrophoenician origin. She begged him to cast the demon out of her daughter. (Mark 7:26)

MARCH 23
Sexual "Others"

It's hard to write about sexuality these days. We are confronted with gay men, lesbians, bisexuals, transsexuals, prostitution. . . . It's only fairly recently that these folks have "come out," and now that they are out, they want to be acknowledged, and if not accepted, then at least tolerated.

I was fortunate in 1999 to be invited to teach one semester of a course entitled "Sexuality: Theology, Ethics, and Pastoral Practice." It was eye-opening. The first half of the semester, we read lots of different theologies of sexuality, and for the mid-term, the students had to write a paper telling me what *their* theology of sexuality was. Given that Vanderbilt's Divinity School is very liberal, I expected that most would say something like, "As long as consenting adults are involved and nobody gets hurt, then it's okay." And I was right; out of thirty students, twenty-five gave me some version of that.

The second half of the semester, we had guest speakers. My intent was to push my students to the edges of their comfort zones. Any theology of sexuality is easy to hold in the classroom, but what happens when theology meets the real world? My first speakers were a lesbian couple. Most of the students found it rather quaint that I would invite them, so settled was this issue for them. The conservative students, on the other hand, found themselves with a theology that condemned homosexuality but also striking evidence that these two women were normal people who had a relationship that was the envy of most married people.

But the liberal students got their turn. I invited "Gary" to come speak to us. He is the publisher of Nashville's sex magazine, the glossy four-color rag that advertises massage parlors and escort services. He was also the manager of one of two swingers' clubs in town. When Gary came to the class, he was obviously ready to have some fun. He wanted to shock the little divinity students. He was arrogant, dismissive, prejudiced, and offensive on almost every level. My poor students, who'd expected an emotional experience much like what they'd had when confronted with the lesbian couple, found themselves in shock. Here was a man who was "moral" according to their theology of sexuality, and yet they loathed him. I had e-mails and phone calls all week long, and so I canceled the next speaker and used the following class period to process the experience of Gary. Everybody who found him creepy had a say. The students needed and got a chance to talk about being with someone so repulsive he had to be experienced to be believed. They needed to voice the shock of learning that their theology of sexuality wasn't sufficient.

And then toward the end of the two-hour class, a student raised his hand. He'd been silent until then. He said, "I have to say I agree with everything everybody has said about Gary. But isn't he just exactly the kind of person Jesus would have hung around?"

Absolute silence followed. And it follows here. What's the answer to that question, and what does that mean for our beliefs about people whose sexuality is different from our own?

And as [Jesus] sat at dinner in the house, many tax collectors and sinners came and were sitting with him and his disciples. (Matthew 9:10)

MARCH 24
Oscar Romero

Oscar Romero is not a saint, not officially, but at the very least he is a prophet, and one whose story can garner respect from even the most jaded atheist. Even people who don't believe in God have to admit that Romero was an amazing man whose courage is extremely rare.

In 1977, Romero was appointed archbishop of El Salvador, a Central American country oppressed by a military government and populated with the poor and persecuted. After his close friend Father Rutillo Grand was assassinated by a paramilitary group for being proactive for the poor, Romero became a vocal advocate for those very same people, rather than trying to "work within the system." From the pulpit, he denounced the evil of state-sanctioned death squads.

In a remarkable move, he refused to participate in any state events until the lot of the oppressed began to change.

Romero was nominated for the Nobel Peace Prize because by his words and actions, he spoke with the voice of Jesus, demanding justice for all people, even the poor. On March 24, 1980, Romero was assassinated as he celebrated the mass.

As a minister, I came to know his story early on. I also heard a detail that may or may not be historically true; in a way it doesn't matter. I heard that Romero had a small, red cross embroidered on his liturgical robes directly over his heart, so the assassin who he knew would eventually come would be able to find the killing spot. Ever since, I have felt called to embroider a similar cross on my own vestments, but I admit with shame that I have not had the courage.

Every person who follows Christ, whether ordained or lay, is called to stand up for justice to the extent that Oscar Romero did. In the United States, it's almost impossible to imagine dying for our faith, but that's the extreme to which we are called by our baptism.

Peace is not the product of terror or fear. Peace is not the silence of cemeteries. Peace is not the silent result of violent repression. Peace is the generous, tranquil contribution of all to the good of all. Peace is dynamism.

Peace is generosity. It is right and it is duty.
(Oscar Romero)

MARCH 25
The Annunciation

Could you say no to an angel? It doesn't seem likely. For one thing, angels are apparently scary. If that weren't the case, they wouldn't have to begin each appearance by saying, "Don't be afraid!" And for another thing, they are carrying a request from God. How can you say no to that package?

But apparently we can. If we read the story of the annunciation closely, we see that Gabriel doesn't zap in, give Mary marching instructions, and zap out. No—he waits. It's not until Mary gives her consent that Gabriel is free to leave.

It's important for us to realize that Mary could have said no. What I mean is that God would have *allowed her* to say no. If that weren't so, then that would mean God was nothing more than a big bully, and Mary an innocent victim.

Once we accept the idea that Mary could have said no to God, then we are given two tremendous gifts that can make our own relationship with God flourish. First, we realize just how brave that young woman had to be. That suggests she might be a very good person to talk to when we're feeling rather frightened by something. And second, we realize that while God has a Plan A for each one of us, and calls us to follow that plan, we are free to say no. If we do, then we aren't discarded; instead, God offers us Plan B. That's a mighty comfort for those who have, at some time in their lives, been pretty certain they've heard God calling but have chosen not to reply. Apparently we get more than one chance.

"Here am I, the servant of the Lord; let it be with me according to your word." (Luke 1:38)

MARCH 26
The Prodigal Son

It was not until seminary that I think I really understood the story of the prodigal son. I studied it in a class on the New Testament, and there, for the first time, paid attention to the context in which it's found. That context gave me new eyes to see what Jesus was trying to say.

This story is one of three Jesus tells in Luke 15, in answer to the Pharisees and scribes who accuse him of welcoming sinners. The first story is that of the shepherd with a hundred sheep: if one gets lost, the shepherd leaves the other ninety-nine and goes after the one. The second is of the woman who has ten silver coins and loses one: she searches carefully until she finds it, and then throws a party to celebrate its discovery. The third story is the prodigal son.

In its context, I realized we should call this the tale of "The Forgiving Father," because in all three stories, the main character—the one who welcomes back the one that's been lost—is a symbol for God. And these stories tell us just how forgiving God can be.

Too many parents of teenagers relate all too well to the story of the prodigal son just on a surface level. Even children raised by good and loving parents can go astray; those parents ache for the lost one until she returns home. That's true even if the lost child is one of ten. And it's true if she's one of a hundred.

While the stories of the prodigal son and the lost coin make sense, the tale of the lost sheep does not. I discovered this by pastoring a rural congregation. No shepherd or cattleman worth his salt will leave ninety-nine animals exposed and in danger to go look for one who is lost. It's a matter of profit and loss. Incredibly impractical. But God doesn't work on the level of profit and loss. For God, every single sinner on earth is equally dear. God will go to extraordinary lengths to bring back to the fold the one who has left the path—even to the extreme of forgiving what many human parents might not be able to forgive.

*"Just so, I tell you, there will be more joy in heaven
over one sinner who repents than over ninety-nine
righteous persons who need no repentance."*
(Luke 15:7)

MARCH 27
Feminists

The time has come to show my age. When I teach
college students who could easily be my children, I
take a day early in the semester for everybody to get
to know each other. Pretty standard stuff: go around
the room, tell us your name, where you're from, what
your major is, why you're taking this class, and what
you hope to do after college. The ones I feel the worst
for are the Women's Studies majors. When they are
speaking, I invariably hear the word whispered:
"Feminist!"

This breaks my heart. I was calling myself a feminist by the time I was sixteen. But it's become a dirty
word these days—a code for a woman who's angry,
ugly, and probably lesbian. The Reverend Pat
Robertson gave us this: "The feminist agenda is not
about equal rights for women. It is about a socialist,
anti-family political movement that encourages

women to leave their husbands, kill their children, practice witchcraft, destroy capitalism and become lesbians."

That's an odd thing for him to say, because Mr. Robertson says he follows the same Lord we do. Only, Jesus didn't think that about women. He honored them greatly. He chose one, Mary, to be the vehicle for becoming a human being, to be his mother. He chose Mary and Martha of Bethany as trusted friends. He chose Mary Magdalene as a close friend and follower; according to the gospels she is the one to whom he first appeared following his resurrection.

There are disagreements today over what a woman is supposed to be. But certainly by now one thing is settled: women are equal co-heirs of God's kingdom, sisters of Jesus Christ, and cherished children of God.

For she is a reflection of eternal light, a spotless mirror of the working of God, and an image of his goodness.
(Wisdom 7:26)

March 28
Unexplainable Horrors

We Americans are lucky to exist in a place and time that means it's normal to live to a ripe old age.

Unlike human beings who lived before the Industrial Revolution and modern medicine, and unlike people today who live without the benefit of these advances, we hope and plan to die only when we've lived seventy, eighty, even ninety years. And the wonderful thing is that many of us get our wish.

But every now and again, the fallen world rears its ugly head. I was a bystander at one of those events when the boyfriend of one of my students died in a hunting accident.

"Joe," twenty-five, was a country boy, and loved many things; two of those were his girlfriend and hunting. One weekend he left the first—for just a short time, he promised—to pursue the second. He and a friend took their bows into the woods and waited for deer to appear near their blinds.

Just as dusk was about to blend into darkness, Joe climbed down from his blind and made his way over to the tree where his friend was. Because in Tennessee bow hunters are not required to wear blaze orange, Joe's childhood friend mistook him for a deer and shot him in the chest. Joe died in minutes; even if he'd been in the middle of town, his wound was so severe an ambulance could not have arrived in time to save him.

I've learned a hard lesson through my years as a pastor: there are times when I must simply say that I don't know the mind of God. There is no way I can

explain why deaths like these occur. It's not a very sat-
isfying answer for grieving people who beg to know
"why?" but it's the best I can do.

I am certain of several things. One, the God we
worship detests death; I know that because of the resurrection, which means the ultimate end of death.
Two, this same God is all good and all-powerful; I
know this because it is simply the nature of God.
Three, on the other side of this life, we'll understand
these mysteries. And four: none of these facts makes
it okay for a young man to die from a misdirected
arrow.

*Why do the wicked live on, reach old age, and grow
mighty in power? (Job 21:7)*

MARCH 29
Natural Disasters

I have a gripe against insurance companies. In
their contracts they speak of natural terrors like earthquakes, floods, tornadoes, and hurricanes as "acts of
God." They are wrong.

All these things *are*, indeed, natural—they are a
part of the ecosystem of the planet on which we live.
All these things are also disasters. But natural disasters

are *not* acts of God. Neither are they a part of God's intent for creation.

Let me put it another way: when God created the universe, there was no such thing as natural disasters. When human beings fell from grace, creation fell with us. While we can't and shouldn't take upon our own shoulders the fault for, say, the recent tornado that killed a family of five, we also need to refrain from putting this responsibility in God's lap. As my spiritual director used to say, "That's not a very nice thing to say about God."

While it's a theme not traditionally emphasized in the western church, scripture and tradition tell us that in the end, when the kingdom of God arrives, not only will people be redeemed, but so will creation. I don't really know what the redemption of creation will look like, but I know it's in God's plan. In the kingdom, there will be no natural disasters and no carnivores. No living thing will suffer—not even the earth.

The wolf shall live with the lamb, the leopard shall lie down with the kid, the calf and the lion and the fatling together, and a little child shall lead them.
(Isaiah 11:6)

MARCH 30
Terrorism

Terrorism, which includes everything from assassination to crashing airplanes into skyscrapers, is evil. I imagine that's a no-brainer for most Christians.

But I think of Dietrich Bonhoeffer, the Protestant German theologian who was imprisoned and executed for planning to assassinate Hitler. If I am honest, I have to say that even though I know his plan was sinful, I think it's unfortunate he did not succeed. The odd thing is that Bonhoeffer, who wrote the stirring book *The Cost of Discipleship,* knew his plan was sinful. I give the man a great deal of credit for refusing to rationalize his own sin; instead, he went ahead, knowing the cost to his relationship with God.

The problem with terrorism, whatever its form, is that it puts us in the place of God, deciding who deserves to live and die. That may seem to contradict my belief that there is such a thing as a just war. But there's a difference between a just war and "just" terrorism. The first is decided to be just by a great many people; the second by only a few. I'm not saying a whole nation or the church can't err in its evaluation of particular instances of planned violence; history shows otherwise. But it's less likely, I think, for the church as a whole, a country as a whole, or the world as a whole to decide poorly than it is for a small group of people or even one individual to do so. As much as I ache over dissension in the church, I also rejoice in it because I know it keeps us from becoming too certain about what's right in each and every situation.

So although terrorism is not a just way to end evil, I wonder if in Bonhoeffer's place I would have made the same decision. Or what if I'd had the chance to assassinate Osama bin Laden long before September 11, 2001?

> *Being evil is worse than doing evil.*
> *(Dietrich Bonhoeffer)*

MARCH 31
The Death of a Child

Every human life includes suffering, but there are some people who get more than their share. During my years as a pastor, I have come to believe that the worst thing that can happen to a human being is the death of a child.

All the psychological evidence backs up my impressionistic belief. Study after study shows that while there are a few couples who are brought closer by the death of a child, most end up getting divorced; the tragedy destroys everything in its path. The other children in the family are damaged by the death, and so is the child's community. The devastation of a child's death is so great that I always press parents to seek out the group Compassionate Friends. No one but people who've had the experience can truly understand what it's like to lose a child to death.

That's why it makes sense to me that God chose to redeem us through the death of a child. God knew that this was the most devastating thing that could possibly happen to a human being, and so chose to join us in suffering the worst. Probably nothing else would have sufficed; after the death of God's son on the cross, no one can turn to the master of the universe and say, "You don't understand my grief. You can't understand how much this hurts. If you knew, you could never allow it to happen." God knows. The resurrection is such a powerful, remarkable thing precisely because it arises out of God's understanding that the depth of human suffering could be redeemed by nothing less.

[Hagar] said, "Do not let me look on the death of the child." And as she sat opposite him, she lifted up her voice and wept. (Genesis 21:16)

April 1
April Fool's Day

It's good to have a day set aside just for laughing. I know I don't do it nearly enough. A half hour of solid laughing can keep me going for several days. I'm sure scientists have done studies that show laughing causes us to produce hormone ABC that "elevates mood." Whatever. It's just good to laugh.

I'm not very good at practical jokes but had an inspiration in seminary. In New Testament class, my professor and now friend Sharyn Dowd was helping us to understand the difficult passage in First Corinthians when Paul says women have to pray with their heads covered. These instructions, she taught us, had nothing to do with men being superior to their wives. Instead, it was a matter of propriety, a custom of the culture at the time—and therefore an instruction limited to that time. She said, "It would be as if I were to go preach in a bikini. It just wouldn't be proper."

My friends and I cut out a picture of a curvaceous woman in a bikini from a women's magazine and used the photocopier to enlarge Sharyn's headshot from the faculty directory. We put her head on top of the model's body, wrote "Sharyn Dowd prepares to preach" at the bottom, and put it in her campus mailbox—anonymously.

The next day, the picture was back in *my* campus mailbox. I rushed it to my co-conspirators' lunch table. "You forgot the most important thing," it said on a sticky-note, and sure enough, taped under the model's arm was a photocopy of a bible.

I'll bet Jesus was laughing right along with us.

Any woman who prays or prophesies with her head unveiled disgraces her head. (1 Corinthians 11:5a)

APRIL 2
War

I want to be a pacifist. I want *desperately* to be a pacifist, and I admire tremendously the brave people who are. But I can't be a pacifist when I think of World War II and Hitler's systematic extermination of God's chosen people. I believe it was right for Americans to go fight in that war.

The theology of the church includes the concept of a "just war," and there's a list of criteria that make a war just. Of course, even people who aren't pacifists can disagree about whether a particular war is just.

War is something I simply have to give up trying to explain. There's scriptural and traditional evidence that God is a pacifist, but there's also the same kind of evidence that God sometimes advocates war. All we faithful people can do, I think, is to study hard everything we can about the theology of war, listen carefully to the church's teachings, pray a lot, follow our consciences, and know that sometimes it's impossible to know the right thing to do.

> *There is a time for war, and a time for peace.*
> *(Ecclesiastes 3:8)*

APRIL 3
The Happy Man

There's a man in Nashville known as "the happy man." To be blunt, he's homeless and he's crazy. For some reason, though, whatever makes most mentally ill people miserable has made the happy man just the opposite.

I see the happy man every couple of weeks, in different parts of town. He'll stand on a busy street corner or, if there's a median, in the very middle of an intersection, and call out happy, joyous praise and exultation. He raises his arms in the air to reach for God when he's not using them to wave to people who drive by. And to credit my fellow Nashvillians, they usually wave back.

Unfortunately, most homeless people aren't as enchanting as the happy man. As I said, they're often mentally ill and that's usually very painful. They may have been living on the streets since they were turned out of mental hospitals in the '70s when the government decided it was abusing someone's civil rights to keep them institutionalized, medicated, fed, and warm against their will. Or they may be folks who've fallen on hard times; the unfortunate thing about that fall is that once you lose your balance, it's hard to get back up again. It's all too rare that someone moves from homelessness to having a home again.

Whatever else we want to say about these homeless men and women, we must first say that they are brothers and sisters of Christ. They are God's beloveds, just as we are. They are made in the image of God, as are we, and if we can't see that image, then we need to get our spiritual eyesight checked.

"Foxes have holes, and birds of the air have nests; but the Son of Man has nowhere to lay his head."
(Matthew 8:20)

April 4
Pilgrimages

For a long time I didn't "get" pilgrimages. I didn't understand how it could help a person's relationship with God to go on a trip. Even if the destination *was* famous or holy, like Israel, wasn't this just a matter of being a tourist?

That was until Tony Dunnavant died and I couldn't go to his funeral. Tony was my mentor in seminary. He was the church history professor, and until my second year in graduate school, I thought I wanted to be a church history professor too. I was Tony's research assistant and student. After seminary, we became friends; he was very pleased when I went to graduate school at his own alma mater.

Christianity celebrates humanity and the individuality of each person because Jesus lowered himself to become one of us. We simply cannot say that material things aren't important, because God became material. We cannot say places aren't important, because God walked on a very specific area of the earth. It is important, somehow, to honor the specificity of our faith by taking the trouble to go to a particular place, with an attitude of mindfulness.

I couldn't make the trip to Lexington on the day of Tony's funeral, but I did it later. I left some flowers on his grave and a trinket he'd once given me.

Going to that particular spot was important. Now I get it.

These all died in faith, not having received the promis-es, but having seen them afar off, and were persuaded of them, and embraced them, and confessed that they were strangers and pilgrims on the earth.
(Hebrews 11:13, KJV)

APRIL 5
The Dentist

I don't know anyone who actually *likes* going to the dentist. There are people who don't mind it very much, but I've never heard anyone say, "Gee, ya know, I haven't been to the dentist in a while and I really miss it." Even if you get laughing gas when you're there, a dentist's visit is *at best* something to get through.

Given how much I hate the dentist's office, I find it remarkable that I go back again and again. It's the responsible, adult thing to do of course. But I think the important aspect of it all is that I put my trust in my dentist. I open up my mouth, where some of the most sensitive nerves in my body dwell, and expect this person to be careful and gentle.

I don't want to say that life is the equivalent of a dentist's appointment—there's too much joy in it for that! But as much as we must trust our dentists, we are called to trust God more. Fact is, there are places in our souls that are a lot more vulnerable than a tooth's nerve, and partly because the possibility of pain in those places is so frightening, we rarely expose them to others or even to ourselves. But God is one in whom we can put our trust. God will be gentle and careful. God knows pain is part of life, but doesn't want to add to it. In fact, God wants to make it better.

My mouth is filled with your praise, and with your glory all day long. (Psalm 71:8)

APRIL 6
Drugs

I hope with all my heart that no one who reads this will ever need to take strong pain-killing drugs. I'm not talking about illegal drugs, but about those given by doctors to provide relief from horrible physical pain.

I wish all human beings could get through life without ever experiencing so much physical pain that they need pain medication. But the sad fact is that things happen in this fallen creation of ours: surgery, accidents, abscessed teeth, kidney stones, childbirth. Thanks be to God those drugs are available when we have to endure that kind of pain.

So I have to ask myself why it is that God doesn't protect us from pain in the first place. I've heard all the lectures about how pain is a warning signal from our bodies to our minds. But there are too many situations in which the message has been delivered and the pain continues long past reason.

I don't have the answer to this one. I do know a few things. I know we experience pain because we and the rest of creation are fallen from the perfection in which God created us. I know someday I'll understand the reason God allows pain, but I also know I won't understand in this lifetime.

I know one, final thing, and this is the most important. I know that God knows what pain is like— both physical and emotional—because Jesus of Nazareth suffered. And somehow God took pain and power and out of them made something that hadn't existed before: resurrection.

So you have pain now; but I will see you again, and your hearts will rejoice, and no one will take your joy from you. (John 16:22)

APRIL 7
Disappointment

Way back in 1987, I embarked on a path that would allow me to become a professor in a seminary or divinity school. I walked down that path because God called me to it. So it took me a while to figure out that while I *was* able to get a Master of Divinity and a Ph.D., I *wasn't* going to be a professor. I went to lots of interviews, but I didn't get a job. All too many of my talented, brilliant friends are in the same situation—all dressed up with hope and nowhere to go.

I know Jesus experienced disappointment. He must have. His closest followers abandoned him in the time of his greatest need. All the people who'd welcomed him to Jerusalem on what we know as Palm Sunday were the same ones who called for Barabbas' release instead of his.

But God works wonders with disappointment. Those cowardly disciples became apostles who gave their lives to preaching the gospel and died martyrs' deaths. Those turncoats were forgiven their sins and became part of the kingdom. I know God will redeem my disappointment and that of my friends. Each and every one of us suffers disappointments, from small ones like a rainy day when we'd hoped to picnic, to big ones like the loss of a dream. Even if we faithfully follow God's call, we'll still have disappointments. Again, Jesus did.

Disappointment is hard, no matter how spiritually mature we may be. And mystery is hard too. Like pain, disappointments often don't make sense. But we can take heart and know that God doesn't waste anything. If we follow God's path, then even our disappointments will be transformed. Into what, I don't know. But Jesus does.

Hope does not disappoint us, because God's love has been poured into our hearts through the Holy Spirit that has been given to us. (Romans 5:5)

APRIL 8
Near Misses

Most people have had brushes with death. Some of those are quite dramatic, as when someone's heart stops beating but is then again started; they are, quite literally, brought back from the dead. Then some of those brushes are pretty trivial, like fender-benders.

I've been in three car accidents in my life. I wasn't seriously injured in any of them. But after each and every one, when I climbed out of the car, I found that I was shaking. I could not stop trembling. A part of me was angry at the other driver for causing the accident, but a part of me was scared—scared of death.

I think that trembling is a good sign. It's the right response to the possibility of dying. I often fool myself and others into thinking that I don't fear death. Partly because I am a faithful person, I know that paradise lies on the other side of death—and who doesn't want to go to paradise? But no matter what I think or feel, apparently a part of me doesn't want to die. It might be the animal part of me, the part that houses the pure instinct to survive.

That's a good thing, though. While we look forward with hope to the kingdom, we are also meant to live as long as God gives us. Life is a precious gift, and it's all too easy to take it for granted. God wants us to be as alive as all the other living creatures on earth, sucking the marrow out of each and every day, loving the experiences that only this short mortal life can bring.

So maybe near misses aren't such a bad thing. If we've been sleepwalking through life, or rushing through it without notice, a near miss can be a wonderful reminder of what it's really all about.

Desire without knowledge is not good, and one who moves too hurriedly misses the way. (Proverbs 19:2)

APRIL 9*
Palm Sunday

When I was in seminary, one of the local rabbis came in and taught a summer school course on contemporary Judaism. It was a strange experience in many ways. We found it incredible that he'd never read the New Testament, and he found it inexplicable that almost everyone who attends Christian worship services actually believes in God. I learned some very important things during that class, but perhaps the most important was this: Most of the Jews didn't believe Jesus was the messiah because the messiah was expected to be a military leader who would drive out the Romans and then reign on earth. They had good reason to believe this—it was in their scripture *and* tradition.

The fact is that Jesus *was* the messiah and *was* a king, but the reality didn't match the expectations. The people in the crowd that welcomed Jesus into Jerusalem put their clothes on the ground, waved palms, and sang "Hosanna." They were expecting a big man, perhaps in armor, riding into the city on a beautiful horse befitting a king. Instead, the person who accepted this royal welcome was an ordinary-looking man who rode, for heaven's sake, on a *donkey*. What kind of a king would ride on a donkey?

Our kind of king, that's who. Our king came to us in weakness, not in strength. He wasn't wealthy, powerful, or invincible. And that was just exactly the point. The entrance into Jerusalem has several layers of meaning. On the surface, there's Jesus on a donkey. Right underneath was the crowd's expectations that would not be fulfilled. But underneath all that was a kind of power and might they couldn't even have imagined. An earthly throne and a lifetime of peace wasn't enough. Instead, through his very vulnerability and powerlessness, Jesus ushered in a kingdom that has no end, a kingdom that's eternal.

"My grace is sufficient for you, for power is made perfect in weakness." (2 Corinthians 12:9)

APRIL 10*
Monday in Holy Week

One of my favorite Shakespearean plays is *King Lear*. King Lear is elderly and a little foolish, but he's basically a good man. His foolishness leads to his earthly downfall but eventual spiritual triumph. In the center of the play Lear, out of his mind with grief over the loss of everything important to him, stumbles out onto the heath and sees the lights burning in the tiny little houses near him. He realizes for the first time that there are hundreds, even thousands of houses just like these in his kingdom. "O, I have ta'en too little care of this," he moans. Lear's redemption comes through the realization that he is human like all others, and that the lowliest human being has at least as much value as he does.

As I said, a tragedy—the classical definition of which is the story of a great man who is brought down by his own flaw. It's an old, old story, one that's been repeated in theater, story, and song pretty much since the beginning of civilization.

But then comes the tragedy of a man named Jesus. He wasn't really a "great" man—not in terms of earthly power, anyway. Certainly he was great in the ways that counted. And he didn't have a flaw; he was without sin. Nonetheless, he was brought down, sentenced to death for sedition, hung on a cross to die, abandoned by his followers, and ridiculed by those who passed by.

To contemplate Jesus on the cross is to open ourselves to the reality of his suffering. If we really allow our protective layers to fall away, we can begin to feel just a bit of what it must have been like for him. We all have suffered, so we can have empathy for him.

But in this instance, God turns tragedy on its head. The lowly man is lifted high—first by the cross and then by resurrection—and the flaws of all human beings, high and low, are forgiven. King Lear's plight can move us deeply, but it is indeed a tragedy. At the end of the play he dies of a broken heart. In Jesus, God did something new, and tragedy has never been the same since.

After mocking him, they stripped him of the robe and put his own clothes on him. Then they led him away to crucify him. (Matthew 27:31)

APRIL 11*
Tuesday in Holy Week

"Father, forgive them. They don't know what they're doing." Jesus spoke these words from the cross, asking God to pardon the very men who were putting the nails through his body.

Forgiveness is a difficult issue for me. When somebody hurts me, my immediate reaction is to strike back, to make them hurt too. Sometimes somebody hurts me so badly I want revenge. There are some things that simply can't be forgiven—or so I tell myself.

Timothy McVeigh coldly calculated the human lives he would end in order to make his point when he detonated the bomb in Oklahoma City. He remained without remorse to the very end. He had killed 168 people, scarred the lives of countless others, broken the heart of a city, and grieved an entire nation. Yet he had no remorse. No surprise, then, that some victims' families put their names in the lottery for seats to watch his execution. It was quite a surprise, though, that a small group of victims' families adamantly opposed McVeigh's execution and worked against it.

It's hard to know what makes the difference between people who can forgive and those who can't. It certainly isn't the degree of the hurt; the evil in McVeigh spread plenty of hurt among those families. I won't say it's spiritual maturity, because that would be a slap in the face to those who have been hurt so badly they can't find forgiveness in themselves no matter how much therapy they get or how much they pray.

I do think forgiveness is a gift of the Holy Spirit. We can cultivate it, of course. We can prepare the ground for it, and ponder the fact that Jesus forgave the men who executed him. We can *want* to forgive, even if we can't get to forgiveness itself. It's like the man who said to Jesus, "I believe, Lord, help my unbelief." Clearly Jesus is the expert on forgiveness, and whether we think we can get there or not, he's the one we'd do best to discuss it with.

Then Jesus said, "Father, forgive them; for they do not know what they are doing." (Luke 23:34)

April 12*
Wednesday in Holy Week

I cannot forget Mary during Holy Week. She doesn't get much Biblical attention in the events surrounding Jesus' last days; John has her at the foot of the cross with the beloved disciple and that's pretty much it. Tradition tells us more, of course, especially in the Stations of the Cross. It's during Holy Week that Mary comes most alive for me. I try to put myself in her place.

What had she thought when Jesus started his ministry? Knowing what Herod's response had been at his birth, she had to be afraid for him. And all her fears were realized, of course, when she looked up at that cross and saw her son hanging there.

Don't you imagine Mary had some very angry conversations with God? I can imagine her pacing around the house, calling for Gabriel to show his face so she could force him to go rescue her son. "You watched over him as a baby. But now, when he really needs you, you won't come?"

How much pain can one woman feel? But I don't think Mary felt one woman's pain. Her son was God; she was the mother of God who had become human, and so in some sense she was the mother of all humans. I think Mary carried inside of her the pain of all women in all times and all places, women from different cultures and faiths, who all knew the indescribable horror of the worst thing imaginable: the death of a child. I don't know how her body or mind stood it. I don't know how she kept from going crazy.

There are some anguishes that only women feel. It hurts both men and women when they can't conceive, for example, but they hurt in different ways. And it's in these hurting-woman times that I turn to Mary for strength, guidance, and understanding. She, of all people, knows the dark side of being a woman.

When Jesus saw his mother and the disciple whom he loved standing beside her, he said to his mother, "Woman, here is your son." (John 19:26)

April 13*
Holy Thursday

This is perhaps the day of the year I am most happy to be a pastor. During worship on this day, I have the honor of standing in the place of Jesus, of walking in his footsteps.

Before I was a pastor, I understood Peter's reluctance to allow Jesus to wash his feet: "Good heavens! You're God! You'll not do such a grubby thing, not if I have anything to say about it!" But now I understand something of what Jesus was going through that night too. In a darkened church I carry a bowl of water and a towel to the first pew, and anyone who is willing comes to the front, sits, and allows me to wash his or her feet.

It is an unaccountably intimate thing to wash someone's feet. I take the foot of someone I know, someone with whom I have in the last year celebrated, grieved, argued, and worshiped, and over it I pour warm water. I see this person's corns and blisters and ingrown toenails, and I am struck dumb. I am overwhelmed by this person's fragility and the depth of the love I feel for them. During the rest of the year I stand in the pulpit and preach God's word to them; I say the words of institution over the elements and feed them the body and blood of Christ. These are privileges that no human being is worthy of. No human, of course, except Jesus. And I marvel at the fact that he exceeds me even in humility. I am just a pastor washing the feet of my parishioners; he was God washing the feet of those who worshiped him.

That night in the upper room, Jesus made it clear how far he was willing to go for those he loved. He would take on the most menial task for them. He would continue to love them despite their faults. He would give his very body and blood so that they could have eternal life.

He poured water into a basin and began to wash the disciples' feet and to wipe them with the towel that was tied around him. (John 13:5)

APRIL 14*
Good Friday

I am so very glad that I was taught the New Testament by a Baptist. They take the scriptures very seriously and so squeeze out of them every possible drop of meaning. There are a hundred things going on during the hours of Good Friday, but one we are usually sheltered from is just what exactly was happening to the body of Jesus. We are embodied creatures. It is the incarnation that is at the center of our faith. And yet too rarely are we given the details of what was going on in that precious body. I know the reason—the details are gruesome. But the better we understand what Jesus endured for us, the better we are able to worship him with gratitude.

First of all, Jesus was crucified naked. It is the modesty of church artists over the last two thousand years that has put a cloth over his genitals. Nakedness was part of the punishment, though.

Crucifixion is a slow, agonizing death. It isn't the nails that get you in the end—those just provide pain and the agony of flies buzzing at the wounds. What kills you is suffocation. If a human being is hung by his hands, breathing becomes harder and harder. But this doesn't happen all at once; it usually takes days for death to come. The crucified man can struggle to a more upright position every once in a while, but he is holding all his weight with his arms. Before long they give out and he must hang again. He can perform this breath-giving pull-up just often enough that he doesn't lose consciousness. People on crosses don't pass out or go into a coma before they die; they are aware of the agony to the very last moment.

There is no shelter from the elements, so if the sun is out, the condemned man burns, and if it storms he is pelted with rain. Because of the time they spent on the crosses and because of the physical rigors their bodies experienced, those who were crucified lost control of their bladders and bowels. They soiled themselves and had to endure that humiliation as well.

Crucifixion was a cruel punishment. It was bad enough to be given a death sentence, but with crucifixion there was no quick beheading or blood-draining knife. Crucifixion went on and on and on.

This is what God went through for us. It's an old saw, but it's true nonetheless. Each time we commit a sin, we drive the nails through our Lord's flesh and into the cross. Were it not for our sin, he would not have been there. As the hymn says, "mine, mine was the transgression, but thine the deadly pain." I am struck each and every Good Friday by the same thought: I don't deserve what Jesus did for me. But then, that's exactly the point, isn't it?

> *What language shall I borrow to thank thee, dearest friend, for this thy dying sorrow, thy pity without end? O make me thine forever; and should I fainting be, O let me never, never outlive my love to thee.*
> *(Bernard of Clairvaux)*

APRIL 15*
Holy Saturday and the Easter Vigil

Over the course of a human life, there are probably dozens of turning points. Some seem major, others minor, and more still aren't really apparent until years later.

"If I give him an ultimatum, will he agree to marry me or will I lose him?" "Which sorority?" "Will the stick turn pink this time, or have I missed another chance to conceive?" "What are the SAT scores hidden in this envelope?" "Did I get in?" "Is there a pink slip in there or just a paycheck?" "I haven't heard from her in decades and now here's a letter. What does she want?" "Boy or girl?" "How did the surgery go?" "Is it malignant?" "Will he be all right?"

These are questions to which we long for answers—as long as the answers are good. If the answers are bad, we dread them. The problem, of course, is that we don't know which is which until we agree to hear them.

The biggest turning point in eternity occurred on this night about two thousand years ago. The funny thing is that very few people remembered there *was* a question: "Will he rise again, as he said, or is he gone forever?" Most of the people who loved Jesus were simply grieving, devastated.

We know differently, of course. We know not only that there's a question, but we know the answer. We know it's a good answer, and we know it changed everything. On Holy Saturday and at the Vigil we wait. We wait for the turning point, for the precise moment when the universe was turned upside down, when evil was defeated, and when the kingdom became reality. We wait in darkness, waiting for the lights and the words: "Allelujah! He is risen!"

And suddenly there was a great earthquake; for an angel of the Lord, descending from heaven, came and rolled back the stone and sat on it. (Matthew 28:2)

April 16*
Easter Day

People always laugh when I tell them that the hardest day of the whole year to preach is Easter. After all, the church is packed with everyone from regulars to the Christmas-and-Easter-only bunch to the curious. The sanctuary is usually decorated beautifully, and the fragrance of Easter lilies fills the air. The choir has practiced their selections for weeks, and there might even be special music or guest musicians, like a trumpet player or guests from the local symphony. Whoever's in charge of selecting lay leaders has made sure the best are at work. Everybody's in a good mood—Lent is over and today is the day everyone gets to immerse themselves in whatever it is they've been without for six weeks. Lots of the women have new dresses and the children are always adorable. It's church at its best.

The problem is that you can't do better than the Easter story itself. With other Biblical passages, the preacher may have to provide a historical background, or explain how something in the text has a different meaning than it did when written. None of that is needed for this passage, though; Easter is the most compelling story ever told. Mary Magdalene goes to Jesus' tomb early on Sunday morning, expecting to grieve, and instead encounters the resurrected Jesus.

He's not just been brought back from the dead, like Lazarus, who would die again—no, he's been changed, permanently. He is a human being, but he is now resurrected and can never die. By going through the hell of the cross, the silence of the tomb, and the experience of resurrection, Jesus became the first— and in being first, opened the way for the rest of us. Because of what happened on the day we remember today, we Christians have the hope that we will live on in resurrected bodies after our earthly death.

How can any embellishment make that story better? All a preacher can do, finally, is tell the tale, marvel at the power and goodness of God, and along with everyone else shout "Alleluia!"

Jesus said to her, "Mary!" She turned and said to him in Hebrew, "Rabbouni!" (which means Teacher).
(John 20:16)

APRIL 17*
Monday After Easter

The denomination in which I was raised had no sense of the liturgical year. One Sunday, out of the blue, you went to church and it was Easter. You knew it was Easter because you usually got a new dress, the Easter Bunny had been by the night before, and Mom had on a corsage, but that was pretty much it. Not a whole lot of buildup, and at church the week following, it was back to business as usual. This mystified me a great deal. If what they talked about on Easter was true, why was everyone so blasé about it?

I love observing the church year, and I love the fact that Easter is not just a day but a season. Having taken seriously the Lenten season and being heartily sick and tired of myself and sin, I want and need more than one day to celebrate what has just happened. I need to chew on Easter—first, to closely examine the resurrection appearances of Jesus for clues about what my life will be like after death, and second, to spend some time being a joyful Christian. The things I contemplated in Lent are certainly real and troubling, but I also have reason to rejoice: in the end, every single one of those concerns will somehow be taken care of.

Easter's not just a day. It's weeks of luxurious basking in the warmth of the resurrection; missing those weeks would be like working all year without a summer vacation.

Mary Magdalene went and announced to the disciples, "I have seen the Lord." (John 20:18a)

APRIL 18*
Tuesday After Easter

So why couldn't Mary Magdalene recognize Jesus at first? In John's account of Easter morning, she mistakes him for the gardener at first. Albrecht Durer has an exquisitely detailed engraving of this encounter. To show that Jesus looks like a gardener, the artist gives him a great big hat that looks an awful lot like today's Stetsons. It's a picture that might make you giggle were the story not so important, but the artist was confronted with the same reality that we are: For some reason, Mary couldn't recognize her Lord at first.

So how could someone as close to Jesus as Mary had been—or the disciples on the road to Emmaus—simply not recognize him? I take this as a tantalizing clue to the mystery of what resurrected life is like. We know he has a human body, because Thomas later touches it, and it carries the wounds he suffered during the crucifixion. But that body is also somehow remarkably different—so different as to be unrecognizable at first.

What will our resurrected bodies look like? Will they be what we would have become had life not taken its toll? Will they somehow show, in a visual way, the state of our souls? And isn't it marvelous that God doesn't simply leave us as wavery spirits unable to enjoy the pleasures of the body? Jesus ate fish on the beach with his disciples. Lots of interesting questions, and probably no way to know the answer until it's our turn. But isn't it wonderful to think about?

Supposing him to be the gardener, she said to him, "Sir, if you have carried him away, tell me where you have laid him, and I will take him away." (John 20:15)

APRIL 19*
Wednesday After Easter

Poor Thomas gets a bad rap. I can't tell you how many homilies and sermons I've heard condemning his lack of faith. I think the story of his encounter with the resurrected Jesus has a quite different meaning.

Thomas is away somewhere when Jesus first appears to the gathered disciples. When he returns, they all tell the same story, but he can't believe it. Who could blame him? He had, after all, seen the crucifixion. Dead is dead—everybody knows that.

Jesus returns a week later and says, "People who haven't seen but come to believe are blessed." That's for certain, and lucky for us, because that gives a blessing to most Christians for the last 2,000 years—

those of us who haven't seen Jesus in a vision, any-how.

But he also allows Thomas to touch him, which is what the disciple said he had to have in order to believe. There's really no condemnation in Jesus' response to the man. This is heartening, because it tells us that Jesus will give us what we need in order to believe. It's different for everybody; some of us believe as children do all our lives; some need signs, miracles, and visions; and some need just the testimony of others. The way we come to belief isn't so important—it's that we do.

Then he said to Thomas, "Put your finger here and see my hands. Reach out your hand and put it in my side. Do not doubt but believe." (John 20:27)

April 20*
Thursday After Easter

The gospels all tell slightly different stories about what happened that first Easter morning. But it's clear that in each, women are involved. Matthew tells us "Mary Magdalene and the other Mary" went to the tomb and encountered the risen Jesus; in Mark, the group consists of Mary Magdalene, Mary the mother of James, and Salome; in Luke, it's Mary

Magdalene, Joanna, Mary the mother of James, and "other women." In John's gospel, Mary Magdalene goes to the tomb on her own and meets her risen Lord.

More than her Lord, I think. All the gospels put Mary Magdalene at the tomb, and John and the extended version of Mark name her as the one to whom he first appeared. After orchestrating the biggest event in all of eternity, it seems unlikely that God would leave to chance something as important as who would first see the resurrected Jesus. I think Jesus and Mary were good friends, maybe even best friends. Once she recognizes him, her first reaction is to try to hug him—something that's apparently not unusual in their relationship—and Jesus has to hold her off for a bit. At the very least, Mary was clearly one of several women who were at the core of Jesus' followers.

The twelve apostles were men, there's no doubt, and so were the four evangelists. I wonder sometimes whether we'd hear more about the role of women if one of the gospel writers had been a woman. In any case, a close reading of what we do have tells us that today, just as on the day of the resurrection, women are important to Jesus and among his closest followers.

Now after he rose early on the first day of the week, he appeared first to Mary Magdalene, from whom he had cast out seven demons. (Mark 16:9)

APRIL 21*
Friday After Easter

The name "Cleopas" appears only in the last chapter of Luke, and he's one of two disciples to whom Jesus appears on the road to Emmaus. Like Mary Magdalene, these followers don't recognize him at first. He falls in with them, listens to their account of recent events, and then teaches them about how the messiah's resurrection was foretold in the writings of the prophets.

When they are about to reach their destination, Jesus starts to leave them, but the disciples beg him to stay and eat with them. Even though they couldn't recognize their teacher, the things this man was teaching them touched them and, as they said, made their hearts burn within them.

Luke describes the moment of recognition. It is "in the breaking of the bread" that Jesus' followers recognize him. The wording Luke uses to describe this event is very close to the New Testament descriptions of the Last Supper. He clearly meant his readers to interpret this meal in that way.

So for every single day in almost two thousand years, Christians have celebrated "the breaking of the bread," and in it found Christ. When we are feeling far from Jesus for one reason or another, we need to take communion, and as often as possible. It's been true for the entire history of the church: in the bread, we will find our Lord.

When he was at the table with them, he took bread, blessed and broke it, and gave it to them. Then their eyes were opened, and they recognized him.
(Luke 24:30-31a)

APRIL 22
Earth Day

On the very first day of creation, God stood back from these two new things called light and darkness, and declared them good. At the end of each day of creation, God called it good. And on the sixth day, after the creation of humankind, God said that creation was *very* good.

Adam and Eve got the deed to our planet. God told them to "fill the earth and subdue it," and gave them "dominion" over the earth. Those words— "subdue" and "dominion"—have brought much grief to this beautiful planet. For most of western Christianity's history, we largely interpreted those words to mean we could regard our planet as nothing but a resource to plunder. The damage of that perception was relatively minor until the Industrial Revolution. Since then, we have devastated the earth. Today, we face the fact that entire species have become extinct, the ozone layer is disappearing, garbage returns to haunt us, nuclear waste is a poison that will be with us for thousands of years to come—and the realization that we have caused these problems ourselves.

I have friends who've abandoned Christianity for the New Age movement because of its emphasis on the environment. What I try to tell them is that Christianity has all the theological foundation it needs for a commission to care for the earth. Our "dominion" over the earth is to be much like the dominion God has over the universe and us: a state of caring, concern, kindness, gentleness, and the use of power of all kinds for restoration, not exploitation.

This love of the earth has been a minor thread in the tradition of the church; St. Francis is the first who comes to mind when we think of those who have cared about the environment. Nonetheless, in this century it took a secular movement to bring the church to awareness of our responsibility. While that makes me feel a little sheepish, it also gives me the energy to work toward a day when the church is the first thing people think of when somebody says "Earth Day."

God blessed them, and God said to them, "Be fruitful and multiply, and fill the earth and subdue it; and have dominion over the fish of the sea and over the birds of the air and over every living thing that moves upon the earth." (Genesis 1:28)

APRIL 23*
Sunday After Easter

One morning after breakfast, Peter and the resurrected Jesus have their famed conversation about feeding the sheep—Jesus' other followers. Three times Jesus asks the question, "Do you love me?" and three times Peter gives the answer, "You know I love you." Biblical scholars fuss and fight about just what this passage means and whether the particular Greek words used are important, but if we give any credit to John as a writer, we must assume his choice of words is intentional.

The first two times Jesus asks his question, he uses the word *agape*. Greek, the language in which the New Testament is written, has more than one word for love. *Agape* love is what we've come to think of as Christian love: a love that will go as far as self-sacrifice. But when Peter answers Jesus, he uses the word *philio*. This is another kind of love, more like the love between siblings. Jesus seems to be calling Peter to a higher kind of love, but the poor man, as much as he loves Jesus, can't do it. So the third time Jesus asks, he switches to the kind of love Peter *can* manage, and asks, "Do you *philio* me?" For the third time, Peter says yes.

This ought to give us pause. Given how important Peter is to the church, isn't it a little discomforting to know he couldn't find in himself the *agape* love Jesus was asking of him? Not really; that day, encountering his recently-risen Lord, all he could manage was *philio*. We shouldn't forget, that in itself is a mighty big change from denial. But as John reminds us, Peter will be martyred because of his faithfulness. That means Peter's love grew. The night before the crucifixion, his fear for his own safety overcame the love he had for Jesus. Later in his life, he died the martyr's death he had feared that earlier, dreadful night.

I like this very much, because I know I don't love Christ very well. I *want* my love to be *agape*, but if I'm honest I have to say that were I threatened with death for my belief in Jesus, I might very well deny him too. I don't like that about myself; I'm just being honest. But Peter's story gives me hope, because it tells me that through my life as a follower of Christ, God will work with me and in me in such a way that someday I *will* be able to *agape*. Maybe I can't get there today, but God isn't finished with me yet, and Peter's story tells me it's possible for me to make a change that deep.

When they had finished breakfast, Jesus said to Simon Peter, "Simon son of John, do you love me more than these?" He said to him, "Yes, Lord; you know that I love you." Jesus said to him, "Feed my lambs."
(John 21:15)

APRIL 24
Spring Flowers

I love the fact that Easter occurs in the spring. Easter comes on the first Sunday after the first full moon that follows the spring equinox. Don't try to figure out the date yourself—it'll make you a little loony. But Easter comes when it does because we know that Jesus' crucifixion and resurrection occurred near the time of the Passover.

Whatever the theological and historical reason, it makes sense to me that Easter comes in the spring.

It's a time of new life; trees bloom, forsythia break into a riot of yellow, and the spring flowers come: crocus first, daffodils, tulips, hyacinth, and on and on. I don't know whether these flowers would seem as beautiful in, say, July, when everything is green and lush. Spring flowers appear against a backdrop of white snow or, at best, brown grass and trees. They are a beautiful and powerful reminder that once again the earth has turned upon its axis and brought us out of the depths of winter and sent life to stir where it appeared there was none.

That's the resurrection, it seems to me. Until that first Easter, death was the end. But since then, death has become a Christian brother's or sister's entrance into the kingdom of God. Yes, we grieve, but it's for ourselves; we rejoice in the fact that our loved ones are resurrected and in the presence of God.

The first crocus begins in me a trickle of hopefulness that becomes a creek and then a raging river. Spring is coming, Easter is coming, heaven is coming.

"Then the sign of the Son of Man will appear in heaven, and then all the tribes of the earth will mourn, and they will see 'the Son of Man coming on the clouds of heaven' with power and great glory."
(Matthew 24:30)

APRIL 25
St. Mark the Evangelist

It's clear from neither scripture nor tradition just who Mark the gospel writer was. Some clues suggest he was closely aligned with Paul; others that he was a student of Peter. In any case, we know most about Mark by the gospel he left us and the way he presented the story of Jesus.

In Mark's gospel, everything happens "immediately"; the word appears no less than twenty-seven times. One gets the sense that the ministry of Jesus, his death, and resurrection are events that took place in a breathless rush. And given the long stretch of human history, those thirty-some years very well could seem like a lightning flash.

One of the most difficult facts about living the Christian life is that God seems to have a time frame that doesn't match mine. While God gives me many good things, I usually have to wait longer than I'd like. St. Mark can be the patron saint of those of us who want things immediately.

Usually we recover from serious illness quite slowly, but occasionally God makes a miracle and we're healed immediately. Normally it takes years for two people to slowly come to know each other, trust each other, and commit to each other for a lifetime, but sometimes God brings together two people who are clearly soulmates. Their quick marriage scandalizes many people until the years go by and it's clear that God knew what was best.

St. Mark's approach to Christianity is something of an audacious one. Things happen fast and furiously. Sometimes that's the way God wants things, and Mark's example can encourage us to ask for things to happen *now*.

Immediately aware that power had gone forth from him, Jesus turned about in the crowd and said, "Who touched my clothes?" (Mark 5:30)

APRIL 26
Falling in Love

There's just something about spring, and poets since ancient times have understood that. Maybe it's the sap rising in the trees, the green blades of flowers pushing their way up to the sky. Maybe it's the extravagance of nature's show, or the exultation of the warm sun on a lightly-covered shoulder. I guess only God knows the reason, but spring is the perfect time to fall in love.

And there's nothing quite like falling in love. It usually comes out of the blue; it's unplanned and serendipitous—from our human perspective, anyway.

There's that inability to sleep or eat, the obsession with that certain someone, the innocently overdone celebration of the discovery that this other person likes ketchup on french fries too! When you fall in love, you can't stop smiling, and you can't wait to see that person. Hours seem like days, days like . . . well, like eternity.

While it would be difficult to have this insight in the midst of falling in love, it is true that the emotions we feel for another person are only a fraction of what we're capable of feeling for God. True—few of us feel passionate about God all the time. But if we read the writings of the saints, we find evidence that sometimes, when we do come to know God well, our experience can be just that giddy.

One of the delightful aspects of all this is the fact that God gives us the experience of falling in love with another human being for a reason. Two reasons, really—first, the joy of the experience itself. And second, so we will have a foretaste of what a love affair with the divine could be.

Ah, you are beautiful, my love; ah, you are beautiful;
your eyes are doves. (Song of Songs 1:15)

APRIL 27
Neighbors

I've had good neighbors and bad. The worst was a man from whom I rented a basement apartment while I was in college. He lived upstairs and was a terrible landlord; he never fixed anything and never responded to any of my complaints. Worst of all, he beat his wife. I knew he beat his wife—all that stood between them and me was a flight of stairs and a flimsy door, locked though it was. I could hear what was going on very clearly. I called the police several times, but back in those days, they wouldn't do anything unless the wife herself made a complaint. I didn't like this neighbor at all; I moved out after three months.

My natural reaction is to love good neighbors and hate the man who beat his wife. But Jesus says I should love my neighbor as myself. That's a tough one. I didn't like this man at all, and even today I can say his *actions* were evil. Nevertheless, I am called to love him. That takes some very difficult work on my part—I have to get inside that man's head. Once I do, I find not only anger and abusiveness, but also a very likely history of being abused and a great deal of unhappiness. When I force myself to see the vulnerable side of this man, it's easier to love him.

My natural tendency is to see things and people as either/or: black or white, evil or good, lovable or worthy of hatred. The real world doesn't work that way, though; only God is purely one thing. God prods me to go beyond either/or to both/and. Any neighbor I happen to have has both good qualities and bad, is a person made in the image of God and also a sinner who does evil things. It's difficult to love a man who abuses his wife, but I am certain that's what God wants me to do. Oddly enough, at this point I can see that it's the worst neighbors who will probably make me grow the most spiritually.

"You shall love your neighbor as yourself."
(Mark 12:31a)

APRIL 28
Dreams

I had the most incredible dream last night. It was very vivid and, while I was having it, seemed very real. I dreamed I was impersonating somebody and that this was a dangerous thing to do; if I were discovered, I would die. My psychodynamically-trained intellect tells me what this dream means: it is soul-killing to try to be someone other than who I am, to live behind a mask.

I once told my spiritual director that I was feeling quite certain about something, but I wasn't sure whether it was God or my unconscious telling me to be so certain. He asked me whether it wasn't possible that God was using my unconscious to speak to me. Light bulb!

Soon after that illumination, I read Morton Kelsey's book *Dreams: A Way to Listen to God*. He suggests exactly what my spiritual director did, that God uses our dreams to speak to us. There is certainly Biblical evidence to support this—perhaps the most famous is Joseph, who interprets the Pharoah's dreams and thereby saves an entire civilization, and his own family, from famine.

So perhaps what's most important about dreams is not what they say, but from whom they come.

And Pharaoh said to Joseph, "I have had a dream, and there is no one who can interpret it. I have heard it said of you that when you hear a dream you can interpret it." Joseph answered Pharaoh, "It is not I; God will give Pharaoh a favorable answer."
(Genesis 41:15-16)

APRIL 29
St. Catherine of Siena

St. Catherine was a remarkable woman in many ways, but one aspect of her life I find intriguing is that she was a tertiary member of the Dominicans. Rather than entering religious life as have so many women saints, she continued to live in the secular world as she followed her vocation. Since God calls most women to secular life, St. Catherine is a marvelous exemplar for us.

The other amazing thing about Catherine is that she had the ear of the pope—of two popes, to be more precise. She was instrumental in moving the papacy from its sojourn in Avignon back to Rome. She offered great comfort and support to Pope Urban VI during the beginning of what was perhaps the most fractious period of the church's history: the great schism of the papacy. While the pope's return to Rome was God's will, it alienated French cardinals, and they set up Clement VII as another pope. Things finally came to the worst when there were three men who claimed to be the pope. Catherine didn't live to see the resolution of this horrible mess in 1417, but it seems clear that she was a great consolation to Urban VI, who had the momentous job of trying to reunite a divided church.

St. Catherine didn't come from a life of poverty, but she didn't live in great riches, either—how could she with twenty-four siblings? She was an ordinary woman with an extraordinary call from God—to take on the indescribable weight of the church's well-being. She had a vision, in fact, in which she saw the church, symbolized as a ship, crushing her. Soon after she had a debilitating stroke and only eight days after that died at the age of thirty-three.

Who among us could imagine writing to the pope, telling him what God wanted? And how less imaginable the idea that the pope would take our advice! Anyone who has spent any time in the church, in any of its manifestations, knows it can be difficult and frustrating. I know I often see myself as a tiny mouse pushing against a huge elephant; such a powerless creature could never have an effect on something so big. Yet St. Catherine's life tells me otherwise; if God calls me to something, then God will give me the strength and whatever else I need to accomplish that task. Even if the task seems audacious.

Treat your possessions as if they were on loan from God.
(St. Catherine of Siena)

APRIL 30
Novels

I love novels. They don't even have to be *good* novels. I have a secret appetite for murder mysteries. But the magic of any book is taking me out of my own surroundings and plopping me down inside someone else's. Whether it's nineteenth-century England and the heroine is as charming as Jane Austen's Emma, or it's twentieth-century California and the heroine as tomboyish as Sue Grafton's Kinsey Millhone, the effect is the same: I'm given the remarkable opportunity to live inside someone else's skin.

That's an important gift, because if we're not able to see things from other people's perspectives, then we're quite unlikely to be able to love them as Christ asks. It takes practice, this mysterious thing called empathy. We're born to consider only our own wants and needs and have to be educated into walking a mile in someone else's moccasins, the way a Native American saying puts it.

I think empathy was a huge part of Jesus' charisma. Of course he was the son of God, was filled with the Holy Spirit, and was sinless. All those things are bound to make someone a compelling person. But one of the ways these facts manifested themselves was through Jesus' ability to put himself in the place of other people. I think of the rich young ruler whom Jesus asks to sell all he has and give the proceeds to the poor. Jesus knew this would be the most difficult thing *this* man could be asked to do. Not everyone would value possessions so much.

Jesus was probably so amazingly empathic because of who he was. We don't have that advantage, but we are able to learn this skill, and one of the ways we can do it is by reading.

> *Nathanael asked him, "Where did you get to know me?" Jesus answered, "I saw you under the fig tree before Philip called you." (John 1:48)*

MAY 1
Work

In the communist countries of the world, May 1 was observed as a celebration of the common worker. The church has designated May 1 as the day of St. Joseph the worker. And before there was a church or communism, people celebrated the equivalent of May 1 as a day of new life—May Day.

I don't have trouble combining work and new life. Sure, work is hard. Too many people have jobs that demand too much of them and pay too little. The poor usually work under horrid conditions, and when I open my eyes wide enough to look inside third-world countries where American corporations have hired workers for pennies a day, I realize just how bad a part of life work can be.

But work, at its best, can also be a very good thing. I like to remember that even *before* the fall, Adam had a job—he was to cultivate the garden of Eden. Work gives me the opportunity to use the gifts and talents God has given me, glimpse a bit of God's perspective by creating new things, and have the satisfaction of providing for myself and those I love. Work—the good kind—helps me grow, keeps me busy, and makes me grateful.

St. Joseph had a call from God: to provide food, shelter, and love to his wife and son, and he did so through his work as a carpenter. Most of us have a similar, commonplace call, and work is probably the best way to answer it. Even when I have a bad day at work, I try to remember all the good things it brings. Or, as a rather plainspoken friend of mine used to say, "Whenever I wonder what I'm doing at work, I just walk past the grocery store."

We are not on earth to guard a museum, but to cultivate a flourishing garden. (Pope John XXIII)

MAY 2
The "Firsts"

There's a very touching scene in the movie *Erin Brockovich*. Erin, for the first time in her life, is working at a job she loves, one that will help innumerable people. Her job requires long hours, though, so her boyfriend watches her children when she's away. One night, driving home, she calls him to find out how the day went, and he tells her that her youngest spoke her first word that day: ball. He goes on and on about how wonderful it was, and while Erin makes the appropriate mm-hmms, we are able to see that she's crying. She missed a very important part of her child's life.

All those firsts are important: the first step, the first word, the first perfect potty-trained day, the first day of school, first part in a play, first date, and on and on . . . through the whole of life, actually. My 103-year-old grandmother saw "firsts" even toward the end of her life: first great-grandchild, first step after a broken hip, first visit of the day. Firsts are important in the lives of people who have them, but they're also important to the people who watch.

It always overwhelms me with gratitude when yet another aspect of life reminds me of just how involved in my life God is. As ecstatic as a mother can be when her child says his first word, God is even more ecstatic when we have our firsts. God pays that much attention. And unlike this broken world where, for example, mothers who must work to support their children may miss the baby's first word, in God's world, nothing gets missed. God takes joy from my firsts. And truth to tell, that's part of what makes a first so important—knowing who it is that made it possible.

God called the light Day, and the darkness he called Night. And there was evening and there was morning, the first day. (Genesis 1:5)

MAY 3
The Post Office

I'm old enough to remember when first-class stamps were six cents, and I grumble every time the rates go up. I complain, too, about how long it can take a letter to get to the other side of town. I grouse when the sorting machinery manhandles a piece of my mail and I get it in a little plastic bag that says, more or less, "oops." I guess the thing I hate the most about my local post office is how long I have to stand in line for service.

I've discovered I can approach this wait two ways: first, I can get angry and snap at the clerk when I finally get to the counter and then leave with an upset stomach, or second, I can marvel at what thirty-four cents can buy me these days. There aren't many places in the world where people can count on the kind of postal service Americans take for granted. All in all, given the huge job it's got, the post office does a pretty good job of being an intermediary between me and the people I love.

I think of the church in kind of the same way. Of course God can come to me personally, and always does. If I'm not hearing God very well, the fault is always my own—for some reason or other, I'm blocking out God's soft voice. So it's good to go to church, which accepts God's message to me and conveys it as an intermediary. Sometimes I can get that message better when it's delivered by another human being than when it comes straight from the source. It cheers me to know that unlike the friends to whom I send letters, God is always right here with me. It's also good to know that when the mailbox of my mind is cluttered with junk mail, God has another avenue to get me the message of love I so badly need.

Ehud came to him, while he was sitting alone in his cool roof chamber, and said, "I have a message from God for you." (Judges 3:20)

MAY 4
Shoes

It's kind of a standard joke: women love shoes. Imelda Marcos will forever be enshrined as the woman who took shoe love to its extreme. Lots of women shop for shoes as a way to brighten their mood.

Quite honestly, I don't get the shoe thing. I don't know why; maybe there's something missing in my femininity gene. I have friends who also don't feel that way about shoes, but it appears most of us collect *something*. For one friend, it's lipstick, for another, nail polish. For me, it's eye shadow. I have green eyes and was told in Home Ec that brown shadow will show them off at their best. So I have four or five shades of brown eye shadow, more greens than I like to think of, and a few major errors like purple.

I see all this as a product of our consumerist culture. Men are subject to it too—it's just that they're fascinated by power tools or golf clubs or whatever else. Some sneaky little voice inside our heads says that if we'll only get the right pair of shoes, the right shade of lipstick or eye shadow, or the right screwdriver, then everything will be okay.

Some people who live in what we call "primitive" cultures have talismans, physical good-luck charms that they count on to make things go well for them.

I don't think I'm any different, really—I'm just too sophisticated to admit the psychological role these things take in my life.

Of course talismans, of any sort, are magic; magic is anything that makes me think I can control God. The opposite of magic is prayer, something that should tell me God is the one who's in charge. I not only can't but *don't have to* purchase a talisman to gain God's good favor; it's already there. I find this quite cheering when I'm contemplating a fifteen-dollar dab of eye shadow at the cosmetics counter. If I can catch myself, I can realize what I'm doing, say, "No thanks," and spend that money on something else.

"The kingdom of heaven is like treasure hidden in a field, which someone found and hid; then in his joy he goes and sells all that he has and buys that field."
(Matthew 13:44)

MAY 5
Cinco de Mayo

These words mean simply "the fifth of May," but they mark an important holiday for people of Mexican and Chicano ancestry in our country. Cinco de Mayo memorializes a Mexican military victory over a larger, invading French force. This isn't Mexican "Independence Day"—that happened September 16, some fifty years earlier. Instead, it's about justice for the weak against the strong.

The Mexicans eventually lost the war, but Cinco de Mayo carries the spirit of not giving up when faced with impossible odds. In the United States, Hispanics from many countries have adopted Cinco de Mayo as a day of celebration.

I understand why that would be. I know a few people who are extremely wealthy and can pretty much make the world run the way they want it to. Most of the people I know, though, including me, live under the tyranny of what Paul calls "principalities and powers." The spirit of Cinco de Mayo tells us all to resist those powers, even when they seem too big to conquer. I try not to forget that all Rosa Parks did was refuse to get out of her bus seat, and from that tiny act of rebellion grew the civil rights movement. And unlike the Mexican army, God will always defeat the powers in the end. We have to live under their rule while we're here on earth, but Cinco de Mayo reminds me that the smallest rebellion against injustice can contribute to a better world here and now.

For we wrestle not against flesh and blood, but against principalities, against powers, against the rulers of the darkness of this world, against spiritual wickedness in high places. (Ephesians 6:12, KJV)

MAY 6
Sewing

Since I've had the label "feminist" attached to me for a great number of years now, a lot of people I meet assume I don't do anything "feminine." It *is* true that I'm not a great cook, but that has more to do with my personal gifts and graces (or lack thereof) than my rebellion against cultural stereotypes about what women are "supposed" to do.

So many people are amazed when they find out I sew. Some of them are quite unbelieving, to the point that I have to drag my sewing machine out of the closet. It's funny to me that something as good as sewing has become a symbol of the oppression of women.

When I sew, I think a lot about God creating the universe. Most of us have been taught that God made creation *ex nihilo*, or out of nothing, but the first chapter of Genesis suggests there was, indeed, something there to work with, chaotic as it was. So as I cut the fabric to match the pattern, I imagine God working with this primordial mess to make planets and stars. When I sew together the side seams of a dress, I imagine God nimbly stitching together the earth and sky. When I come to a particularly difficult part, like setting in a sleeve or putting in a lining, I think of all the care and patience God had to take in making the creatures who inhabit our world—including us.

We're pretty familiar with the image of God as a potter, shaping us and the world out of clay. But in sewing, I find an image not to exchange for that of potter, but to add to it: God as seamstress.

For everything there is a season, and a time for every matter under heaven . . . a time to tear, and a time to sew. (Ecclesiastes 3:1,7)

MAY 7
The Symphony

While I grew up listening to rock and roll, I love classical music. I especially love going to hear the symphony orchestra live. I close my eyes and let the music wash over me. It amazes me that scores of people are up on that stage, playing separate instruments, and yet when they're put all together, they create one beautiful sound. Sure, there are different levels to a piece of classical music, and that's one of the reasons to listen to it over and over again. But anyone who's ever been to a recital can testify that all it takes is one instrument to go wrong and the whole thing is affected negatively.

I wish human life were more like an orchestra. We all play different instruments with our lives. There are big groups—like the violinists; and small groups—like the harpists; but if there are hard feelings among those groups, I'm never aware of it during a concert. Unlike real life, a rebel group of oboists never goes off on its own during a concert. Why is it that a group of human beings as small as a committee, a neighborhood group, or a class can fuss and fight and hate each other, but a group as large and complex as an orchestra can get along?

I guess the difference is that the orchestra has a conductor. Each of the musicians puts aside his or her own desires to follow the conductor, who takes all the different instruments and makes them into one beautiful sound. The symphony reminds me that if we were only willing to put aside our willful selves and follow Jesus, we humans, as a race, could make beautiful music together.

Raise a song, sound the tambourine, the sweet lyre with the harp. (Psalm 81:2)

MAY 8
Making the Bed

Even if I don't remember my dreams any particular morning, I can usually tell how good or bad they were by the state the bed is in. If I've had peaceful, sweet dreams, the covers are barely disturbed, and all it takes is a pull here and a tug there to put the whole thing back together. But if I've had a bad night . . . well, sometimes it's so bad I have to strip the whole thing down and start from the beginning.

Still, the final product is the same: a nice, neat, pretty bed. In life it's all too easy for me to be pessimistic and assume that difficult times are going to be the end of me. But if I sit down and add everything up, I see that's not the case. God watches out for me and works in my life so frequently that most of the time, my life's equivalent of a ripped-up bed ends up restored to order and neatness. Again, it doesn't always work out that way; sometimes a pillow goes missing forever or the bedspread gets changed completely. But most of the time, God sees to it that the sheets are smoothed, the blankets straightened, and the pillows plumped.

In all your ways acknowledge him, and he will make straight your paths. (Proverbs 3:6)

MAY 9
Coloring Books

Sometimes it's fun to get down off the couch and flatten out on the floor with the children and color. The crayons have a familiar smell that reminds me of my own happy childhood days, and there's something soothing about the back and forth motion of coloring, filling in the different blocks of the pictures in the coloring book.

The frustration for children, of course, is learning how to color inside the lines. Watch the refrigerator art gallery in any home, and you'll see the movement from wild swatches of color that seem to have no relation to the picture itself all the way to beautifully-colored pages that could be illustrations in a children's book. The psychologist in me says that coloring helps children develop their motor skills, and the evidence of that growth is there for the eye to see.

It's kind of a shame, though, that I find myself as an adult continuing to color inside the lines. I mean, there's nothing *wrong* with coloring outside the lines—it's just different. But so often I accept the way it's "supposed" to be and just go along following the rules.

God's not like that. The Holy Spirit has colored outside the lines for all of eternity. That Spirit is the one who has kept me on my toes while I grow as a

Christian. It's so easy for me to fall back into the atmosphere of my childhood religion, where the focus was on following rules and doing things "right." Then along comes a homily that tells me if Jesus were here today he wouldn't be hanging around with good church people. He'd be out with the sinners—the people I try so hard *not* to be like.

I guess that childhood religious instruction was very powerful, because I need this lesson again and again and again: coloring inside the lines doesn't make me a good Christian. Even God doesn't color inside the lines.

Then [Jesus] said to them, "The sabbath was made for humankind, and not humankind for the sabbath."
(Mark 2:27)

MAY 10*
Mother's Day

(Observed the Second Sunday in May)

Mothers have the holiest work in the world: like God, they create life. Then, also like God, they work nonstop. They feed, diaper, clean, teach, hug, bandage, and on and on. Trying to make a job description for a mother is very much like trying to make one for

God—the job's just too big. My own mother often shared a saying with me when I was young: Man may work from dusk to dawn, but woman's work is never done. I think that saying is right, but I think it should read "mother's" instead. Women without children simply *are* able to stop working. Mothers can't.

Although I grieve because I don't have children, I'm also able to recognize that my barrenness allows me to measure the sacrifice mothers make in ways they can't. Having a child means sacrificing one's self. That's it, plain and simple. Even a mother who gives her child up for adoption sacrifices her body's resources during pregnancy and the joys of watching that child grow to adulthood. Most mothers sacrifice again and again, for years and years, putting the best interests of the child ahead of their own.

Women who have children usually do realize that they make sacrifices, but they often make light of them because their sacrifices are tempered with love. I think that I, a woman without children, might be more objective about the extent of a mother's sacrifice than they.

When people say, "God is like a mother" these days, this is one of the first things I think of—the willingness to sacrifice. It's an awe-inspiring quality in God, and it should be in mothers too.

*He gives the barren woman a home, making her the
joyous mother of children. Praise the Lord!*
(Psalm 113:9)

MAY 11
Chin Hairs

I remember as a child seeing women with long, thick, curly hairs growing out of their chins. It always gave me the creeps, and I always thanked God *I* didn't have that problem.

Then I got a little older and my friends started making jokes about it. "We've promised each other we'll go to the same retirement home and pluck each others' chin hairs." And then came that horrible day: my first. When I pulled on it, I discovered it was fully an inch long. It was dark brown and apparently usually curled up under my neck. As I scrambled for the tweezers I wondered how many people had seen that hair and been disgusted by it.

So many times in my life I find I'm like the Pharisee who prays at the same time as the sinner. The Pharisee in me thanks God I'm not like other people, in things as minor as chin hairs and as major as big sins. It's so easy to feel smug. But this is one of the reasons I'm convinced God has an immense sense of humor: sooner or later, that quality or behavior I saw and condemned sprouts in me. Sometimes it's inside and invisible to everyone except me and God—a first taste of horrible jealousy, perhaps. Sometimes it's on the outside, like chin hairs. Lord, keep me from saying any prayers that begin, "At least I don't. . . ."

"The Pharisee, standing by himself, was praying thus, 'God, I thank you that I am not like other people: thieves, rogues, adulterers, or even like this tax collector.'" (Luke 18:11)

MAY 12
Saying "No"

I am a life-long student of learning to say no. As I was growing up I somehow came to believe that my value as a person increased in direct proportion to the number of times I said "yes" to somebody's request. All too often I've said yes too much, and ended up tired and cranky—burned out, in other words. If I let it go on too long, I get so bad that whoever has sought that "yes" from me wishes she'd never asked.

I think our culture teaches women to say yes most of the time. Just look at the ratio of men to women volunteers in, say, the church. Of course volunteering is a good thing, as are most of the things we're asked to agree to. But I know very few women who aren't cruelly overextended. And I also know that when I am so taxed, even in good works, that I can't "give cheerfully," then it's time to start saying no.

It's a difficult discipline for a woman, I think. It helps to remember that Jesus said no quite often. When the demands of the crowds and his ministry got too heavy, he went off by himself. It also helps to remember he didn't give excuses, as I do so often when I guiltily say no. Miss Manners, Judith Martin, assures me that all I have to say when I refuse is something like, "Oh, I'm so terribly sorry, but I just can't." If the asker presses further, I should say, "It's just impossible right now. Maybe another time." I don't have to justify saying no as often as it takes to keep myself healthy, cheerful, and willing to give. After all and once again: Jesus didn't.

But Jesus refused. (Mark 5:19a)

MAY 13
Children's Birthdays

I was astounded when I first learned that my ex-husband had never had a birthday party. My mother made our birthdays extravagant occasions. There was always a party with lots of friends and games. She always made a cake related to whatever it was we were fascinated with at the moment: Batman, princesses,

Snoopy, football. We always got presents and were encouraged to unwrap them with glee. All in all, my sisters and I always felt that we were queen for a day on our birthdays.

I know there are some parents who go too far with children's birthday parties. Sometimes it becomes a competition between parents to see who can give the best parties; the entertainment can escalate from games to a clown to outings to theme restaurants or parks. I'm not advocating that kind of excess.

But I do believe all children need to be told, at least once a year and in a celebratory way, that the people in their lives are happy they were born. Everything about Christianity tells us that God knows us individually, cares for us individually, and saves us individually. The individual matters in Christianity, and that's largely because our faith is focused on an individual rather than a pantheon of gods or some abstract principle. Jesus was an individual, the son of God, and our children are daughters and sons of God.

It's possible to spoil children, sure. But celebrating their very existence with birthday parties isn't spoiling them—it's just reminding them of how important they are in the eyes of God.

For [God] strengthens the bars of your gates; he blesses your children within you. (Psalm 147:13)

MAY 14
Eating Out

One of the most memorable evenings of my life was when a bunch of friends pooled their money and took me to one of the swankiest restaurants in Nashville. At The Mad Platter it's easy to spend fifty dollars a person on dinner. But the food . . . oh, the food. I ate things I'd never heard of before that night, but every bite made me quiver, it was so good. We also had one waiter to ourselves; when he wasn't busy doing something for us, he simply stood quietly to the side, watching for a glass that needed filling or an empty plate wanting to return to the kitchen.

I don't know many people who can afford eating out like that very often. But on those rare occasions that it's possible, it's good to enjoy every possible aspect of the event. At the center is the food and taste buds rejoicing at new flavors. Then there's being in the company of beloved friends. And there's the opportunity to have a foretaste of the kingdom.

Given how wonderful that night at The Mad Platter was, it's hard for me to imagine that what awaits me in God's kingdom is better. But clearly that's the case. Jesus compared the kingdom to extravagant dinner parties quite often. I suppose the food will taste better than the finest delicacies on earth, and the service—given by angels, perhaps?—

will surpass that of the most attentive waiter here. But the best part of all will be the company at the table, because it will include not only family and friends, but Christ.

He brought me to the banqueting house, and his intention toward me was love. (Song of Songs 2:4)

MAY 15
Pumping Iron

Odd as it may seem, I like lifting weights. It does have its negative aspects: blisters, too many men, and beautiful young women in spandex. But lifting weights makes me feel strong. When I leave the YMCA I feel a foot taller. I like the strength it gives me in the rest of my life. While it's always nice to have help with groceries or the three-gallon jugs of purified water I buy, it's also good to know I can fend for myself if I have to.

I was introduced to weights by a friend who was quite a fanatic; he was in the gym every day. Of course, he had to work different parts of his body every day, because when you lift weights, you're supposed to give your muscles a day of rest between bouts. That's because lifting actually tears muscle tissue; when it grows back—which it needs a day to do—then it grows back stronger and—if you're going for bulk—bigger.

That's a mighty powerful metaphor for life. Nietzsche said, "What does not kill me makes me stronger," but I prefer to think of this in a Christian way. Given that life is full of events that will tear us up a little or a lot, it is wonderful that God uses those events to mend us into stronger people. Personally, I'd rather avoid getting torn up and arrive at my dotage nice and soft, but that's not the way the world works. It's not as if I'm given a choice. It tickles me that my YMCA has painted a quotation from Ecclesiastes over the weight room door, but overall I think they're right.

[There is] a time to break down, and a time to build up. (Ecclesiastes 3:3b)

MAY 16
The Good China

One of the memories I have around the holidays is of my mother's "good" china. It was white with a narrow gold band around the edge, and when I held it up to the light I could see my hand through it. The good china didn't go in the dishwasher, so I also have memories of doing a lot of dishes by hand. They're holiday memories, in particular, because my mother used her good china and the silver only on special occasions—Thanksgiving, Christmas, Easter, and dinner parties with important guests.

I don't have a set of china; when I got married it made more sense to me to register for more practical things like a toaster oven and a crockpot. But I do have odds and ends of china. I pick up place settings or tea cups and saucers at garage sales and flea markets, just because I think they're pretty. And I use them every day. Sure, I break something every now and again, but that's just exactly the point: God didn't keep back the best because it would get broken. The best, of course, was Jesus. Like us and like good china, he was fragile. It took the Romans just a few nails and a couple of wooden beams to do him in.

Again and again I'm overwhelmed by the fact that God has squandered so much quality on me; I surely don't deserve it, and frequently I abuse and break it. It makes no sense that God would sacrifice Jesus for my eternal well-being. But that's a measure of God's grace—only the best for us, and an infinite supply of it.

Give no thought to your possessions, for the best of all the land of Egypt is yours. (Genesis 45:20)

MAY 17
Jeans in Church

There are hugely important theological issues that can cause dissension in a church, but for a really nasty fight in a Protestant congregation, you've got to have people wearing jeans to church. I realize this is probably unfathomable to my Catholic sisters; the invitation to Mass seems to be "come as you are." But not so in my tradition.

There are all sorts of reasons, of course, that people dress up to go to church on Sunday mornings. Older folks will tell you they want to dress their best "for the Lord," and find jeans disrespectful. In some churches, Sunday morning is an unannounced competition between women, to see who has the nicest clothes. Historically, in many denominations like my own, joining a particular church meant moving up the ladder of social status, and people naturally wanted to show off their prosperity. Clearly the first argument is the best.

I understand the desire of folks who want to dress their best for God, but I fear it can convey a subtle message: this one, single hour on Sunday morning is holy and we must wear special clothes to appear before God. But that suggests we are *not* appearing before God the other 167 hours of the week. Dressing as one always does in order to attend church suggests at a deep level that while the particular activity of worship is especially holy, it's not the church building that makes it sacred. It also suggests that we don't need to pretty ourselves up in order to face God. That's good theology, because God sees right straight through our clothes to our souls, anyway.

I don't think it's *wrong* to dress up for church, and I have always encouraged the older folks in my congregations who see this as important to do so. But I also hope they can see that if wearing jeans during the week isn't disrespectful to God, it isn't at church either.

O Lord, our Sovereign, how majestic is your name in all the earth! You have set your glory above the heavens. (Psalm 8:1)

MAY 18
The "Replacement"

I drove thirty miles north to Springfield, Tennessee, yesterday to have lunch with a former parishioner. While we visited at the only tea room in town, we ran into the new minister of the congregation. I'd heard about him for months, and was glad to finally meet him. I told him—truthfully—that I pray daily for his ministry and its success, not only among the members of the congregation, but the entire community.

But I have to confess there was also a strange little feeling in the pit of my stomach. I've had it when I've returned to other churches and job sites. It's a nasty little sentiment that whispers in my ear, "See, they don't need you! They're getting along just fine without you!" In other words, my pride gets a little wounded.

The best part of me wants Canaan, the new minister, to have a wonderful ministry at Central. I really do hope he can lead these people I love so much through the difficult changes they're facing, and on into a renewed sense of calling to be the body of Christ.

But when I hear that little voice in my head, I have to remind myself that there's nobody in this world who can't be replaced at work. I remember that what's special about me, what sets me apart from everybody else, is not the job I have—it's who I am as a person. God loves me just the same no matter where I work or how "well" I perform. I like a quote that a friend borrowed from someone: God doesn't ask for success. God asks for faithfulness. When I can see things that way, then I'm able to shush that little part of me that's worried that somebody else is going to get loved more than me, and wish the best for my replacement.

Let no one despise your youth, but set the believers an example in speech and conduct, in love, in faith, in purity. (1 Timothy 4:12)

MAY 19
"Are We There Yet?"

I heard these words from a friend's child when a bunch of us were on our way to a state park about an hour away from Nashville. I laughed because I remember very well when those same words came out of my young mouth.

Time crept along when I was a child. That was good sometimes—summer vacation, for instance. But it wasn't good on long car trips. Children just don't have the inner resources to occupy themselves for hours away from their playthings. I don't care how much license plate bingo you play—for a child, a long car trip is hell. They want desperately to be there, wherever "there" is. They want to arrive; they have no taste for the journey.

As I opened myself to these memories from my own childhood, I realized that I often approach life this way as an adult too. While I'm better able to amuse myself and now actually *like* trips in the car, I'm often impatient for whatever goal or event I'm anticipating. I can't wait for vacation; I can't wait to lose another dress size; I can't wait for the book to be published; I can't wait to meet the right man and fall madly in love. There's nothing wrong with looking forward to things—anticipation is a gift unique to human beings, and it increases the pleasure of happy events.

The danger, though, is focusing too much on the goal and missing the gifts on the road to it. God fills each and every day of our lives with good things. Like Celie in *The Color Purple*, I think it disappoints God when we rush right past the "ordinary" things of day-to-day life: flowers and trees, the glorious process of "wasting time" with friends and family, or a perfect spring day.

I admit that though I use different words, I sometimes whine because "we aren't there yet." But when I've got my head on straight, I remember that while the goal of life—heaven—is wonderful, so too is the journey to it. I don't expect a child to be able to treasure life's process in and of itself, but I'm a much happier camper, as an adult, when *I* do.

So they resumed their journey, putting the little ones, the livestock, and the goods in front of them.
(Judges 18:21)

May 20
Clerical Collars

Clergy in my denomination don't usually wear clerical collars, but I have one I wear in two situations: first, when I'm attending a public event like a rally in my role as a pastor, and second, when I'm visiting someone in the hospital in a small, rural town. I learned the need for the second a long time ago. The nurse behind the desk wouldn't give me the full access to a patient that clergy are usually accorded because she didn't believe there was such a thing as a woman minister. When I went back wearing the collar, she let me pass. People just know the formula: clerical collar = minister.

I have clergy friends in many denominations, and among the ones whose traditions demand clerical collars, they run the gamut from overuse to underuse. I once overheard someone say a colleague "probably wears her collar in the shower," and I have a friend who takes his collar off the second he leaves church property.

I like clerical collars. I mean that I like to see people wearing them. I like to see someone in a clerical collar pumping gas, at the grocery store, even at the liquor store. That collar quickly takes my thoughts to God, and I like having visual reminders that God is around when I'm picking through the string beans just as much as when I'm praying in a chapel. I like them, too, because our culture is rapidly becoming a secularized one, and I think all of us—Christians or not—need to be reminded that the church is here and has a place in community life.

It's been a long time since I saw someone wearing a clerical collar at Wal-Mart. Maybe I need to encourage my friends who wear them to keep them on when they do "non-holy" things like shop.

The Lord has sworn and will not change his mind,
"You are a priest forever according to the order of
Melchizedek." (Psalm 110:4)

MAY 21
Oh, My Aching Back

For the fourth day in a row now, I've been awakened not by my alarm clock but by my back. It hurts so much I have to get up and take some pain pills; by the time they take effect, I'm awake. So not only do I have a backache, I'm sleep-deprived and cranky too.

Millions of Americans have back problems, so I know I'm not the only one. I do know, though, that I've caused this particular ache myself. I've been pushing myself in the weight room, upping the weights too quickly. And my body is telling me to stop.

While what I've done certainly isn't smart, it's not "sinful" either. It's easy for me to forget that while all human beings are sinners, which is bad, we're also all *limited* creatures, which isn't bad. I'm not God; I'm not all-powerful, and I can't just decide how much weight my back is going to take. My body and its limits get that decision. Of course I don't like this; the sinful part of me hates the fact that I'm limited. That part wants to be all-powerful, all-knowing, eternal . . . in other words, God.

Being a creature with limits isn't a bad thing in itself. The problems arise when I forget about those limitations or my pride tries to take control. I'm letting myself off the hook for this particular backache—I think I just got too enthusiastic. But it's a good reminder to be gentle to myself and not to expect too much of a body that wasn't created to be superwoman.

In fulfillment of his own purpose he gave us birth by the word of truth, so that we would become a kind of first fruits of his creatures. (James 1:18)

May 22
Buzz's Den

Buzz was four years old when he came to live with me. Before then, he lived in a puppy mill, where he was the stud. It wasn't a happy life . . . except for the times when he was "working," he lived in a cage those entire four years. A saintly woman named Cindy Heron (www.furry-friends.org) rescued him, as she does so many dogs.

Buzz is a pretty happy guy these days, but he does have some psychological scars from his earlier life. The first time I took him to be groomed, being put in the kennel to dry after his bath made him so depressed he couldn't raise his head for three days. He can't understand me, but I've sworn to him he'll never, ever be in a cage again.

Most dogs, who spend their puppy time with loving families, come to regard their kennel, or cage, as their "den," and it's their safe place. Whenever things become overwhelming or the dog feels endangered, she retreats to her den. Buzz obviously doesn't have a cage for a den, but he has adopted the space underneath the rocking chair where I spend a lot of time reading. I make a point of never forcing anything on him when he's in his safe place.

We human beings need safe places, too, even if they aren't confined to a few particular square feet. Maybe a particular room in the house, or a friend's house, or some other space becomes the place where we know nothing can hurt us. I like to envision my own safe place surrounded by God's hands, deflecting anything that will harm me. Theologically, I know

God is a continuous presence in my life and protects me wherever I go. But it's also good to have a place where I can relax completely and feel that everything will be okay.

To those who are called, who are beloved in God the Father and kept safe for Jesus Christ: May mercy, peace, and love be yours in abundance. (Jude 1:1b-2)

MAY 23
Big Mistakes

I teach part-time in the anthropology department at Vanderbilt University, and my status means I don't know my faculty colleagues very well. But last year I started to get to know a young woman who'd come from the Northeast to be our physical anthropologist. I liked her a lot, and was sad when I found out the next year that she'd left, gone back north.

I was shocked too. The academic market is depressed these days; tenure-track positions are hard to come by. I've not been able to get one since my graduation in 1996. So I was amazed that this woman would give up a job at a prestigious university.

But I knew she wasn't happy. She had shared with me many times her sense of feeling displaced. A life-long Yankee, she felt completely afloat in Southern culture. She said to me once, as if reporting a murder, "I've had *seven* people ask me where I go to church!"

It would be easy to second-guess her decision to leave. She should have stayed longer, given it a better try. She's damaged her academic career. And on and on. But to tell the truth, I think she did the right thing. It was clear to her that she'd made a big mistake taking the position she did, and rather than trying to pretend everything was fine when she was miserable, she saw the mistake for what it was and fixed it, despite the unarguably high cost.

Although this woman clearly wasn't a church-goer, she taught me something important about God. Apparently God allows us to back out of our mistakes. It's okay to say, "Lord, I thought I heard you calling me down this path, but apparently I was wrong." I believe that, but I'm afraid I don't usually live as if I do. My tendency is to think that once I've committed myself to something, there's no turning back. It took a "godless Yankee" to remind me God is more gracious than that.

Then Saul said, "I have done wrong; come back, my son David, for I will never harm you again, because my life was precious in your sight today; I have been a fool, and have made a great mistake."
(1 Samuel 26:21)

MAY 24
Graduation

My friends' children are starting to graduate from college. That most assuredly makes me feel old. On the other hand, it's a marvel to see young men and women that I may have known as babies finish the first big stage of life and move on to the adult world of work and marriage. As boring as graduation ceremonies can be, I attend them anyway because for the thirty seconds it takes the person I know to walk across the stage and get a diploma, I am proud and happy and moved, all at the same time.

I like to think of death as a kind of graduation. Of course I fear death as everyone does, but given my firm belief that the afterlife is a spectacular place to be, I try to find images for death that are a little humorous rather than scary. So when I go to a graduation, I spend the downtime—the commencement address, the other 999 graduates—on a fanciful daydream. I imagine my family and friends who've died before me all gathered on a sunny, green field when I die. I suspect I would be a bit confused, not quite certain what I'm doing there. I seem to have memories of participating in all the graduations a person could possibly have: kindergarten, high school, seminary, and graduate school. I certainly know what to do in a graduation, so when it comes my turn, I go up on the stage. Instead of the college president, though, I shake the hand of St. Peter. He welcomes me into heaven and suddenly I realize what's happened: I've graduated from life.

That might seem morbid to someone else, thinking about death on a day that's focused on celebrating a young person's movement into a new stage of life. But that's just exactly the point. I think of myself at my various graduations, and remember how I felt: relieved, excited, a little nervous, and happy, happy, happy. I really like the idea of approaching my last earthly graduation the way I did the others. After all, when I die, I will be moving into a new stage of my—now—eternal life.

Listen, I will tell you a mystery! We will not all die, but we will all be changed, in a moment, in the twinkling of an eye. (1 Corinthians 15:51-52a)

MAY 25
Cleaning the Coffeemaker

While I was wiping off the coffeemaker, I accidentally knocked it on its side and saw, for the first time since I bought it a year ago, the bottom of the part where the coffee comes out. Talk about disgusting! The whole thing was stained with splashes from coffee, and I had to use the scrubbing side of my sponge to get it all off. But the worst part was the circular part in the middle, where all the water that's been through the coffee grounds and filter drips into the pot. Those twenty-or-so little holes were all surrounded by black crud. I finally had to take an old toothbrush to it, and while I was doing so I tried not to think about the effects of this mess on all the cups of coffee I've made, unaware that the filth was there.

I find there are parts of me like that too. I mean parts of me that are not only filthy—sinful—but hidden as well. I'm not usually aware of them. While I'm conscious of many of my sins, I've repressed awareness of others so well that they only show dirt during "accidents." Maybe I say a particularly nasty thing about someone and think, "Now where did *that* come from?" On reflection I discover some envy I didn't know was there. Maybe I find myself spending twenty minutes describing one friend's new car to another. When the listening friend yawns, I ask myself, "Why am I going on and on about this?" Aha!—some covetousness I've hidden away.

While it's most definitely good for me to dig out these hidden sins and wash them away, it also scares me a bit. If I didn't know these were there, doesn't that suggest there are probably others I don't know about? It does indeed. Like the grime under my coffeemaker, I wonder what damage these sins cause while I'm clueless.

Thank God—and I mean that quite literally—that God is the one in final charge of cleaning my soul. Unlike me, God is aware of every single sin, every dirty spot whether big or small. While I use a toothbrush to clean my coffeemaker, and prayer, repentance, and absolution to clean particular sins away, God uses the blood of Jesus to completely cleanse my sinful *nature*. That cleaning fluid is unbelievably mighty: it can take a sin-riddled person like me and make me shiny, clean, and new, even in the hidden, dark recesses. Most remarkable, I guess, is the fact that this "detailing" is free; all I have to do is ask for it.

You have already been cleansed by the word that I have spoken to you. (John 15:3)

MAY 26
All-Nighters

It's around this time of year that towns in middle Tennessee hold their version of the Relay for Life, a program of the American Cancer Society. The Relay usually begins around 6 or 7 p.m. and goes for twenty-four hours. Teams from local businesses, churches and civic organizations decorate their campsites according to a theme, with a prize going to the most original. Funds are raised by team members gathering pledges from friends and neighbors—not for number of miles walked, but simply for participating in the Relay. That's because for twenty-four straight hours, each team keeps at least one person walking around a track lit by luminarias dedicated to people who have had cancer. The challenge is to stay up all night long. Cancer never sleeps, the organizers say, so for one night a year, neither will the people who want to end it.

At my first Relay—the first time in my life I'd stayed up all night—I found out *why* staying up all night is such a big deal. Bodies *hate* it. The hour between 3 and 4 a.m. seemed endless, and not long before the final ceremonies at 7 a.m. I found myself feeling kind of sick and quite cranky.

It astounds me to realize that God keeps watch over us all night, every night. Of course, God doesn't have a body and so isn't prone to all the unpleasantness an embodied creature experiences without sleep. Nevertheless, without sleep, twenty-four hours makes for a long day. And God does this 365 days a year, year after year. I can preach that in a sermon or teach it to a Sunday School class and toss it off quite casually, but one single night of no sleep reminds me just how magnificent that depth of care is.

My soul waits for the Lord more than those who watch for the morning, more than those who watch for the morning. (Psalm 130:6)

MAY 27
Therapists

My therapist finally returned from three weeks of vacation. I was really glad to see him. After almost four years of weekly conversations, three weeks without him seemed an eternity. Because of Phil Chanin, I am a much saner person than I was a few years ago.

Many people find it shameful to go to a therapist. Having trained to be one, I know this from the other side. The first several visits are usually heavy with the person who's seeking help struggling to feel okay about having resorted to what seems an extreme measure.

It's an odd prejudice, of course. Nobody with a broken leg would think twice about visiting an M.D., but folks with depression—an equally physical malady—often suffer for ages before they finally see a therapist. We speak of God as the Great Physician, and rightly so. All healing has its source in God. But God has given us doctors to help heal our bodies, and we are grateful for them. God has given us clergy to help us heal our souls, and we're grateful for them. I am also grateful for my therapist, and all the others who serve as conduits for God's healing power and help God's beloved children overcome terrible emotional wounds.

Perhaps there would be less distaste for therapists if we called them "counselors," a word that's in scripture. Handel's great piece of music that is often performed around Christmas, *The Messiah*, sings with power about the One who is coming to save us. Among his titles: Wonderful Counselor. However ambivalent our culture may be about therapists, I know I thank God daily for mine.

For a child has been born for us, a son given to us;
authority rests upon his shoulders; and he is named
Wonderful Counselor, Mighty God, Everlasting Father,
Prince of Peace. (Isaiah 9:6)

MAY 28
A Rotten Day

I had one of "those" days yesterday. It was Saturday, my one day off during the week. I'd planned to meet a friend for lunch, run a couple of fun errands, and then hide from the world for a while as I read a trashy novel or watched a mindless video. Not a very exciting day off, but I didn't even get that.

My landlord called early, waking me up, and told me he'd be at my place in an hour to install a new (to me) refrigerator. I ran around getting dressed, tending to Buzz's morning needs, and clearing a path from the door to the fridge. Then I sat down to wait—which I did until 1 p.m., hours later. I emptied the refrigerator, packed my perishables with ice in the sink, and retreated to my bedroom for the hour the landlord had estimated it would take him to exchange the appliances. Four hours later he finally left. The rest of the stuff that happened yesterday was just as petty, but I was mighty crabby by the end of the day because it hadn't at all turned into the kind of day I'd wanted.

I get like this when I forget that just a few years ago I would have given anything for a day like yesterday. In the midst of chemotherapy and a six-month prognosis, every day was one of grief, extreme exhaustion, and pain. I sometimes listened to people complain about their days, ones like I just described, and while I didn't say it out loud, I did think it: "Hey, wanna trade lives?"

I'm not saying it's not okay to be crabby, or to resent an intrusion that disrupts my plans. What I am saying is that everything's relative. I just wonder sometimes what God thinks when I whine about days like the one I just had. Despite the disappointments, there were also many gifts: my friend came over and visited, I got to watch my video, and I got a new(er) refrigerator, one I don't have to defrost. Maybe in the future I can see all this in the midst of my frustration and do myself the favor of taking it all a little less seriously.

For he will hide me in his shelter in the day of trouble; he will conceal me under the cover of his tent; he will set me high on a rock. (Psalm 27:5)

MAY 29*
Memorial Day

(Observed fourth Monday of May)

I'm afraid that children growing up these days probably see Memorial Day as another three-day weekend, one in which they're likely to have a cookout, and if they're lucky, make a visit to some body of water. I suspect very few of them know what Memorial Day is really about.

Because my father was a career Army man, there's no way I could have misunderstood Memorial Day. Because he spent a year in Vietnam, I knew the costs involved when soldiers are away from their families, and I prayed nightly that we wouldn't get that notification every active duty soldier's family dreads.

Each Memorial Day I try to do something to remember the men and women who died in combat. I don't like anything that suggests God is an American, or that God prefers the United States over any other country, but I do think God wants us to remember our dead, the ones who gave their lives for us.

After all, isn't that what Jesus did? He wasn't a soldier; ironically, the anticipated messiah was expected to be one, a great military leader who would free the Jews from Roman occupation. Christ turned out to be much more like a lamb led to slaughter. Jesus was a man of peace and tenderness, but also one who was willing to give his life for the people he loved, which in his case just happened to be all of humankind. Just as we remember his sacrifice every Sunday—the Lord's Day—it makes sense to me to remember the sacrifices made by our military men and women on Memorial Day.

The Lord goes forth like a soldier, like a warrior he stirs up his fury; he cries out, he shouts aloud, he shows himself mighty against his foes. (Isaiah 42:13)

MAY 30
Pooper Scooper

As I was trying to occupy myself in the pet warehouse while waiting for Buzz to be groomed, I happened to wander down the aisle dedicated to what they euphemistically call "waste disposal." I found something very original and useful, an invention that uses the plastic bags every supermarket in the country has these days. The invention was clever, but what was most interesting to me was the inventor: a ten-year-old boy.

I don't know anything about this boy, but I'm guessing he's not a genius. Child prodigies tend to devote themselves to math, music, and science, not dog poop. The scenario that makes most sense to me is a pretty standard ten-year-old with the chore of walking and cleaning up after the family dog. Like most children, he didn't automatically do things the "normal" way, because children don't necessarily know what normal is.

I think this is part of what Jesus was talking about when he recommended the faith of children to his followers. The standard interpretation of "childlike" faith is one that doesn't question. But the children I know aren't like that; they question everything, up one side and down the other. What they *are* able to do—the ability too many of us lose as we age—is view things from a very practical, very fresh perspective. In one area of life, that means the invention of a new kind of pooper scooper. In the arena of faith, it means taking in what we adults tell them about God and Jesus, asking questions, and then accepting the most reasonable explanation of everything they've heard: God must love them very, very much.

Out of the mouths of babes.

"Truly I tell you, whoever does not receive the kingdom
of God as a little child will never enter it."
(Mark 10:15)

MAY 31
The Visitation

I don't think it's a coincidence that Mary visited Elizabeth. What we tend to focus on when we read the story of the visitation is that Elizabeth's baby leapt in joy and that Mary spoke the beautiful, moving words we now know as the Magnificat.

But let's not forget that Gabriel told Mary that Elizabeth was pregnant. Mary certainly knew how old Elizabeth was, so she knew what a miracle it would be should she be pregnant—as much of a miracle as what Gabriel had told Mary was going to happen to her.

Clearly Mary believed Gabriel, and clearly she accepted God's desires in a humble and faithful way. But she also hot-footed it to Elizabeth's house, because there she would see what would confirm what she'd just been told: her pregnant, elderly relative.

We can believe the promises God makes to us and *also* want the added encouragement of other Christians who can tell us from personal experience that God's promises do come true. That's one of the reasons community is so important to a Christian. When the faith of one person wanes, the faith of the community waxes. Sometimes in our darkest days it becomes very difficult to believe that what God has promised will come to pass. In days like those, like Mary, we do well to seek out the company of people who already know this truth through experience; until we recover the depth of our faith, they can believe for us.

When Elizabeth heard Mary's greeting, the child leaped in her womb. And Elizabeth was filled with the Holy Spirit. (Luke 1:41)

JUNE 1
Random Acts of Kindness

I was rushing through the grocery store the other day. All I needed was milk, and the only time I was able to get there was that busy hour when everyone was on the way home from work. I stood in line at the U-Scan-It, scanned and bagged my gallon of milk, and tried to put a five dollar bill in the bill receiver. But it wouldn't go in. The cashier called me over and told me that the woman who'd used the scanner before me had paid for my milk.

I was speechless. I was certain I didn't know this woman; I'd had a good look at her—besides the tabloids, there's not much else to do in lines but check out the other customers. I was quite certain I'd never seen her before in my life. And yet she paid for my milk.

Now, in the grand scheme of things, this was a small kindness. I guess it added less than $2.50 to her bill. But people don't usually do things like that.

I've heard the slogan, "Commit random acts of kindness and senseless beauty," but I've never before experienced its benefits. Or I guess I should say I've never experienced it in quite this way. The fact is that I actually experience kindness and senseless beauty every day. God has filled my life with innumerable blessings, and I am well aware that most people in the world haven't been given a fraction of what I have. I'm also aware that God didn't have to make this world so beautiful; it could have functioned just as well without red and orange sunsets. What that woman did was remind me—and I so often need to be reminded—of the extent to which I am the recipient of kindness and beauty. The only difference is that the comparable gifts of God aren't random at all.

Whoever pursues righteousness and kindness will find life and honor. (Proverbs 21:21)

JUNE 2
"My, Haven't You Grown?"

I used to hate it when I heard that from relatives I hadn't seen in a while. It seemed like a complete inanity. But I said much the same thing to my nieces recently.

I made the five-hour trip to Cincinnati to see the girls, along with their mother, my sister, and her husband. I haven't seen them for months, and I was amazed at the changes in my nieces. Yes, they'd both grown quite a bit. The younger is a couple of inches taller and the older looks as if she's just beginning to enter the very first stages of puberty. Both girls are reading books far beyond the norm for their ages, and the personalities I could glimpse in them even when they were infants are now in full bloom.

I want to put the brakes on all this! I would rather keep them young, right about preschool age, and if it were up to me, I'd slow their growth and changes by a factor of four or five. I starve for the uniqueness of their company, but the realities of life mean I don't see nearly as much of them as I'd like. God surely knows this about me, but also knows that deep down, I want what's best for them. And "best for them" is what God is doing with them: adding pounds, inches, knowledge, wisdom, charm, and on and on. It reminds me of that one little sentence in the New Testament that covers the entire life of Jesus between the ages of twelve and thirty.

My nephew is five hours away in a different direction. I think I'd better get there soon.

And Jesus increased in wisdom and in years, and in divine and human favor. (Luke 2:52)

JUNE 3
Old Age

I saw the movie *Logan's Run* on video recently. It's a hokey sci-fi movie from the '70s, set in the twenty-third century. People live in a vast, domed city and are provided with every sensuous luxury possible. There's no such thing as marriage or family—just lots of sex. The only problem is that nobody lives past the age of thirty. The hero, Logan, and the love interest, Jenny, escape the city to "outside," where they make their way to the crumbled, vine-covered monuments of Washington, D.C. There they meet an old man who is apparently the last survivor of humans who continued living outside the city. Jenny asks him, "Do those cracks in your face hurt?"

Logan and Jenny realize they must return to the city and tell the people that they don't have to die at thirty. That's what they do, and in the process the city blows up and thousands of young people come flowing out of the domes toward the old man who's waiting outside.

I used to worry about getting old. I traded moans and jokes with my friends about the process, but underneath I knew none of us was very happy about it. That's despite the fact that the Bible regards long life as a gift, and despite the apparent fact that the majority of life is lived in old age.

Then I got a terminal diagnosis, and when I saw old people, I'd think to myself, "That's what I hope to be one day." So these days, when I hear somebody complaining about getting older, I say, "Hey—old age is one of my goals!"

Do not ignore the discourse of the aged, for they themselves learned from their parents; from them you learn how to understand and to give an answer when the need arises. (Sirach 8:9)

JUNE 4
Weddings

For years and years I couldn't figure out why people cry at weddings. After all, it's a wonderful day, isn't it? I don't mean the bride and groom or members of their immediate families. All those people are experiencing very strong emotions, so tears make sense. But the other guests—why do they cry?

I finally formed a theory when I attended a wedding I wasn't officiating, so I could allow myself the luxury of my own feelings. As I sat listening to the familiar words of the ceremony, my mind naturally went back to my own wedding. I remembered my state that day: scared, full of anticipation, full of love for my about-to-be husband, and full of dreams, too, of what our life would be like.

That's when I started crying. People who are marrying for the first time don't have a realistic view of married life. They have an idealized, romanticized picture, and as the years pass, those unrealistic dreams will be erased, bit by bit. I am *not* being cynical here, just realistic.

It's kind of like a little girl who finally understands there's no such thing as fairies. The fact is there are other marvelous and magical things in this world, some even more enchanting than fairies. But still, the loss of a dream is the loss of a dream. At a wedding, I weep for the loss of innocence . . . mine, in the past, and the bride's, in the immediate future.

I weep, too, with deep gratitude that no matter how unrealistically we may approach marriage, God unfolds for us all the possibilities inherent in what is a profound human relationship. It could be all disappointment, but God won't leave it at that. God lets us have our childish dreams, and then, as we struggle to leave those dreams behind piece by piece, puts in their place a wondrous reality we were, at the beginning of marriage, too innocent to imagine.

[Jesus said,] "For this reason a man shall leave his father and mother and be joined to his wife, and the two shall become one flesh." (Matthew 19:5)

JUNE 5
A Glass of Champagne

I am a minister in a denomination that gave birth to the prohibitionist Carrie Nation. Since the nineteenth century, my church has viewed alcohol with suspicion. More than that, I live in the South, which is heavily populated by people who aren't *suspicious* of alcohol but are convinced it's demonic. Believe it or not, in Nashville it is illegal to sell beer within 500 yards of a church. The city had to make an exception when they realized their new indoor stadium was only 400-and-something yards from First Baptist Church.

So I end up missing a lot of wedding receptions. The plain fact is that although most people in these parts express disapproval of alcohol, they want to have it at wedding receptions. The problem is me, the minister. If I perform the ceremony, then of course the couple feels they have to invite me to the reception. Everybody assumes—quite wrongly—that I, a minister, am against Demon Rum. That means they don't break out the champagne until I leave. Because I know all this, and because I want people to have a good time, I usually spend about ten minutes at wedding receptions. But it hardly seems fair.

I hope you're smiling as you read this; I mean it to be funny. Of course I'm aware of all the problems alcohol can cause. But in moderation, wine, for example, is a delightful part of human life. Ben Franklin said "Beer is proof that God loves us and wants us to enjoy ourselves." And Jesus, of course, turned water into wine at Cana. But please believe me when I tell you there are millions of people who think that "wine" was grape juice.

So the next time you enjoy a glass of champagne at a wedding reception, thank God for the delight of it. I'll be enjoying mine at home.

"Come, eat of my bread and drink of the wine I have mixed." (Proverbs 9:5)

JUNE 6
The Lotto

As I write, the news is full of stories about people buying lotto tickets. The jackpot is up to $300 million. I understand the temptation—even though Uncle Sam takes half, $150 million is still a lot of money.

Funny thing, though. Everything I've read about lottery winners shows the money doesn't make them happy—quite the opposite, actually. A sizeable portion of lottery winners say they wish they'd never won.

How in the world can that possibly be? While money can't buy happiness, it's very difficult to be happy without it. I've read stories of poverty-stricken homes full of love, but I'm willing to bet not a single one of those families would have refused enough money for heat, food, and clothing. More than that, in the Bible God often rewards good people with wealth.

But the Bible also teaches about the dangers of money. When I allow my fantasies to take over, I see what would happen if I suddenly became wealthy: I would buy a house—and not just any old house, but my dream house. That would mean spending days and days visiting houses with a realtor. And maybe I couldn't find exactly what I wanted, and would decide to build. That would probably take a year, and I'd be consumed with making sure everything went right. I'd have to choose materials and paint colors and wallpaper. I'd have to shop for new furniture because what I have isn't going to work in my dream house.

Suddenly, my fantasy life has taken me to a situation in which I'm consumed by the things money can buy. When would I find the time to teach, to write? When would I have the time to see my friends and family? Wouldn't it just be easier to skip church? And wouldn't time for prayer get harder and harder to find?

I'm willing to say there are people in this world who handle lots of money wisely, but I'm not so sure I'd be one of them. Maybe God knows what's best when arranging my life in such a way that millions don't fall in my lap.

"It is easier for a camel to go through the eye of a needle than for someone who is rich to enter the kingdom of God." (Mark 10:25)

JUNE 7
Baby at Work

A colleague made her first appearance at the office since the birth of her son, and she brought him along. In a mere thirty seconds, there were six women hovering around the two-month-old boy. I wasn't lucky enough to get a chance to hold him; I had to be content with putting my finger in the palm of his hand and feeling him squeeze it as he searched out my eyes. Swoon.

There's just something about a baby; it's primal. Although it's a controversial thing to say these days, I'll go ahead and say it: there's a maternal instinct. Other mothers instantly remember the too-short infant stage of their own little children, even if those children have kids of their own by now. Young women look in a baby's eyes and see what they hope is their own future. Women who can't have children but desperately want them feel a tremendous internal ache, and women who don't want them find themselves avoiding the maternal circle like the plague. Mostly positive, sometimes negative, the feelings that babies stir in us are strong. I've known very few women who are blasé about babies.

This is as it should be, I think. Babies are one of God's billboards that read something like this: "Life is good. Hope for the future. You thought you could never feel love this deep? Believe it or not, my love for you is a hundred times as strong." A bit of a miracle in itself that something so small and so vulnerable can telegraph such an important message. But then again, isn't that just like the God we know?

Now the man knew his wife Eve, and she conceived and bore Cain, saying, "I have produced a man with the help of the Lord." (Genesis 4:1)

JUNE 8
The Face of Jesus

Sunday's paper carried a story about a local woman who used a white towel to clean the mud off her dog's feet, then glanced at the towel and saw in it the face of Jesus. She immediately called her husband, and he also saw it right away. Somehow, this towel came to the attention of a reporter.

These things happen in Tennessee. A couple of years ago, a rural woman saw the face of Jesus in the rust patterning the side of the refrigerator that sat on her front porch. Newspaper subscribers got a picture of that one too.

Quite honestly, I can't see it. Maybe the photos don't accurately convey the details that would make the face clear. Or maybe, as I heard a couple of people suggesting in the corner coffee shop, the woman is a nut case.

My friend Volney Gay, who is a professor of religion, anthropology, and psychiatry at Vanderbilt, was interviewed by *The Tennessean*. I suspect the reporter sided with the coffee drinkers and wanted somebody to give a psychological explanation of exactly what kind of craziness caused these things. If that's the case, he was gravely disappointed.

Instead, Volney said, "It has always occurred. It's not a delusion. It's part of religious life—not just Christianity but all religions. What does a tree produce?" he said, referring to a Biblical passage. "You judge a tree by its fruits, not its roots. What is the outcome of her religious experience? How has her life changed? That is what's important. It sounds like it has changed for the better."

Many people would find Volney's comments astounding, given that he's a psychoanalyst and critical of religion. For him, the woman's experience was real and important, whatever its source. Those of us who believe in God—whether we see the face or not—must allow the possibility that the source is divine. But the wonderful thing about all this is that God has created human beings in such a way that whether faces like these are carefully drawn by an angel's hand or form themselves in the God-created minds of some who see it, the source is always God.

"No good tree bears bad fruit, nor again does a bad tree bear good fruit." (Luke 6:43)

June 9
Bumper Stickers

My friend Paul is loaning me his car for an out-of-town trip. Since mine's about ten years old, I don't feel very safe driving it long distances. Paul will drive my car while I have his, but it's not the engine he's worried about—it's the bumper stickers.

The rear end of my car is fairly well-plastered. Back when I was a minister in a small town where everybody knew my car, I didn't feel free to express my quirky opinions on my bumper; some of my parishioners would have been mortified to be identified with some of my beliefs. So since then, I may have gone a little overboard to compensate. Anyhow, here are the sayings on the back of my car: "Save Tibet." "First they burn books. Then they burn people." "Goddess Bless." "I'd rather be driving—NC Zen Center." "Vanderbilt University Faculty Parking Permit."

I admit it's not a middle-of-the-road group of sentiments. I'm not a middle-of-the-road person. For many, many years, I thought everyone had to like me for me to be a "good" person. Turns out that's not the case. I discovered that no matter who I am— unless I'm a completely blank slate—I'm going to offend *someone*, so I may as well be who I am. I heartily believe God affirms this approach to life. After all, God's the one who made me this way.

Some of the remarks I get about my bumper stickers are positive; others are about as rude as remarks can get. But that's okay; not everybody liked Jesus of Nazareth either. I don't have to be liked—I just have to be who God means for me to be.

And he said, "Truly I tell you, no prophet is accepted in the prophet's hometown." (Luke 4:24)

JUNE 10
Children at the YMCA

Since I'm more or less self-employed, I have the luxury of setting my own schedule. That means I can go to the YMCA when it's least crowded, in the middle of the day. I'm always glad, though, when school lets out, because then the Y is teeming with children.

I teach at a university, I write at home. I go to movies during the day and the grocery store late at night. One side effect of this life is that I'm rarely around children. I don't like that; there's something about it that just feels wrong. It's not right to move in a world where everyone's an adult.

For most of human history, people lived in communities that included everyone from newborn babies to the most ancient elders. I suspect God intends it that way, because when I find myself cut off from either end of the age spectrum, I start getting a little hinky.

I need the enthusiasm, innocence, and curiosity of children to keep me from getting old. I need the wisdom, peace, and perspective of old folks to keep me from forgetting the long view. Unfortunately, American culture is leaning toward segregation of the ages. Old folks don't die at home anymore; they go to retirement communities and nursing homes. There are apartment complexes that ban children. Even

Jesus' disciples thought some events were "adults only" and tried to keep children from "bothering" the Lord. He made it very clear they had it wrong; and the main place I find my age-variegated community is at church.

A university campus is an exciting place to be in many ways, but it's not the real world. I need a dose of children on a regular basis. That's why I like it when they get out of school for the summer and play "Marco Polo" in my lap lane.

> *How very good and pleasant it is when kindred live together in unity! (Psalm 133:1)*

JUNE 11
Laughter

I have a friend, "Sam," who can't laugh. He can smile and he can chuckle, but when it comes to a deep down belly laugh, the kind that makes your stomach hurt, he's laughter-impaired. He had a rough childhood in many ways, and so it's good he's in therapy. He says one of the ways he'll know he's better is when he's able to laugh.

There's a contemporary religious artist who has painted a picture called "Laughing Christ." I found it a little unsettling at first. Almost every picture I've seen of Jesus shows him either in great distress or gazing off into the distance with a thoughtful look on his face. But surely Jesus laughed. He wouldn't have been human if he hadn't. There's nothing in this life that doesn't have a humorous side, dark though it may be. It shouldn't surprise us that funeral directors are known for telling jokes. ("How's business, Tom?" "Good, good—they're dying to see me.") Scientific studies have shown that laughter does our body good in multiple ways, and we know from experience that laughing is good for the soul. After the first shock wears off, the "Laughing Christ" makes a lot of good sense.

"Blessed are you who weep now, for you will laugh."
(Luke 6:21b)

JUNE 12
Bad Drivers

I don't do well with bad drivers. I get angry, I swear at them, I honk my horn. I am able to believe that serial killers have a chance to get into heaven, but not bad drivers. If I were God, they'd spend eons in the lowest rung of purgatory.

It's a good thing I'm not God, then, isn't it? And if, for instance, it makes *you* angry when women get bossy, then it's a good thing for me that *you're* not God. People don't like the idea of judgment these days—"You're being judgmental!"—and there are scripture passages to support that distaste. But no matter how "liberal" our Christianity may be, we can't really get past the fact that there will be a judgment some day. Jesus spoke of it, scripture writers assumed it, and the church has always taught it. The reason the idea of judgment scares me so much is my experience. I've had others judge me, and I've judged other people. There's no human being on earth—including me—whose judgment I'm willing to trust.

The good news about judgment is that it is *God* who does the judging. You and I can fuss and fight and debate about whether something is a sin, but in the final analysis, God is the one who decides all that. I am certain that when I meet my maker, I will be confronted with every single sin I have committed, and I'm sure I'll have to agree with the charges. But my faith tells me I have an advocate, a defense attorney who will argue my case and in the closing summation offer up his life for my freedom. At that point, I don't want anyone but God making the decision on what I'm going to be doing for the rest of eternity. I want that so badly, I'm even willing to let God have the final word on bad drivers.

Therefore you have no excuse, whoever you are, when you judge others; for in passing judgment on another you condemn yourself, because you, the judge, are doing the very same things. (Romans 2:1)

JUNE 13
HMO Horror Stories

I once had a friend named Carolyn Smith. She had been working thirty years in a hunger ministry for slave wages when she was diagnosed with ovarian cancer. Her HMO refused to cover an investigative treatment that might have saved her life, and she died. Carolyn died not because of a lack in modern medicine. She died because of the way health insurance works these days.

I can't pretend to have the answer to this mess we're in. All I know is this is *not* what God has in mind. Jesus didn't heal the paralytic halfway and leave him to drag himself home with one good leg. He didn't tell the woman with a hemorrhage she had a pre-existing condition that disqualified her for healing.

Physical healing is central to the Christian faith. It's so central, in fact, that the Greek words for healing also mean salvation. God doesn't care only about our souls; if that were the case, then Jesus wouldn't have wasted so much time and energy dealing with sick people. Our

God wants us to be well in body, mind, and spirit. Anything that stands in the way of that wellness is evil. I don't know anybody who's going to argue with me when I say cancer, for example, is evil. It's a lot more controversial to say lack of health care is evil, but that's what I believe. I could be wrong, of course. I always have to allow that possibility. But if I'm right, then what's God going to have to say to the people responsible for Carolyn Smith's death?

The centurion answered, "Lord, I am not worthy to have you come under my roof; but only speak the word, and my servant will be healed." (Matthew 8:8)

June 14
Blast From the Past

I picked up the phone this morning and on the other end was an old friend. Sherry and I were friends when I was attending seminary in Lexington, Kentucky. We had the same spiritual director and he introduced us. We were close then, and Sherry was the best possible combination of friend, older sister, and mother. We haven't stayed in close touch since I left, but fifteen minutes into our phone conversation it was as if we'd had lunch last week.

I'm beginning to suspect that God is not a linear being. My tendency—and I think the tendency of most Westerners—is to think of life as a straight line that has a past, present, and future. I don't think that's right. It's not a circle, either, because I don't and can't have the same experiences again and again. Life with God is most like a spiral; while I go forward and leave behind people and questions and passions, I often find myself encountering them again. That second encounter always has a different texture to it, because I've changed in the meantime and so have the others. But many times these beloved people and I have changed in parallel ways, so we can pick up a friendship that's different from the earlier one but perhaps even better.

I'm just beginning to get a glimpse of the way God works with our lives. I suspect that at the end of my life I'll be able to look back and see nothing was wasted or lost. Instead every friend and every experience gets added to the swirl of that spiral. I don't have a full vision of it yet, but I'm starting to see that in a very important way, we never really lose anyone. That's how generous a God we have.

When they were satisfied, he told his disciples, "Gather up the fragments left over, so that nothing may be lost." (John 6:12)

JUNE 15
Please, Please, Please?

During every registration period, I have one or two students who call or visit my office to make a breathless plea. "Hi Dr. Stroup my name is Carla and I'm a senior and I need your class to graduate and I tried to register for it but it's closed and. . . ." I have taken to stopping them before they get very far into the story. What they want is to get in my class. The registrar, not me, is the one who decides the maximum number of students for my classes, and the way I look at it, the more the merrier. These students always gush gratitude, because from their perspective, I've given them something they thought was difficult to get.

It reminds me of a story about Alexander the Great. He had a practice of hearing requests from ordinary subjects on occasion. One day, a poor farmer came in and boldly asked for a dowry for his daughter, an education for his son, and more land for himself. Alexander granted his requests immediately. His courtiers were astounded and asked him why he was so generous to someone so pushy. Alexander roared, "I'm tired of people asking me for pennies. That man treated me like a king. He asked for what he knew a king could grant."

I admit that sometimes my prayer goes something like this: "Well, God, I don't expect the best, and I don't expect the most, but I wonder if you could please just give me the teeniest, tiniest second-hand version?" I think God is much more like Alexander and wants to shower me with blessings. It's a bit insulting to God to ask for a little bit because it assumes God has little to give. If I can so easily give my students something they need, then doesn't it make sense that it's only easier for God?

The righteous will surround me, for you will deal bountifully with me. (Psalm 142:7b)

June 16
Life Coaching

I only recently heard of a person called a "life balance coach." I was a little skeptical at first because it sounded a little goofy, but Thelma is the least goofy woman I've ever met. She's a savvy businesswoman who knows there's more to life than money.

I think most of the people Thelma works with are successful middle-aged men and women who sit back, realize they've attained their goals, and ask, "Is that it?" She helps people decide not so much what kind of work they want to do, but what kind of life they want to live. What, she asks, are your priorities now?

The search for meaning? Achievement? Or play and creativity?

I think this process is great, but it rankles me that our culture has had to invent a position for someone who offers this kind of help. In old-fashioned language, Thelma is helping people discern their vocations. She doesn't use religious language, but that's what she's doing, and she has a clientele because apparently the church doesn't do this much any more.

That's a shame because everyone, not just clergy and religious, has a vocation. God has a call for everyone. It takes time and thought and prayer to discern what a particular person's call is. I've used spiritual direction for this process, and I know that without the insights I've gained, I'd be floundering around and very unhappy.

Thelma is a wonderful person and she's doing good work. I just wish the church would start emphasizing this aspect of the Christian life. Imagine a congregation's brochure or web site that says, "What does God want from you? Come worship with us, and we'll help you figure it out." In the meantime, try www.thelmakidd.com.

He has told you, O mortal, what is good; and what does the Lord require of you but to do justice, and to love kindness, and to walk humbly with your God?
(Micah 6:8)

June 17
The Garden's Bounty

There is simply no substitute for corn on the cob that's been picked just hours before it hits the boiling water. A little butter, some salt and pepper, cute handles to put in each end if you're fussy. That's all it takes to create heaven on earth.

Or homegrown tomatoes. Red, firm, juicy, tangy. All it takes is a slice of a big, beefy tomato sprinkled with salt and pepper between two slices of fresh bread slathered with mayo. Eat it over the kitchen sink and listen for the angels groaning in envy because they don't have taste buds.

One of the great delights of civilization is the restaurant. A chef takes exotic ingredients I never considered combining and out of them makes a delicious meal. It's easy to spend $50 or $100 on a meal at a really good restaurant.

But when a four-star restaurant isn't in the budget—and it rarely is in mine—there's the consolation of produce from the garden. Simple, plain produce, barely tampered with. I do believe God's simplest creations rival the finest gourmet cooking. Or maybe that's another way to look at it: our God is the ultimate chef.

Then [Jesus] said to his disciples, "The harvest is plentiful, but the laborers are few." (Matthew 9:37)

JUNE 18*
Father's Day

(Observed third Sunday of June)

I feel sorry for fathers these days. They still live with the stereotype of fathers as distant men who earn the money to support their family but who aren't really invested in their children. On television, they're portrayed as buffoons. I can't count the number of sitcoms in which the father is a clueless idiot.

That's really too bad, because fathering is an extremely important job. A father's contribution doesn't end with the provision of sperm. Real, actual fathers hang in there with their wives, work hard, and are as involved in their children's lives as are their mothers. Just as mothers give unique gifts to children, so, too, do fathers.

Boys get a role model, someone who teaches them how to be men. Girls get a loving, caring, gentle male who teaches them how they should be treated by the men in their lives when *they* are adults. It's not that another man can't give some of this to children; they can. But it's profoundly important for children that this kind of acceptance and approval comes from their fathers. Dad isn't just any man—he's *the* standard by which boys will measure themselves and girls will measure the men in their future.

Children also get their first pictures of God from their fathers. In church they hear God spoken of as "Father," and so their experience of their own fathers gives them a gut-level belief about what God is like. Lucky children with good fathers accrue a picture of a God who is loving, kind, supportive, and protective.

No human father can be completely like God the Father. In theological terms, it's not that God is like men and so we call him father; rather, it's that God is the perfect father from whom human fathers are to learn how to be good fathers. Today is a good day to thank fathers for what they've given us. It wouldn't hurt to also tell them how much they taught us about God.

> *The father of the righteous will greatly rejoice.*
> *(Proverbs 23:24a)*

JUNE 19
"Girl" Magicians

I met a woman magician the other day. Though neither of us had any statistics, we both agreed that magic—the commercial kind, at least—seems to be a man's field. All the way from sleight-of-hand to illusions, almost every magician I remember seeing on television or in the movies was a man. There was often a woman present during these performances, but she was the one in the box who got sawed in half, or the one in the box that had swords stuck into it, or . . . well, you get the idea.

I doubt there's anyone out there making a serious philosophic argument that women shouldn't be magicians. That just seems to be the way it's turned out. I'm not saying that discrimination against women in the workplace is over, but compared to thirty years ago, women have unprecedented access to any kind of job they want.

Or that they're called to. And I think that's the point. God has a vocation in mind for each one of us. Sometimes that's what we think of as a "job"—something to get paid for. Sometimes vocations are other things: friend, wife, mother, community activist, Girl Scout troop leader. For every woman—and every man, for that matter—God has a plan in mind. I like to think of it as an invitation, because God rarely *forces* people into anything. But I'll be happiest when I'm living out the vocation God has chosen for me, simply because God created me for it—fashioned me in such a way that there's a near-perfect fit between me and my vocation. Sometimes women have to work hard to break into stereotypically male vocations, but if God is the one who's calling, then the effort is bound to be worth it.

*Now the Lord came and stood there, calling as before,
"Samuel! Samuel!" And Samuel said, "Speak, for
your servant is listening." (1 Samuel 3:10)*

JUNE 20
Modesty

When I was visiting my sister recently, a bunch of us gathered around the dining room table for brunch, and then stayed to talk—one of my family's favorite activities. My brother-in-law decided to go take a shower. After a while their youngest decided she had to ask Daddy something and whipped open the bathroom door to do so—just when he was standing there in his birthday suit. He yelled, she closed the door and ran back to us, eyes big as saucers, and we all laughed. We exchanged stories of our first memories of seeing the opposite sex naked. My eight-year-old niece contributed to the discussion and said, "Well, I saw Daddy once without his pants on, and let me tell you, it was not a pretty sight." You can imagine the laughter that followed.

Children are naturally curious about other peoples' bodies—those of their friends, the opposite sex, grownup women and adult men. That's why the game of "doctor" is so popular. But adult bodies are quite different from their own, and boys' bodies are quite different from girls'. Like most of us, children seem to assume that they are the norm—anyone who differs is weird.

Maybe one way to say it is that appreciation of the bodies of the opposite sex is an acquired taste. And God is the one who puts in us the drive to acquire it. At adolescence our hormones kick in and all of a sudden, the bodies of them—whether boys or girls— become exceedingly attractive. It's good this happens, or the human race would have died out a long time ago. Once again, it appears that God has arranged things just right.

Upon my bed at night I sought him whom my soul loves; I sought him, but found him not; I called him, but he gave no answer. (Song of Songs 3:1)

JUNE 21*
Summer Solstice

This is the longest day of the year. If you talk to people who live in extreme northern lands, they'll tell you that on this day there is no night at all—just daylight. For most of us the day isn't quite that dramatic, but it's a good day to mark nonetheless.

It makes sense to me that the pagans of old worshiped the sun. It is the sun, after all, that keeps our planet warm enough to live on. Human life couldn't exist on earth without the sun. But even if it could, earth would be a pretty dismal place without the sun to warm us after a dip in the pool, make the flowers grow, and dispel the frightening tentacles of darkness that reach into our dreams and haunt us.

There is also great comfort in the fact that each and every morning, the sun rises. Many ancient cultures have myths about some hero who stops an evil being from keeping the sun hidden. While it hardly has the power of an ancient myth, the line from the song in the musical *Annie* conveys the same sentiment: "The sun will come out tomorrow." On a symbolic level, humans over the centuries have seen the sun as a force of hope.

While the old pagans had the source of the sun wrong, they were absolutely right about its importance to us on both physical and psychological levels. We know that it is our God, Yahweh, who set the planets in motion around our sun and created a luxurious habitat for a new kind of creature called human being. The solstice is a good day to remember that fact and celebrate it.

Then the righteous will shine like the sun in the kingdom of their Father. (Matthew 13:43a)

JUNE 22
Volcanoes

When I was a teenager, my parents took us one summer on vacation to "the big island" of Hawaii, where there is an active volcano crater. Every few years it has an eruption; lava snakes down to the sea, where the meeting of molten rock and water creates steam and new land. When we visited, the volcano had erupted just a few months before, and we were one of the first groups allowed to tour the new lava flow.

We learned that there are several different kinds of lava. Some thick lava belches out of the earth so slowly a child could easily outrun it. Other lava is as liquid as water and runs just as quickly. It's very difficult to understand just what a volcano is until you've had the experience. When we made our tour, the newly-created ground had cooled enough to give us a safe, solid place to walk, but it was still so hot that at the end, the treads on my sneakers had melted into a smooth, slick surface.

THAT is the sort of thing that makes your stomach do flip-flops. That flip-flop feeling is awe. It's a sudden, overwhelming realization that the world is so big and the forces of nature so powerful that human beings are just grains of sand in comparison. I need to feel awe on occasion, because it reminds me just how powerful God is. And the remarkable thing about that power is that God uses it for my good. Were it not for God's powerful hands holding this beautiful planet together, volcanoes would be spewing lava everywhere, all the time, and I would be nothing but a little crisp. There's quite a drama going on around me on the cosmic level, every single day. But it takes something as unusual as walking on a volcano to give me the appropriate feeling of awe.

Then Job answered the Lord: "See, I am of small account; what shall I answer you? I lay my hand on my mouth." (Job 40:3-4)

JUNE 23
Firefighters

Since he was two, my nephew has had a thing for what toy makers like to call "rescue heroes." Those are police officers, firefighters, EMTs, people who run the "jaws of life," and so on. And while the little boy likes all the rescue heroes, he is particularly fond of firefighters.

He's on to something. Just what exactly is there NOT to like about a firefighter? Of course these people are human and have faults. They live next door, and so we know they're like the rest of us. They are normal, average men and women; unlike celebrities, we don't think twice about seeing them in the grocery store or at church. But the remarkable thing is that every single day, they risk their lives for the rest of us.

I am convinced that firefighters are powered by the Holy Spirit. The whole enterprise doesn't make sense otherwise. Why else would people who have a normal survival instinct rush into a burning building to rescue others? It might make sense if those "others" were family, but total strangers? It really and truly defies logic; I don't usually think about that because I'm so used to seeing firefighters. But I realize that these men and women are, in some way, offering themselves to God as sacrifices. In order to do the good work of God, they are willing to die.

It doesn't surprise me, then, that after the terrorist attacks on the World Trade Center and Pentagon, children started thinking of firefighters as heroes. My nephew had it right all along.

And war broke out in heaven; Michael and his angels fought against the dragon. (Revelation 12:7a)

JUNE 24
Birth of St. John the Baptist

Luke tells us that Mary and Elizabeth, John's mother, were relatives. That makes John and Jesus cousins, I guess—to one degree or another. It's weird for me to read the stories of John appearing out of the wilderness, heralding the arrival of the messiah, and realize that John had grown up with that messiah. Whether he knew as a child who Jesus was we can't know, but it seems reasonable to imagine that they were well acquainted, especially since they were just six months apart in age.

My imagination takes me back to some reunion of the Mary/Elizabeth clan, when the boys are, say, eight or nine. As women seem to do at functions like this, they gather in a group that allows them to chat but also to keep an eye on the kids. I imagine the women waiting until Mary and Elizabeth have left the group. Then the gossip starts: "Oh, can you believe that John? He's a beast! Can't his mother keep him under control? I guess you can't expect otherwise given her age. But the boy eats bugs, for crying out loud. Don't they notice how weird he is?" Then I imagine this group turning its attention to Mary's son. "Now that Jesus, he's a good boy. Not a lick of trouble to his parents. He's quiet, he works hard in his father's shop, smart as a whistle and polite too."

The women's conclusion on all this: in the future, John's parents will grieve their crazy son, but Jesus' will bask in the comfort of a good Jewish boy.

I go to this length because I often need to remind myself that God's ways are mysterious to me. Had I been one of the women in that group, I, too, would have foreseen trouble for John and a comfortable life for Jesus. But God knew that even though John would sacrifice the comfort of home for the wilderness, prophesy the coming of the messiah, and baptize people for repentance of their sins, it was Jesus who was going to seem crazy to a lot of people.

You just never know what God's up to. Perhaps John's prophetic personality *did* make him a difficult child. But God would take that seemingly disturbed boy and turn him into the most important herald the world has ever known.

Now John wore clothing of camel's hair with a leather belt around his waist, and his food was locusts and wild honey. (Matthew 3:4)

JUNE 25
Potluck Dinners

One of the things I like best about church has nothing to do with belief or worship. It's the fact that we love potluck dinners. As a minister, I have been to more potlucks than I can remember, and the extra pounds I carry with me are my souvenirs. A potluck is simply marvelous: everyone brings her best food (okay, okay, sometimes "his," but it's usually "her"), plunks it on the table next to everybody else's best food, and the result easily rivals an outrageously expensive dinner in the finest gourmet restaurant.

I wish the church worked like potlucks in other areas of its life. I wish that all Christians would bring their best and plunk it down next to everybody else's. I wish all Christians would prepare their offerings so they're big enough to make up for the contribution some non-cook couldn't make. I wish all Christians would take at least a little bit of everybody else's offering and proclaim it good. I wish all Christians would take a spoonful of old Mrs. Yancy's horrible tuna Jell-O mold and discreetly dump it in the trash with their paper plates so her feelings wouldn't be hurt. And I wish all people would help clean up, even just a tiny bit.

I've heard the church described as a ship, a mother, a house. I've never heard it described as a potluck dinner. All I know is that while I can't steer a ship, can't have children, and can't build a house, I can bring something to a potluck dinner.

"So have no fear; I myself will provide for you and your little ones." (Genesis 50:21a)

JUNE 26
Former Students

I recently ran into a former student. She rushed up to me and wanted to know whether I was teaching in the anthropology department again. My answer was yes, but I had dozens of questions about her. I couldn't ask them all, of course, but they were there. How was your semester abroad? Did your thumb heal after you burned it welding a sculpture? Do you like your work? Have you found someone to love for a lifetime? Have you been blessed with children? Did you find your life's passion, and if you did, what is it?

I did ask my student to keep in touch, and pressed my business card in her hand so she'd have my e-mail address. I do this with all my students. I invite them to write me and let me know what they're doing. Only two or three from each class do. I am always delighted to hear from those few, but wonder about the others and miss them. When I said this to one of my former students, she said, "Dr. Stroup, nobody thinks you really mean it."

I was stunned. Of course I mean it. I come to care for every student over the course of a semester. In their weekly two-page papers they write not only about anthropology but also their hopes, their dreams, their disappointments. I will never forget a single one of them.

It occurs to me, though, that I'm not immune to the student mindset that so disappoints me. When I imagine God taking as much interest in me as I do in all my students, I don't believe it. Oh, I *believe* it—I mean I think this is true. But it's hard to feel. It's too easy to feel insignificant, just one of billions that God can't be bothered with. It was good for me to run into my former student. She stirred up feelings in me that I simply must admit God feels for me. That stunned me too.

But the steadfast love of the Lord is from everlasting to everlasting. (Psalm 103:17a)

JUNE 27
Class Reunions

My high school recently held our class's twenty-fifth reunion. I was lucky to attend high school in Hawaii, but unlucky to be stuck on the mainland without the funds to travel to the reunion. I did talk at length with friends who were able to get there. I found myself hungry for information about people I hadn't seen in a quarter century.

Class reunions must be very similar, because in our culture we already "know" what a reunion is going to be like—whether that's a real one or one in the movies. The girls who were beautiful but stuck-up in high school are still beautiful but unhappy down deep. The nerds who were miserable in high school are now successful businesspeople. Everybody's aged, although there's always one or two folks who look like they did decades ago. And the major theme of class reunions is this: wanting to impress everyone with what you've made of yourself.

One of the pictures I conjure in my mind when someone has died is of the heavenly reunion that he or she is going through. Not only will that person be with family and friends, but also with God. And the remarkable thing about the *real* reunion is that no one is a failure, no one is a nerd, no one needs to impress anybody else. That's because in the "final reunion," we will be cleansed of all the trappings of this life, and we'll live as God intended us to live—without sin, in the joyful company of others, and the always-apparent presence of God.

Maybe I'll make it to my thirtieth class reunion. Maybe by then I'll have grown enough as a Christian to not worry about how I look or how people will perceive me. Maybe by then I'll be more focused on the real reunion—the reunion with God.

And I heard a loud voice from the throne saying, "See, the home of God is among mortals. He will dwell with them as their God." (Revelation 21:3a)

JUNE 28
Do I Hafta?

If the classes I teach at Vanderbilt are small enough, I usually ask each student to make a presentation on the work she or he has been doing during the semester. These presentations always come at the end of the semester—partly so the students can gather as much information as possible, but also to give the teacher a much-needed rest from lecturing.

The first time I did this, I started getting phone calls and e-mails from students the Friday before presentations were to start. They wanted to postpone their presentations. Everybody had excuses; one was good (a death in the family). The others were along the lines of "my boyfriend broke up with me," "there's one more thing I want to research," and "I'm hung over." To all but the first student, I said this: "You all have known about these presentations since the first day of class. They were on the syllabus. I'm sorry you've got difficult stuff going on in your life, but part of being an adult means doing things you've committed to even if you don't feel like it."

That probably makes me sound like a mean teacher, but I think it's true. And I'm not unsympathetic. I've asked "Do I hafta?" many times myself. When I start that kind of whining, though, I remember that Jesus asked basically the same question in the garden at Gethsemane. God's answer to him was "yes."

So when I find myself asking God, "Do I hafta?" I usually catch myself and figure it out without an appearance from an angel. Then I go and do what it means to be an adult . . . or what it means to be a Christian.

But Jonah set out to flee to Tarshish from the presence of the Lord. He went down to Joppa and found a ship going to Tarshish; so he paid his fare and went on board, to go with them to Tarshish, away from the presence of the Lord. (Jonah 1:3)

JUNE 29
Sts. Peter and Paul

It makes sense to me that Peter and Paul should be remembered on the same day. It's not just some coincidence that they shared a day of martyrdom. Peter and Paul complemented each other, and we need both of them in the church today.

Peter was a simple man, a fisherman by trade, when Jesus called him. Paul, on the other hand, was a Pharisee, highly educated and even a citizen of Rome, which was an unusual honor for a Jew. After

Jesus' death, Peter is cautious; he wants to be sure to obey the Law so far as God wishes it. It takes a vision for Peter to finally agree that the Jews can eat what was previously considered unclean food. Paul, on the other hand, is almost bubbly in his willingness to give up the old. Everything he was before Jesus entered his life, he says, counts as nothing. Peter's ministry was largely to the Jews and Paul's to the gentiles.

The church today needs the spirits of both great apostles. It needs the traditionalism of Peter's descendants, the papacy, and it also needs the wildness of the Holy Spirit found in Paul's spiritual children. Without Peter, the church would fall into ruins because the tornado that is the Holy Spirit would tear it up without the strong pillars of tradition the Peters have built. Without Paul, the church becomes outdated, intransigent, and complacent.

Jesus asked Peter to tend his sheep, and the risen Christ asked Paul to stop persecuting his people and become one of them. I wonder sometimes how the two got along; they were quite different men. But the fact that the church remains two thousand years later—and not only remains but has prospered—is evidence that whatever their differences, they were able to work them out for the good of all. Not a bad example for parish councils or church boards who can't stop fussing among themselves.

*Then after three years I did go up to Jerusalem to visit
Cephas and stayed with him fifteen days.
(Galatians 1:18)*

JUNE 30
Invisible People

There was a time in my life when I had to work two jobs to pay the bills. One of them was to go early Saturday morning to a store called "A Southern Season" to wax their brick floors. The store was a ritzy place in a ritzy town, and they had lots of people in early to bake the fresh bread they sold each day and stock the shelves with kitchen tools from the other side of the world.

I started at 4 a.m. at one end of the store, and by the time the store opened at 10 a.m., I'd be finished and head home for a nap. At 5 a.m. the bakers came in, and the salespeople at 9 a.m. I've got to admit that when I was waxing brick, I wasn't wearing my nicest clothes. So it shouldn't have surprised me that when the sales staff came in, they ignored me and the other cleaning people. They not only didn't speak to us, they'd look straight at us and their eyes didn't see us. It was very strange to have the experience of being invisible.

One day I got up from my post-waxing nap and went to do my Saturday chores, one of which was buying my favorite tea at A Southern Season. When I walked in the store I wasn't wearing anything special—just regular errand-running clothes. But my hair was clean and I had makeup on. And when I walked in the door, the salespeople jumped all over me: "May I help you, ma'am?" These were the very same salespeople to whom I'd been invisible earlier that morning, and to whom I would still be invisible the next Saturday morning when I was there waxing brick.

Being invisible changed my outlook on the world. I don't claim any moral superiority for it, because if I hadn't had this experience, I would have been as clueless as most of my middle- and upper-class friends are. But here is what I learned: God sees the invisible people in our world just as clearly as the visible ones. And to be a Christian, so should I.

"He has brought down the powerful from their thrones, and lifted up the lowly." (Luke 1:52)

JULY 1
Fine Wine

There's a story that comes from the Hassidic rabbis. A wealthy man had a neighbor who was poor.

Every year at Passover, he sent over some money so the poor man and his family could have their Passover meal and a little extra to tide them over. The rich man had a son, and when he got to a certain age, the father started sending the son over with the money. One year the son came back, the money still in his hand. The father asked him what happened. "I was going over there to take them the money," he said, "when I happened to look in the window. And our neighbor, the man who's supposed to be poor, was sitting there drinking a very expensive bottle of wine."

The father took the money back from his son, opened his wallet, and pulled out more bills. He gave the money back to the boy and said, "Our neighbor must have once been a very wealthy man to have developed a taste for such fine wine. From now on, we'll give him twice as much. Run on, now."

I want to grow in spirit and faith and understanding to the point that my first reaction to the son's revelation is not a feeling that someone's been cheating. I want to grow into the wisdom and generosity of the rabbi who told this tale, and that of the God we both worship. Enough said.

You cause the grass to grow for the cattle, and plants for people to use, to bring forth food from the earth, and wine to gladden the human heart.
(Psalm 104:14-15a)

July 2
Broken Toys

Buzz's favorite dog toy of all time is the cheapest available at the local mega-pet store: a thin plastic ball that squeaks. These balls cost ninety-nine cents apiece, and I do stock up on them. Though he's a little guy and has tiny teeth, Buzz plays so enthusiastically that eventually he'll rip a hole in his ball and it won't squeak any more. And for some reason I'll probably only learn from St. Francis, the squeak is the most important part about it.

So I've created a system. I have a stock of balls hidden away, on standby. When one ball suffers terminal injuries, I bring another out of the stock while Buzz is napping. He never searches for the old balls; he's too enamored of the new ball's fresh squeakiness.

I have preached many a time against treating God like a vending machine: you put in a certain number of good deeds and prayers, and out pops whatever it is you requested. But the fact is that God does give us gift after gift after gift. Some we've asked for. Some come in a form that doesn't precisely match what we had in mind. But the fact is that the vast majority of the gifts God gives us are things we don't think twice about. It's not just that we take these things for granted—though we do—it's that God is constantly giving, when we don't even know we need something.

I guess Buzz would miss his squeaky ball only if his dog mommy neglected to replace the one that's fading. And I think I wouldn't notice the remarkable gifts in my own life until they were missing: the feeling of safety I have in my elfin attic apartment; the way the full moon shines right through my skylights during the winter; the way it feels when I put my hands in clay and make something so beautiful it shocks me.

This isn't the first time I've made this point in this collection of meditations. It probably won't be the last, either. That's because if you're anything like me, you need to be reminded on a regular basis of just how generous God has been to you.

The steadfast love of the Lord never ceases, his mercies never come to an end; they are new every morning; great is your faithfulness. (Lamentations 3:22-23)

JULY 3
St. Thomas, Apostle

St. Thomas' big claim to fame is being the disciple who refused to believe that Jesus had been resurrected until he could put his hands in the wounds his savior had suffered. He got his request, and as I said in the meditation for April 19, I think Thomas has gotten a bad rap for that.

Tradition tells us that Thomas evangelized India. There are legends about his work that are impossible to prove and seem highly unlikely. But it is an undisputed fact that along the Malabar Coast of India, there is a large group of native Christians who call themselves "the Christians of St. Thomas." We don't know much about them before the sixteenth century, but the people themselves have an ancient tradition that St. Thomas established seven churches in Malabar and then went eastward to the Coromandel Coast, where he was martyred.

So often I find myself wondering if I will have a legacy after my death. I've done nothing spectacular, had no children. I imagine Thomas wondered the same about himself. He encountered huge numbers of Hindu people; most of them were indifferent to his message, some were hostile, and a few believed him. I imagine that when he died, he thought his little band of Christians would be swallowed up by the native faith of India in no time. But two thousand years later, they're still here.

That's why I take heart when I wonder about my legacy. St. Thomas reminds me that God can take what I think is a tiny little seed and make it into something big and marvelous.

*"If you then, who are evil, know how to give good gifts
to your children, how much more will your Father in
heaven give good things to those who ask him!"*
(Matthew 7:11)

JULY 4
Independence Day

I'm an Army brat and I've probably seen more
parades than a dozen civilian kids put together. I've
heard the national anthem so many times and at such
meaningful events that I have to take control of
myself when I sing it, or I'll end up crying. Even
when I think this country is headed in the wrong
direction, I still love it. I wouldn't want to live anywhere else in the world. There's no country that's
even a close second.

God has been remarkably kind to us as a nation.
God's providence combined people and events in
such a way that we are very blessed. Of course we
have tremendous national resources—from the
mountains, to the prairies, to the oceans white with
foam—but we have remarkable political resources as
well. We have the freedom of speech and the freedom
to worship as we wish. We have the opportunity to

affect the way this country is run. We have a remarkable mandate of tolerance that will, I think, perhaps be the greatest gift we give to the other nations of the world.

Thanks, God, for being so good to the good old U.S.A.

God bless America, land that I love. Stand beside her, and guide her, through the night with the light from above. From the mountains, to the prairies, to the oceans white with foam, God bless America, my home sweet home. God bless America, my home sweet home.
(Irving Berlin)

JULY 5
Spooning

I'm not talking about courting, as our grandparents did when they spoke of "spooning." I'm talking about a man and a woman nestled together in bed, his front to her back, like a couple of spoons in the silverware drawer.

It's a talent, spooning is. Not everyone can do it. The couple has to have a good combination of heights so her hair isn't tickling his face all the time, and so she can sleep comfortably on his arm without making it fall asleep. When it doesn't work, it's miserable; when it does, it's heaven. At least for women, it's heaven. In public, if men speak of it at all, it's as something they do to please their wives.

Spooning is heaven for most women for several reasons. First, it adds another full dimension to the term "sleeping together." When a couple spoons, it means that sleeping with each other is more than having sex. It's an intimate activity in and of itself. And spooning gives most women a wonderful feeling of security.

We're all most vulnerable when we're asleep, and having a man "cover our backs," quite literally, can contribute to a feeling of safety. I've seen several versions of sculptures showing a child nestled into a big hand.

Problem is, I don't know anyone who's ever found a hand big enough to nestle in—child or adult. Spooning is as close as we can get in this world, I think, to experiencing the reality of God's continual protection and care.

See, I have inscribed you on the palms of my hands.
(Isaiah 49:16a)

JULY 6
"Idols"

I regret to recall that when I was young, the leaders in my denomination taught us that Catholics were "idol worshipers." The evidence was clear, according to them—after all, look at all those statues. And we knew worshiping idols was one of the *big* sins.

I regret to say that there are probably some ministers in my denomination today who still utter similar hateful and misguided remarks. The fact is that statues are not only *not* idols, they are positively good for us.

Part of the problem with our faith is that we have a God who is invisible. We can see evidence of her existence, yes, but we don't know what God looks like. It's hard to be in a relationship with such an abstract being.

The flip side of that invisibility and transcendence is the incarnation. In Jesus, God became human, changed the rules of eternity, and left us with many consolations until the time we are to be reunited with God. The sacraments are some of those consolations, but so, too, are things we call "sacramentals"—not sacraments in and of themselves, but objects that do similar things the sacraments do: serve as an outward and visible sign of an inward and invisible grace.

Because we're embodied, we live through our five senses. It's very difficult for me as a sense-dependent being to understand and relate to someone I cannot see, hear, taste, touch, or smell. That's where statues come in—as do rosaries, icons, medals, and holy water. They give me something tangible as a channel to reach God.

Quite frankly, I think all churches could use a few statues or icons. Otherwise, we leave our believers crippled in their search for the holy. Idols, indeed!

For while we live, we are always being given up to death for Jesus' sake, so that the life of Jesus may be made visible in our mortal flesh. (2 Corinthians 4:11)

JULY 7
Coincidence

I was at a meeting of the board of trustees of my denomination's historical society when I got to chatting with one of the new trustees. He was from east Tennessee, he told me. I was amazed to hear that because, I told him, I have a sister who lives in east Tennessee. What town did he live in? Johnson City, he said, and I replied, even more amazed: That's wild—my sister lives in Elizabethton (just a couple of miles from Johnson City). He said he did, too, actually—he just told people Johnson City because no one had ever heard of Elizabethton. Well, we went on like this until we discovered that he lived half a block away from my sister. An amazing coincidence.

Of course I want to make some sort of sense out of it; I want to understand how such a thing could happen, and "coincidence" just doesn't do it for me. Freud would tell me that it was a coincidence only because my unconscious mind linked the two together. Jung would say this was an example of synchronicity—a non-causal principle of connection. And a hundred other thinkers would give me a hundred other explanations of this coincidence, along with all the others I've encountered.

To tell the truth, I like this explanation the best: Coincidence is when God chooses to remain anonymous.

The word "coincidence" does not appear in the Bible.
(Anonymous)

JULY 8
Clergy

I've served two churches as an interim minister, pastoring them while they searched for a permanent pastor. Denominations without bishops to appoint clergy to congregations have search committees that look at the resumes of dozens of candidates, interview many, and finally offer a call to one. It's usually a long process, because it's pretty hard to please everyone on a search committee. Even folks who have their clergy appointed know that no pastor can please every parishioner.

So I liked the story of one candidate. Every single church he'd been in had grown. He'd taken several churches from just a handful of people to attendance in the hundreds, even thousands. He had a good education, was on the young side of middle age, and so had the best of both worlds: experience *and* energy. He had glowing recommendations from the highest muckety-mucks in the denomination down to the lowest child in a local congregation. And churches all over the place wanted him.

But there was a down side. The search committee had to get past three things. First, he wasn't married. Although no one ever accused him of any hanky-panky, there was a young man who traveled with him from church to church. Second, he had a serious medical condition. And third, he'd spent time in jail.

The candidate, of course, was St. Paul. It's embarrassing, from both sides of the pulpit, to realize that Paul would probably have a hard time getting work as a pastor today. Evidence from his letters makes it pretty clear he was a controversial figure even in the churches he himself planted.

There's no such thing as a perfect pastor, priest, minister, or preacher. No member of the clergy can please every person in a congregation—and he or she shouldn't be expected to. If she does, then there's too much "comforting of the afflicted" going on, and not enough "afflicting the comfortable."

Three times I was beaten with rods. Once I received a stoning. Three times I was shipwrecked; for a night and a day I was adrift at sea. (2 Corinthians 11:25)

JULY 9
The Fashion Police

Several years ago, I decided that clothes really have only two purposes: to cover and protect our bodies, and to serve as costumes. That changed the way I dressed, quite dramatically. I might wear a brown swing jacket decorated with African designs and cowry shells. Or sneakers covered with red sequins and "There's no place like home" written around the rubber edge. Or a floor-length black chiffon skirt with a yellow cotton T-shirt. In other words, I play with clothes.

As you might imagine, I get a lot of weird looks. I've been astounded by the number of people who feel quite free to comment on my looks. There are some positive comments, yes—"Cool jacket"—but most of them are rather negative: "You'd better run, dear. The fashion police are coming."

This always reminds me of C. S. Lewis' vision of heaven. No one will wear clothes, he said, because there will be no use for them and nobody will be ashamed at their nakedness. He said that since people in heaven are "neither married nor given in marriage," we'll still have genitals but they will serve as mere decoration.

I may not agree with that last sentiment, but overall I think Lewis had it right. In that one perfect place, the only thing that will matter to our eyes is spiritual beauty. I don't know how spiritual beauty will manifest itself in our resurrected bodies. But I *do* know there are no fashion police in heaven. So I continue to costume myself each day, and every time I get a shocked or curious look, I'm reminded of the time and place where no one will care that my shoes—should I choose to wear them—don't come from Italy.

If through delight in the beauty of these things people assumed them to be gods, let them know how much better than these is their Lord, for the author of beauty created them. (Wisdom 13:3)

JULY 10
Children's Art

My apartment is so small that my dining room table serves as my work area as well. Truth to tell, there's more room there for clay, beads, paint, fabric, and everything else than there is for eating. On this table I have a lamp, and leaning against the base of the lamp, in a place of honor, is the oddest "sculpture" you've ever seen.

It's made of clay . . . several colors of clay that have been mixed together just enough to create swirls. It's a sculpture of a woman, but she has no hands and her legs look more like cones than anything else. The only reason I have this sculpture there is because it was made by my beloved niece.

Everyone who's ever had children or even liked them a little bit has been the recipient of their artwork. Refrigerators often serve as art galleries with revolving exhibitions. Objectively, this art is . . . well, it's childish. But when it's created with love and seen through the eyes of love, it's more beautiful than anything Rembrandt could paint or Rodin could sculpt.

I think God sees our work that way. After all, God's own handiwork—nature—has some pretty odd-looking creations. Duck-billed platypus and walruses are, by our aesthetics, ugly. Whether we're artists or not, we all create things: families, gardens, non-profits, homeless shelters, and on and on. And no matter what any human thinks of this work, including ourselves, God sees it as beautiful. And that's because, just like my niece's sculpture, our work is made with love and seen through the eyes of love.

"Look at Behemoth, which I made just as I made you; it eats grass like an ox." (Job 40:15)

July 11
St. Benedict

Benedict is rightly known as the man who first established a monastic order. Although I've long had a fascination with monasticism and have often sought silence and the presence of God in monasteries and convents, I'm afraid some people don't like monasticism. All too often I've heard comments like, "What a waste. Think of all the good works that could be done by people who've locked themselves up in religious orders. What a life—must be nice to feel holy and not have to *do* anything."

I sometimes fear that such friends think prayer isn't "work" because it doesn't "do" anything. But anybody who's cultivated a regular prayer life knows otherwise. Stay with a monastic community for a week, keep the hours with them, and you'll definitely know prayer is work. And prayer *does* do things. When I was very sick with cancer, I could tell that friends had asked religious in five different convents or monasteries to pray for me. Me—little old me! I *felt* the power of that prayer.

My skeptical friends would be comforted to know that Benedict himself gave alms and food to the poor and tended to their illnesses. But I'm going to be stubborn and maintain that the biggest gift Benedict gave all of us is the heritage of all those voices raised in prayer—every day, many times a day. Skeptics always ask for the proof that such prayer does anything. My answer is always this: What would our world be like if all that prayer *hadn't* been offered? Thank you, Benedict.

When beginning any good work, pray fervently that God may complete it. (St. Benedict)

JULY 12
Gardening

I don't have a green thumb. I've tried, but it seems to be the case that either you're a gardener or you're not.

If I'm honest with myself, I know that's not true. I have a neighbor who keeps a yard and beautiful gardens, and it's by watching Harriet that I've discovered the secret to gardens: hard work. I see a lot of her when I walk my dog, and very rarely is she sitting on her porch sipping lemonade and admiring her handiwork. She's usually on her hands and knees or behind a mower, working her tail off. The woman doesn't quit. I don't know where she gets the energy, but I have finally figured out that the secret of green thumbs is hard work. Despite common belief, even the garden of Eden needed tending!

In many ways, it's the same with our spiritual lives. I'm not talking about our salvation—that's in the hands of God and only in the hands of God. While our relationship with God is suffused with grace, it also takes a lot of hard work.

Plain and simple, there's nothing better than daily prayer. It's hard to get in the habit, I know, and easy to get out of it. My daily life is rushed and filled with important tasks. It can seem almost impossible to pray every single day for even fifteen minutes. But if I'm honest with myself, I realize how much time I devote to television, the Internet, and all the other wonderful distractions of modern life. Surely I can cut back just a bit and give that time to God.

The result, I think, is a garden like Harriet's— lush, beautiful, and sustaining.

The Lord God took the man and put him in the garden of Eden to till it and keep it. (Genesis 2:15)

JULY 13
Tattoos

I don't have a tattoo, and don't intend to get one. I've been tempted only a couple of times. I once saw a photo of a woman who'd had the scar from her mastectomy tattooed with a flowering vine. And since my eyebrows never really recovered after chemotherapy, I've wondered whether it's possible to have them tattooed on.

I haven't taken the step, but I don't have a problem with people who have. I know a lot of parents are horrified when their children—now past the legal age of consent—get tattoos. "Just imagine," they say. "When you're seventy years old, you'll still have that tattoo of a butterfly on your ankle.

They're permanent. You can't get rid of them without expensive laser surgery!"

This strikes me as funny, because the folks who protest have often allowed themselves to be tattooed. It's not a visible tattoo, but when at baptism the priest makes the sign of the cross on the person's head, it marks one forever and always as belonging to Christ. And even with the most advanced cosmetic surgery, that tattoo can't be removed.

That's rather reassuring to me. Maybe I'll get a visible tattoo myself one day—the day I use my 105th eyebrow pencil. But in the meantime, I like knowing that I am marked as Christ's own, forever.

For in the one Spirit we were all baptized into one body—Jews or Greeks, slaves or free—and we were all made to drink of one Spirit. (1 Corinthians 12:13)

July 14
Bl. Kateri Tekakwitha

Kateri was the first Native American Christian to receive the status of "blessed" from the church. Her life was short and filled with tragedy. When she was four, smallpox wiped out her family and left her disfigured. When she was baptized into the Christian faith at twenty, she was cast out of her tribe. At just twenty-four she died, partly because her bout with smallpox had left her with bad health, and partly because she inflicted many penances on herself. Throughout her life and in common with many Native Americans, Kateri felt a close connection to nature.

It's a shame that Kateri's devotion to the created world didn't extend to her own body. Sadly, in her time, people thought that punishing one's body in repentance was a sign of close relationship to God. Today we understand that God takes no pleasure from pain and suffering we inflict on ourselves. But many of the church's saints did and said things that would horrify modern believers. It's important to view Kateri in the context of her own time and understand that she thought she was doing what God asked.

Kateri's greatest deed was to follow Christ when it alienated her from her own people. That's more than enough for anyone to endure, and it is from *this* act that I can learn from her. "My" people are already Christians. Sometimes I do and say things to alienate even them. An example is the blessing with which I end every worship service: "May the blessing of the Father, the Son, and the Holy Spirit, one God and Mother of us all, be with you today and remain with you always." I truly believe that this blessing accurately represents the God we worship; others don't agree and so shut me out. Any time we modern Christians defy the popular culture—sacred or secular—and live as we believe Christ is leading us, then we are likely to experience rejection, just as did Kateri. And just as the Lord she followed.

"Jesus, I love you." (Last words of Bl. Kateri Tekakwitha)

JULY 15
Perfection

I don't think advertising companies would like to hear that I doubt they'll ever come up with a way to make their junk look like real mail. That's because the very best software is missing something: the human element. I know that when I write something by hand, it's quite obvious it came from me. I mess up some of the letters as I write. The pressure of my pen actually dents the paper, more deeply here, lightly there. When I put on the stamp and the return address label, they're always off-kilter.

It is these small clues that tell us whether something or someone is authentic. Real people make mistakes; real people aren't one hundred percent consistent in *anything* they do. I'm suspicious of anyone or anything that's too perfect. It makes me suspect they're up to no good, because normal people don't take the time and energy to make everything perfect—or, wisely, even to try.

Sometimes the fakers I meet are as insignificant as bulk mailers. Others are sophisticated con artists, others still just plain folks who've decided for some reason that they have to look perfect. You know the people I'm talking about; check out the covers of women's magazines the next time you're killing time in a drug store.

Strange as it may sound, I'm always glad when someone's imperfections start popping up. It tells me they are authentic, real. It tells me it's okay if *my* imperfections come out. And it tells me that like snowflakes, God didn't make a single one of us billions of human beings exactly like any of the others.

Indeed, there have to be factions among you, for only so will it become clear who among you are genuine.
(1 Corinthians 11:19)

JULY 16
Music

There are squabbles aplenty in many churches today, and some of the most intense are about music. One group wants "traditional worship music" and another wants "contemporary." Some congregations approach this split by blending the different styles of music in the same service. It can lead to some rather bizarre musical events.

But I do understand why people feel so strongly about music, especially in church. Music reaches us in a way words cannot, even the most eloquent words. Some people are so musically inclined, in fact, that they go to worship services expressly for the music. For them, listening to music *is* worship.

The problem with that, many clergy will tell you, is that music is not precise. Even words spoken in worship can be interpreted in many different ways. That's only more the case with music. But my inclination is to trust the music. Just as I've never heard of any human society that has no religion, neither have I heard of one that has no music. Just as God created humans to be creatures who worship, so are we created to be musical.

Would it be possible to hold a worship service that was nothing but music? I think so. I need words as well, but just listening to some pieces of music away from church puts me in touch with God in some very profound ways. The best news seems to be that we have multiple ways of finding God, and music is an important one.

They were all under the direction of their father for the music in the house of the Lord with cymbals, harps, and lyres for the service of the house of God.
(1 Chronicles 25:6a)

JULY 17
Scary Movies

I am something of a movie buff, and Alfred Hitchcock is one of my favorite directors. He was able to create in his viewers an extremely high level of suspense with very little of the blood and gore that peppers so many movies today.

I like other suspense movies too. I get so wrapped up in them that even though I may know the ending, I still have the emotions of suspense during the film. I think most people are like that, or suspense movies wouldn't sell so well. But when you stop to think about it, it's a rather strange phenomenon.

Why in the world would I pay five-plus dollars and spend two hours of my time in order to make myself feel frightened? I know I'm not a masochist, so it's not that I seek pain. Truth to tell, I think I like scary movies because they help me believe in God.

Face it—some horrible things happen in this world. Almost every human who lives on this planet incurs suffering. We know quite well what it feels like to be sad, frightened, and in pain. What we don't know as well is the experience of having those difficult feelings translated into joy. Certainly that's what God does with the resurrection—takes the most horrible feelings any human could feel, and turns them into joy. But while I know that in my head, I need to experience it too—over and over again.

So when I watch a scary movie, I feel distressing emotions, just as I do in my "real" life. But since most scary movies have a happy ending, I get relief from those emotions, all in the space of two hours. God's translation of my whole life into joy is, I hope, rather far in the future. In the meantime, I need to experience that translation again and again to believe it. Of course no movie can come even close to what God will do with me when I die, but the resolution of scary movies is the closest I can come to that experience.

Weeping may linger for the night, but joy comes with the morning. (Psalm 30:5b)

July 18
Teen Rebels

Many of my friends' children are in their teen years now, and from the sidelines I watch the parents go waaay up and waaay down, as if they're on a roller coaster. When sixteen-year-old Sam is winning awards at the school banquet, his parents fly high. When fourteen-year-old Suzi tries smoking, her parents crash.

The plain fact is that while the teen years are among the most idealistic in the human life span, they are also the most rebellious. In this stage of life, teens practice separating from mom and dad. They know that in the not-too-distant future, they'll be on their own and will have to act like adults. The rebellions of adolescence are experiments with freedom.

As a therapist, I tell parents of teenagers this: The two things they need from you are overwhelming assurance of your love and very clear rules. The teenage way of maturing is pushing *away*. If mom and dad are loose with their rules, the kids don't have anything solid against which to push. One day rebellious teenagers will come back to their parents; having proven to themselves and their parents that they're capable of living as adults, they are then free to enjoy the warmth of parental love.

As a minister, I tell parents of teenagers something else: Rebellion isn't always bad. Some of it is—taking drugs, drinking, promiscuity—and falls in the category of what we call sin. But some of it—most of it, we hope—is simply a matter of exercising the free will God has given them. Parents of course want to keep their children from making the same mistakes they made, but it doesn't work that way. Each generation has to figure it out for themselves.

So it's difficult to be the parent of a teen. But if I look carefully, I can see something important in the midst of all the arguing, curfew violations, bad grades, blue hair, piercings, and tattoos: the ability to see myself through God's eyes. I am like the rebellious teen and God is like the patient and concerned parent. Most of the time I take my own side, but parenting a teen—or watching one's friends parent a teen—helps me understand an awful lot about God.

Even children make themselves known by their acts, by whether what they do is pure and right.
(Proverbs 20:11)

JULY 19
Beads

One of my hobbies is making bracelets and necklaces out of beads. I like to buy big lots of mixed beads and divide them in different ways: color family, size, shape. Then begins the process of making, say, a necklace. First I choose the beads. Which colors should I use together? Which shapes? Do I want a uniform, formal look, or something more casual and mixed up? I string the beads and then set about making knots between them—the way pearl necklaces are knotted. It's a long and tedious process in many ways, but it has a very practical virtue: if the necklace breaks, you'll only lose a couple of beads.

All this has spiritual virtue as well. I suppose there's a reason that one of the stereotypical pictures of psychiatric hospitals is patients stringing beads. It *is* calming—or can be, if I allow myself to get into the spirit of the thing and stop worrying about everything else I have to do. The rest of the world slips away as I focus my attention more and more on what my hands are doing: sliding beads down the string and making the knots between them. Since I often use beads of different sizes, that means the size of the holes in them is different, too. Sometimes one knot is sufficient to hold a bead in place, but if it's a big bead with a big hole, I may have to double- or even triple-knot the string to keep it in place.

It startled me one day to realize that God is much like a good bead-stringer. Patient. Careful to choose individuals—and just exactly the right individuals. Making allowances for differences. Creating something beautiful. Making knots so we can't be lost.

I think about the annual crafts fair held here, and as I mentally travel the different booths, I see more images of God: the potter, the weaver, the painter, the welder, the sculptor. I've never had this thought before, so it will be interesting to keep it in mind at the next craft show. How many faces of God can I find among the artisans?

Yet, O Lord, you are our Father; we are the clay, and you are our potter; we are all the work of your hand.
(Isaiah 64:8)

July 20
No Free Lunch

One of my earliest memories is of pestering my father to stay home more instead of going to work. It must have been early in the year, because his response—which I am certain came out of his preoccupation with something—was, "Well, somebody has to pay for all those presents you got at Christmas." Today as an adult, I feel great compassion for that young father who couldn't know that an offhand, frustrated remark could so powerfully shape his daughter's spirituality.

My memories of that conversation are very vague, but I do remember thinking that if my parents had to pay Santa Claus for all those presents, then it wasn't nearly such a big deal that he brought them. If they had to pay, Santa was just a delivery man.

Of course I grew up and learned the adult version of what my father had taught me years earlier: there's no such thing as a free lunch. As a young woman I tried to believe that wasn't true, and got burned badly a couple of times before I grew a thick skin of skepticism about anything that sounds too good to be true.

The only problem with all this is that "no free lunches" applies to every part of life *except* God. With God, it's *all* free lunches. We don't have to pay for our salvation in any way—Jesus covered that price. But we're so used to the fact that outside of relationship with God there are no free lunches, it's hard for us to believe it, at a gut level, about God.

I don't have a quick fix for this problem. We can't teach our children to expect that they'll be handed everything on a silver platter; that would cripple them for adult life. So I make do. Every time I see or read or hear about something that promises something too good to be true, my cynicism kicks in. It says, "Remember: no free lunches!" I try to remember to add an automatic additional step to that thought process and say, "Except with God. With God, it's all free."

For the judgment following one trespass brought condemnation, but the free gift following many trespasses brings justification. (Romans 5:16b)

July 21
It's Not the Heat . . .

It's true in Nashville. It's *not* the heat . . . it's the humidity. There's nothing quite like a steamy day in July when the temp is 96, the humidity 98, and the temp index at 115 or so. I've seen ads for special gadgets that promise to cool you off with intermittent mists of water. These gadgets were obviously created by someone who's never been in the south. The last thing we need is more water, unless it's a great big body of it like a pool or lake.

On especially nasty days, churches in the area will take out big ads in the paper that say something like, "You think it's hot now? Wait until hell." The idea, I guess, is to evoke fear in people from the traditional visions of hell as a place of heat, fire, and brimstone.

It's quite ironic, then, that these churches in their literalism actually underplay the nastiness of hell. If heaven means living in the presence of God, then hell is the complete absence of God. Nothing could be worse. Occasionally I dig around until I find those places in my soul that feel abandoned by God and then experiment by trying to imagine what it would be like to feel completely like that, all the time, with no hope of it ever changing. Now, *that's* a nightmare.

It's true that I don't like summer weather in these parts. I survive by rushing from one air-conditioned place to the next and looking forward to autumn. But summer isn't hell. I can handle summer. Hell I can't.

O my God, I cry by day, but you do not answer; and by night, but find no rest. (Psalm 22:2)

JULY 22
St. Mary Magdalene

Poor Mary Magdalene. She's been unjustly accused of more sin than just about anyone in Christian history. Scripture tells us very little about her: that she came from Magdala; that Jesus at one time had cast seven demons out of her; that she traveled with the group of women who followed Jesus and financially supported his ministry; and that she was the first witness to the resurrection.

But tradition has put this Mary in other roles she doesn't deserve. There's no evidence, for example, that she was a prostitute. There's no evidence that she was the woman who anointed Jesus with oil, on his head or feet, depending on which gospel you're reading. But tradition has made her a scarlet woman, all the way through Nikos Kazantzakis' version in *The Last Temptation of Christ*.

I think there's a reason that happened. Mary, Jesus' mother, is a remarkable woman. She is both a virgin and a mother—a status no other woman can possibly have. Mary carries all of our good feelings about motherhood.

What this means is that we who worship Jesus Christ see one woman in his life who is, quite literally, the madonna. No other woman is so completely pure, though, so psychologically we need to expand our symbols of womanhood. That means Mary Magdalene is stuck with being the whore.

That's a shame in many ways, because as I said, we have no scriptural evidence that her "demons" were sexual in nature. If we give Mary Magdalene over to the whore tradition, we women lose a very important role model. This Mary was apparently quite close to Jesus. It was she to whom he first appeared after his resurrection, and the fact that he has to tell her, "Don't cling to me" means that in their former relationship, it was usual for them to hug. This all suggests a deep friendship between Jesus and Mary. It's a friendship we twenty-first-century women can have too. I'd like to reclaim Mary Magdalene and use her as a reminder of how an ordinary woman—both good and bad, like us—can have an extraordinarily close friendship with Jesus, the Christ.

Jesus said to her, "Do not hold on to me, because I have not yet ascended to the Father. But go to my brothers and say to them, 'I am ascending to my Father and your Father, to my God and your God.'" (John 20:17)

JULY 23
Santa Claus

A friend's eight-year-old was asking her about Santa Claus the other day. She hemmed and hawed and told him yes, Santa Claus is real. He skipped off, reassured, and she has questioned herself ever since, wondering whether she did the right thing. She also asked me, "Why in the world is he thinking about Santa Claus in July?"

To tell the truth, I think it's because all of us, not only children, think about Santa Claus all through the year. Those of us who are adults, of course, aren't worried about the actual Santa, because we know he doesn't exist. But I have found that I often end up thinking about a God who is a whole lot like Santa.

He knows when you are sleeping, he knows when you're awake. He knows if you've been bad or good, so be good for goodness' sake! I have in my mind a picture of God sitting in heaven, with a sharp pencil and a notepad. And God says, "Ooooh, not good. Didn't go to church today. That's one on the bad side. Mmmmm hmmmmm. Talked to the weirdo woman who frequents the library. One on the good side. Oh, yelled at her husband. Bad. Uh-oh. Kissed a man who isn't her husband. Bad. Very bad."

It is true that God knows everything I do, and it's also true that God doesn't like it when I sin. But there are no lists. Jesus Christ took both those lists and tore them up. It's not a matter of lists anymore. It's not how many marks in the "good" column, how many in the "bad." It's not a matter of the things I have to do to make God love me, numbered one through ten. There aren't any! All that's there is Jesus Christ, born, lived, died, resurrected. All to get rid of those lists.

"See, I am coming soon; my reward is with me, to repay according to everyone's work."
(Revelation 22:12)

JULY 24
But I'm Special

I had a call from a friend who once had an affair with a married man, while she was married too. They both divorced their spouses and got married. A couple of years later, she's discovered that he's cheating on her. I got her calmed down, but she kept saying, "I just don't understand how he could do this to me." Of course the first five or ten times she said this I agreed; I comforted her. But finally I answered, "Well, he did it *with* you, didn't he?" All she could say was, "Yes." "Then why wouldn't he do it with someone else?" And she burst into tears again and said, "Because I'm special!"

She is, indeed, special, and so am I. So are you. But there's a nasty little underside to believing that we're special, and that's narcissism. When I'm narcissistic, I think I should get special treatment because I'm different from everybody else—better, in fact. Realizing I do this starts me on the road to flogging myself until I realize that being narcissistic makes me not only a sinner but rather pitiful.

When I am narcissistic, I start believing that God loves me because I'm special. Because I obey the rules, or have very good reasons for breaking them. Because I'm a minister, for heaven's sake. Because I tithe. But to think along these lines means believing that my relationship with God is a matter of who I am, of how I act; that the quality of the relationship rests on me, not on God.

But thank heavens that's not the case. I am special and God has a one-to-one relationship with me. But that's not because I'm specially chosen over other people or because I live a good life. It's because God has decided to love me and be in relationship with me, to treat me as a treasured daughter and not a disgusting sinner, by sending Jesus to earth. Once the resurrection occurred, the responsibility for any human-God relationship moved from the human to the divine side. What that means for me, today, is that I don't have to be special.

Beloved, we are God's children now; what we will be has not yet been revealed. What we do know is this: when he is revealed, we will be like him, for we will see him as he is. (1 John 3:2)

JULY 25
How Could You?

A good friend died this week. She was young—only thirty-two—and had three beautiful little girls who are all under ten. She and her husband adored each other, and she was one of the backbones of my church's volunteer program. If it hadn't been for "Jane," a hundred Sunday bulletins would never have happened. She was a good friend too. She always remembered my birthday and—unlike some of my closest friends and even my family—the anniversary of my own diagnosis with cancer. I cannot believe that I am still here and Jane is gone.

Here is one version of my many prayers this week: "This isn't right, Lord. This isn't the way it's supposed to work. Why did you let this happen? You S.O.B."

At Jane's funeral the minister said we weren't to question God. He said God works in ways too mysterious for us to understand. He certainly wouldn't approve of my prayer.

I do, foundationally, believe that God is in charge and that in the end, all will turn out for the best and that my limited human understanding will be expanded so I can see things from God's perspective. But in the meantime, I reserve the right to yell at God. Many people I know think this is sinful, but when I look at the Bible, I see plenty of examples of very holy people doing the same. And I think God's big enough to take my anger.

A rabbi friend once said the first thing he was going to do on reaching heaven was grab God by the beard and demand some explanations. I know what he means.

> *Why, O Lord, do you stand far off? Why do you hide yourself in times of trouble? (Psalm 10:1)*

JULY 26
Vampires

Everybody has their dirty little secrets, and one of mine is vampires. I love Anne Rice's vampire books and watch some vampire movies. I love vampires because I understand them: They drink the blood of humans to survive. They come out only at night. They can be killed only by a stake through the heart or exposure to sunlight. They attack the innocent. And they are evil. That's the real reason I like vampires: they are evil, period. In vampire stories, things are black or white, good or evil, either/or.

My human heart wants things to be either/or. It's easier if things work this way. But despite my occasional escape from real life, I know the world isn't an either/or place. It's both/and. Even the world of God is both/and. We are body *and* soul. We are each unique creations of God, and yet we also need community to ripen into the fullness of who we're supposed to be. God has given us freedom *and* limitation.

Life is stable *and* life is chaotic. There's life *and* there's death. We are good *and* we are evil. That's where the world of God and the world of vampires come crashing into each other.

I often wish the world were as simple as either/or. I know I'd choose the good side, and I know I could hate the evil side. But human life has more nuance than that. Maybe that's why I particularly like Anne Rice's vampires. Unlike Bram Stoker's Count Dracula, they have some good in them. So here I am, all mixed up. I like to take mind-vacations to places where things are either/or, but I also like things that reflect the fact that the world is both/and.

Then the Lord God said, "See, the man has become like one of us, knowing good and evil; and now, he might reach out his hand and take also from the tree of life, and eat, and live forever." (Genesis 3:22)

JULY 27
Straight Talk

My dear friend, pastor, and former professor Liston Mills is one of the wisest people I've ever known. When I was in grad school, I was one of the few students who wasn't afraid of him. I think he liked that about me, so we got along pretty well. Liston taught by lecture, of course, but once in a while he'd stop and put forth pithy little sayings that we started calling "Liston's Laws." One of my favorites is this: "Neurosis is the sinner's response to the frightfulness of being alive."

As a therapist, Liston thought therapy was a good idea. But unlike a lot of therapists, he knew that therapy—as good as it can be—is only one of many human solutions to pain. Liston knew that nothing a human being comes up with is going to fix things completely. The human response to suffering of any kind is to do anything we can to avoid it.

But Christ chose the opposite. In obedience to God, he allowed himself to be crucified. He could have chosen not to do it. He seemed to know it was coming up. He himself said he could call angels to come and save him. But in obedience, he chose to be crucified.

That's not to say we should pursue pain and suffering. That's just exactly the point: we don't have to. Jesus has done it once and for always. We don't have to do it again.

Once I realize that Christ has already done the ultimate fix on my sin-filled and suffering-filled human life, then I can freely choose to pursue helpful human aids like therapy. There's nothing wrong or shameful about therapy—not as long as I stay clear on who the ultimate healer is.

O God, you have rejected us, broken our defenses; you have been angry; now restore us! (Psalm 60:1)

July 28
Overnight Success

I don't want to be a name-dropper, but here I go anyway. I have a good friend named Dave Krinsky. I met Dave when we were both students at the University of North Carolina at Chapel Hill. We were in just about every creative writing class together, and as long as I've known Dave, he's wanted to write comedy. That's all he's ever wanted to do. So the day after graduation, he and his writing partner John loaded up their cars and moved to California. Happy ending: he and John are co-executive producers for the hit animated sitcom *King of the Hill.*

But Dave didn't have overnight success. Until just a few years ago, he lived on about $12,000 a year, money that came from an investment. For ten solid years, he worked and worked and worked to make it in comedy. I admire him tremendously, because I have never worked at something for so long without success.

Dave is a constant reminder to me of God's faithfulness. I think of Abraham and Sarah too. They were one hundred and ninety when they had the child God had promised them. I don't know what it is that enabled Dave and Abraham and Sarah to keep working and hoping when it looked like the promise was never going to arrive.

I have dreams too. I've wanted to write the Great American Novel as long as I can remember. But I've given up, time and again, when faced with rejection. My frailty is that I want overnight success in order to keep trying. What I need is what brought Dave his "overnight" success: faith.

Courage is the price that life exacts for granting peace.
(Amelia Earhart)

July 29
St. Martha

I think St. Martha's been treated poorly by the Christian tradition. The homily I've heard time and time again holds her up as the wrong way to approach the Christian life. While good Mary sat at the feet of Jesus and listened, bad Martha hustled and bustled, preparing dinner and even getting huffy because

Mary wouldn't help. Jesus and all those preachers have told me that Mary "had chosen the better part."

But that's not the only story about Martha. In John, Mary and Martha send word to Jesus that their brother Lazarus is dying. Jesus delays long enough that Lazarus does die. When the sisters hear that Jesus is on his way, Mary stays at home and cries, but Martha sets out on the road to meet him. She shows him her anger: "If you'd gotten your act in gear, Lazarus wouldn't be dead." Jesus tells her that Lazarus will rise again, and Martha says, "I know he will rise again in the resurrection." Jesus answers, "I am the resurrection and the life. Those who believe in me, even though they die, will live, and everyone who lives and believes in me will never die. Do you believe this?" And she does something amazing: She makes the first full confession of faith in Jesus that occurs in John's gospel. That's a mighty fine legacy to leave for believers to come.

Something about Martha helped her understand who Jesus was. I like that, because I know that the church's history has been full of Marthas, most of them women. It is women who have cleaned the churches, washed the linens for the altar, sewed the priests' robes. It is Marthas who have taught innumerable children, fixed food for the potlucks, and made sure the altar wine was ordered.

Yes, Mary had the better part: she sat and listened to Jesus and got the message straight from his lips. But Martha had a pretty good part too: something in the way she lived her life—a life of service to others— helped her become the first one in John's gospel to truly understand just who exactly this friend of theirs named Jesus really was.

[Martha said] "Yes, Lord, I believe that you are the Messiah, the Son of God, the one coming into the world." (John 11:27)

July 30
Warranties

Remember back when warranties were a sort of promise? You bought something with the expectation that it was going to last a good long while, and the manufacturers clearly thought so too, because they'd give you a warranty of three or five years. If you had a problem with your gadget, whatever it was, you took it to the store where you bought it and they fixed it for you. If it was a big gadget, like a console TV or a washing machine, they came out and fixed it. And during the warranty period, repairs were free.

Times have definitely changed. Sure, you can still get repair service on big items like cars and appliances.

But the warranty periods have grown shorter and shorter. A year seems to be standard, and if you're buying a telephone or a can opener, you're lucky to get 90 days. And let's say that can opener breaks. They tell you to mail it—in the original carton, mind you—back to the manufacturer. You're supposed to include a check for $15 for something like a "processing fee," and if you wait two or three months, you might get your can opener back. Problem is, the thing only cost $20 to start with.

I've got to be fair—it's not just manufacturers who have weakened on keeping their promises. Politicians, married people, and students all break promises they make. I have to admit I've broken one or two myself, and I feel rotten about it.

Every time I encounter a broken promise, I think of God's covenantal promise to love us. No matter what I do—even break my promises to God—God continues to love me, to care for me, to draw me back to the straight and narrow.

If only God would start making small electronics.

I will not violate my covenant, or alter the word that went forth from my lips. (Psalm 89:34)

July 31
Big Sinners

People in my congregations often think I'm just trying to make a point when I say in a sermon or during a meeting that I'm a Big Sinner. That's not the case, though. I have sinned big. There are a lot of good Christian people who go through their lives sinning the little tiny sins that we all sin because we're fallen. These folks are sinful people, yes, as all of us are, but they've never committed any of the big, bad sins.

I'm not one of those people. I'll refrain from sharing the details, but I've done some things that would cause me a great deal of shame if people found out about them. I'm not recommending being a Big Sinner, but we major league sinners do have an advantage. I can't pretend that I'm righteous; I can't pretend I'm perfect; I can't pretend I don't need God's love and forgiveness.

So I think I have an advantage over the little sinners. They can fool themselves sometimes into thinking they've got it all together. I, on the other hand, know that my only hope is to throw myself on the mercy of God. The good news is my faith tells me that mercy is infinite. And the other good news is that I don't have to walk around trying to maintain the façade that I'm a "good Christian."

Paul said he was the biggest sinner around. I won't go that far, because in a backward way, there's some pride in saying that. But I've got to say—I understand what he means.

The saying is sure and worthy of full acceptance, that Christ Jesus came into the world to save sinners—of whom I am the foremost. (1 Timothy 1:15)

August 1
My Enemies

I don't like to think that I've got enemies, but I do. There are a few folks in the world of academia who have probably gained quite a bit of satisfaction from the fact that my teaching career has gone nowhere. And I know there are some folks in my denomination who can't say they're sorry that despite showing so much early promise, I've not amounted to anything in our small Christian family. And then there are the people who are my enemies not because they know me, but because of what I am. There are people who hate the idea of women ministers and do everything possible to block their congregations from hiring them.

Do I pray for my enemies? Sure I do . . . because, as St. Paul tells the Christians in Rome, it heaps burning coals on their heads. What's harder is acknowledging that they are good Christians. Whenever I preach the story of the Good Samaritan, I wiggle and squirm because it tells me that Jesus says being a good neighbor means doing the right things, not liking or disliking people. And I've got to admit that my enemies, every one of them, have given of themselves to churches and communities and seminaries and divinity schools. Apparently the fact that someone dislikes me doesn't bar them from God's kingdom.

Often I wish it did. It hurts when my enemies do nasty things to me or when I know they're celebrating my latest failure. I want God to be on *my* side. What Jesus reminds me, though, is that God is on *our* side—the side of the entire human race.

No, "if your enemies are hungry, feed them; if they are thirsty, give them something to drink; for by doing this you will heap burning coals on their heads."
(Romans 12:20)

AUGUST 2
South Africa

It's been some years since the evil system of apartheid ended in South Africa. What's interesting is the way the black majority has dealt with the white minority that oppressed them for so many years.

The new government established something called "The Truth and Reconciliation Commission." The basic idea is that somebody from the old white government, often a military man, will come in front of the Commission and confess everything he did back in the bad old days of apartheid. And then the Commission forgives him. No trial. No jail time. He's forgiven.

Not surprisingly, there are people in South Africa who aren't crazy about the Commission. Some black South Africans want revenge, and who can blame them? Some of the whites hate having to confess wrongdoing when they were only "following orders." On the whole, though, the Truth and Reconciliation Commission seems to work.

For the life of me, I can't imagine anything like this working in the United States. I can't really say why I'm so skeptical, but when I ask other people about this, they agree. What is it about us that keeps us from dealing with harm—grievous, serious harm—in this way? I imagine Jesus wholeheartedly approves of what they're doing in South Africa, because basically, they're following the core of the Christian message: repent of your sins and be forgiven.

Is it possible that we in this country aren't quite as Christian as we think we are?

"Whenever you stand praying, forgive, if you have anything against anyone; so that your Father in heaven may also forgive you your trespasses." (Mark 11:25)

AUGUST 3
"Expert" Christians

The biggest compliment anyone can ever give me about a sermon is, "I understood everything you said." I like that—it's what I aim for. What smarts a little bit is that the person usually follows up by saying something like, "Back when Reverend Smith was here, I never understood a word he said. He sure was smart." The implication is that I am not so smart. Ouch.

It is true that some of our Christian sisters and brothers like to impress us with the depth of their knowledge and the number of multisyllabic words they can squeeze into one sentence. I think the most intimidating religious experts are canon lawyers. I wouldn't go head-to-head with any of them—all I'd do is embarrass myself.

But the fact is that being smart, as much as we value it, doesn't do anybody one whit of good when it comes to getting into heaven. When you get down to the bottom line, there's only one thing I, or anybody else, has to know: that Jesus is the Christ, the son of the living God, Lord and Savior of the world, and my own personal Savior. When I realize that a five-year-old child can know the most important information in the universe as well as I do, it's pretty easy to stay humble.

Knowledge puffs up, but love builds up.
(1 Corinthians 8:1b)

AUGUST 4
A Joyful Noise

I once belonged to a big church that had a fantastic choir and an incredible organist. You had to audition for the choir; there was a waiting list to be in it, and people who didn't even go to that church came and sang in the choir. Let me tell you, they sang some incredible music. The choir director used to say that the only people who would have jobs in heaven would be theologians and musicians. There I was, at the time a lowly church secretary, so where did that leave me? Sitting and listening to him play the organ and the choir sing for the rest of eternity, I guess.

Thank goodness that choir director—who shall remain nameless, bless his pompous little heart—was wrong on both counts. First of all, theologians won't have jobs in heaven—everybody will know everything there is to know about God and the universe. Everything will be perfectly plain to the simplest person. And the fact is that scripture does not command us to make a "beautiful" noise to the Lord, but a "joyful" one. That means my off-key hymn-singing, done enthusiastically, counts more than a perfect but emotionless rendition of Bach's Mass in B minor.

Don't get me wrong; I don't have anything against beautiful music. I love it. When I'm having a good year financially, I buy season tickets to the Nashville Symphony. But it is true that the church I attend now doesn't require auditions for the choir. The choir director weeps with joy if someone volunteers. Their quality can't come even close to the choir of that church I used to attend. But they sing lustily, happily, joyfully. And that's what matters.

Make a joyful noise to the Lord, all the earth; break forth into joyous song and sing praises. (Psalm 98:4)

AUGUST 5
The Hope of Heaven

One year in seminary, I attended a large church and helped out occasionally during worship. It was Easter morning and the senior minister and I were in his office putting on our robes for the service. He sighed real big and said, "Oh, I hate Easter!" I was stunned. Hate Easter? I asked him why. "Because I hate preaching something I don't believe in." He was, of course, referring to the resurrection.

One of the dirty little secrets of the mainline churches is that a lot of its clergy don't believe in the resurrection. I know that's hard to believe, but trust me—it's true. I don't write this to shock people or to start a witch-hunt for unbelieving clergy. I write it because sometimes it's difficult to remember that as hard as this life is, as awful as death is, there is something better waiting for us on the other side. I know I need to hear that fact again and again; I need to be reminded of it often. And if my minister doesn't believe in the resurrection, I'm not going to get the reminders I need.

I want to be very clear about this: the center of the Christian faith is that Jesus of Nazareth was the son of God. He was born as a human being, lived and taught, and was crucified on the cross. Three days after he died, he rose from the dead, and ever since that day, all Christians trust that Jesus' saving actions mean we get to go to heaven when we die.

I've gotten to the point of asking ministers for a resurrection sermon when I haven't heard one in a while. Trust me—unlike disc jockeys, clergy get very few requests, so they're quite receptive to them. Give it a try . . . ask the person who speaks in your pulpit to spin that golden oldie, "The Hope of Heaven."

The same day some Sadducees came to him, saying there is no resurrection. (Matthew 22:23a)

AUGUST 6
The Transfiguration

I like Mark's account of what happened at the transfiguration, when Jesus took Peter, James, and John and went up on a mountain. They saw him in the light of his true nature and in the company of Elijah and Moses.

Of course at first the disciples are filled with fear. But once that initial fear passes, Peter wants to build "booths" for each of the three. He wants Moses and Elijah to stick around, and for Jesus to stay in his transfigured state. Making each a hut is Peter's way to tempt the three to forget the problems and worries of day-to-day life and to stay on the mountaintop.

If we're lucky, each of us will have several mountaintop experiences in our lives. Some of those may be religious, others not. But eventually, we all have to leave the mountaintop and come back down to sea level.

I counsel all the young people I know to relish the mountaintop experiences in their lives, but nobody ever listens to this old fogey. I was in seminary with a woman who graduated one Friday in May, was married Saturday, and then on Sunday was ordained. She took off two whole weeks, then, before her husband's ordination.

I'm not saying that's *bad* to do. I'm sure she had a spectacular couple of weeks there. But especially once we grow up, mountaintop experiences come all too rarely. Of course, there are those who go on to win Nobel prizes and McArthur genius fellowships, but most of us aren't that lucky.

Then Peter said to Jesus, "Rabbi, it is good for us to be here; let us make three dwellings, one for you, one for Moses, and one for Elijah." (Mark 9:5)

August 7
Nursing Homes

As a pastor, I have visited far too many nursing homes and seen far too many elderly people wasting away, with no company other than the poorly-paid aides who don't stay long because of the low pay and the hard work involved in the job. But I cannot condemn the people who put these elders in nursing homes.

In an ideal world, elderly people could live at home until they died. In that ideal world there would be, in the home, one or two full-time caretakers for children and elders. But that ideal world doesn't exist—except for a very few wealthy people who can hire full-time, in-home caretakers. There are other families that have committed themselves to their extended family so much that grown children have chosen to stay in their hometown and live in close proximity to their elderly parents. Neither option is financially viable for most people.

One of the common entreaties Paul made to the young Christian churches was to care for the "widows and orphans." The idea was that the church, as a whole, could provide sustenance and companionship to people on both ends of the age spectrum who had been left without their usual sources of support.

I know of very few people who gladly put their parents in nursing homes. Usually it's a choice attended by a great deal of anguish. I'd like to suggest that the church could step up and have a hand in this ministry.

I'm not talking church-run nursing homes. Those we have. But what about a small community of elders, physically and emotionally troubled, who live together and are cared for by nurses and attendants paid by a local congregation that includes their adult children? Rather than farm elders out to various nursing homes, then, churches could provide small, homelike environments for their elderly.

It might seem like there's not much here for a spiritual meditation. But remember: most of us will end up aged; some of us will end up infirm. How would we wish to live in that case?

Let the elders who rule well be considered worthy of double honor. (1 Timothy 5:17a)

August 8
Gifts Without Strings

A friend of mine named Debbie is a single mother and worked for years to buy her own house. She and her son managed to squeak by on her librarian's salary. One of Debbie's dreams was to have some patio furniture, so they could sit out on the patio when the weather was nice, chat, and eat ice cream.

One day a truck from K-Mart pulled up to her house. The driver asked her name, and when she told him, he unloaded a full set of patio furniture in her back yard. She protested that she hadn't ordered it, but the delivery guy kept saying, "That's what the order says, ma'am, to deliver this all to you."

To this day, Debbie doesn't know who sent her the patio furniture. Whoever it was, though, really understood what a "gift" is. A real gift comes without strings attached—even the strings of an expected "thank you" and, in the case of a large gift, a continuing feeling of obligation to the giver. Not many of us are able to give this freely, without strings. We want something in return, even if it's just gratitude. The person who made this gift is a very mature Christian—whatever his or her age.

It's nice when things like this happen because they remind us that God's love comes with no strings attached. Yes, God *likes* to be thanked. God would *prefer* that someone who's been overwhelmed with blessings would recognize Christ as the source and live their lives accordingly. But for some reason, even a lack of gratitude doesn't dissuade our God. The gifts just keep on coming. All of us, whether we realize it and admit it or not, are receivers of gifts without strings.

"Or who has given a gift to him, to receive a gift in return?" (Romans 11:35)

AUGUST 9
Pruning

It might seem years away at this point in the summer, but fall is definitely coming, and I need to get out there and do my pruning. In what seems to be a contradiction in logic, I cut plants back so they will grow bigger, better, or more the next spring.

Human beings need pruning too—we all have qualities that must be cut off in order to allow the godly qualities to grow. A man in one of my former congregations was a banker. He was a man with many gifts for ministry, and when I see people like that, I tend to bug them about it. He told me he really liked the idea of ministry, but it would mean a huge cut in his standard of living, and he just couldn't do that. He didn't know how he could survive without his nice car and house, without the prestige of living in the best neighborhood in town. One day, out of the blue, he lost his job and couldn't find anything else for nine months. The family had to cut back on all extras just to survive. One day he finally got a job offer from another bank, but he sat down with his wife and told her that wasn't what he really wanted. What he wanted was to go to seminary and be a minister. And so he did. He'll say this himself, though: before he could grow into the person God intended him to be, he had to be pruned of his love for money and need for security.

The trouble with pruning people, as opposed to trees, is that it hurts. And I'm not saying God does nasty things to people, like take that banker's job away from him, in order to prune them. But given the fact that life is what it is—an existence that includes suffering—God takes that suffering and uses it to prune away the ungodly qualities we've allowed to grow in our souls. Again, being pruned hurts. And it's okay to complain during the process. But in the end, it will serve us best.

"Every branch that bears fruit he prunes to make it bear more fruit." (John 15:2b)

AUGUST 10
Nerds

The term for nerds changes every few years, but as far as I can tell by watching from the outside, those nerds, whatever they're called, still exist—in grade school, junior high, and high school. College is a bit kinder to nerds, because they can usually find some like-minded folks to hang out with. But on the whole, life is tough on the nerdy ones.

That's why I think that some of the biggest heroes and heroines I know are high school students. I know these teenagers from my work in churches they attend, through friendships with their parents, and from my work as a teacher. These brave souls yearn to be popular, just as everyone does. And yet they know that to be with the "in" group, you've got to act a certain way. Whatever makes you cool changes from school to school, year to year. But one of the things you've got to do if you want to be popular is to join everybody else in rejecting the nerds.

The teen heroes I know refuse to do that. They won't join in that kind of cruelty. And they've paid the price. They'll never be in the Homecoming Court, and they won't be among the most popular. They won't get to go to all the dances, they won't be elected as class officers, they won't get the premier places on the sports teams.

But I call these young people heroes because they are doing something very important: preaching with their lives. They may never say the word "Jesus" in their school, but the way they live teaches any and all who care to look that the usual clique-centered system isn't the only way to make it in school.

I wish more teenagers could preach with their lives—then maybe the Columbine killers wouldn't have felt so hated. And I wish more adults could preach with our lives too. What a different world it would be.

> *Preach always. When necessary, use words.*
> *(St. Francis of Assisi)*

AUGUST 11
St. Clare of Assisi

St. Francis is one of the world's favorite saints, and with good reason. My complaint is that St. Clare doesn't get nearly as much good press.

Francis, of course, is known for his love of the created world as much as he is for his stance on poverty. But Clare's life offers a clearer focus.

Clare first felt called by God when she heard Francis preach. Against the wishes of her family, she went to the tiny group of Franciscan friars and asked for admission. Of course, given the conventions at the time, the sexes had to be separated, so Clare was received and eventually made the leader of the women's order, the "Poor Clares."

Clare had a radical view of poverty. Many monastic orders—then and now—prohibit their members from owning anything themselves, but as a whole have vast holdings. I learned this once when a Benedictine monk, who had come to our seminary for a semester, had the most up-to-date laptop computer on campus. I asked him how this could be so and he explained: the laptop wasn't *his*. It belonged to the order. He was only given permission to use it.

I'm not saying that's bad. I'm saying that Clare took another path. She fought hard to keep her order from being forced to own property. Eventually she prevailed, and so the Clares, aptly named after their founder, are also truly "poor." Any religious makes a tremendous sacrifice when he or she enters a monastic order, but the members of the Poor Clares perhaps sacrifice the most.

This kind of radical poverty is difficult for Americans to grasp. Our culture sends us countless messages saying the "good life" means to buy, buy, buy and to own, own, own. St. Clare left a heritage that stands as a corrective—perhaps a salvific corrective—to any American who encounters it.

Contemplate . . . the poverty of him who lay in the manger, wrapped in swaddling clothes. What marvelous humility and astonishing poverty! (St. Clare)

AUGUST 12
Religious Satire

The Door, or *The Wittenburg Door* as it was previously known, calls itself "pretty much the world's only religious satire magazine." Not surprisingly, *The Door* struggles to stay afloat. Not many people know about it, and many are offended by it. I like it for two reasons. First, no religious group is immune; they satirize everyone from Baptists to Catholics to New Agers. And second, they allow us to laugh about our faith.

The Door gathers religious news from around the world that is a bit . . . well, odd. For instance, they reported on a woman who created "a life-size Madonna and child sculpture out of dryer lint."

The Door also features strange but true advertisements from the merchandising side of Christianity. The one I remember most vividly was what you might call a "combo" communion cup. The idea is this: As each worshiper enters the sanctuary, they are given a combo. It is hermetically sealed in plastic and so is guaranteed to be germ-free. When it comes time in the service for communion, the worshipers open their combos, eat the little piece of bread that's nested underneath the cup, and drink the sip of grape juice. Then everything's disposable!

One of the reasons I love *The Door* so much is that try as they might, they can't come up with anything better than the real stuff. We Christians get some pretty wild ideas sometimes, and it's very, very good to be able to laugh at ourselves on occasion.

> *It is hard not to write satire.*
> *(Decimus Junius Juvenalis)*

AUGUST 13
Health Food

There's a great big health food store just a half mile from me; it's as big as a regular supermarket. I buy a few things there, but the sad truth seems to be that eating healthy means eating expensive.

I'm not even talking about vitamins or supplements or special herbs or anything. I mean just plain old food. At the store they sell organic produce—no pesticides, natural fertilizer, no wax. This store isn't just for vegetarians, either. They sell milk from cows that are guaranteed not to have been given rBGH or antibiotics. The meat is from free-range animals that have been fed the kind of food they were originally designed to eat. They also haven't been pumped full of additives that make it easier to farm.

I have a great deal of sympathy with the natural food movement. I would like to eat "natural" food all the time. It seems to me that God was pretty wise about creation, and while we can use our brains to make farming easier (milking machines, for instance), we don't really need to be pumping our food full of medications and hormones that God didn't put in them. It's an odd way to think about it, but eating organic would mean eating Biblical.

That's one of the problems with living in a civilization. Scientific progress has come up with all sorts of tricks to create higher yield, whatever the crop or animal being raised. It's just sort of strange that I have to go to a special store and pay higher prices to eat the kind of food God intended for me to eat.

Be patient, therefore, beloved, until the coming of the Lord. The farmer waits for the precious crop from the earth, being patient with it until it receives the early and the late rains. (James 5:7)

AUGUST 14
St. Maximilian Kolbe

I don't know of anyone my age who can comprehend the horror that sprouted in Germany and sent its tentacles all through Europe in the 1930s and '40s. I make a point of watching documentaries about the Holocaust; the survivors are correct that we must never forget what happened. If we forget, then it can happen again.

While Hitler's main focus was the Jews, he also tried to exterminate homosexuals and gypsies. Into the midst of all that horror came a priest named Maximilian Kolbe. He was imprisoned because, unlike most religious leaders of the time, he was an outspoken opponent of Nazism and published his views. At Auschwitz, he continued to minister to his fellow prisoners; for Christians he even held Mass in secret using smuggled bread and wine.

But the most remarkable thing Kolbe did was live out what Jesus taught about love: "No one has greater love than this, to lay down one's life for one's friends" (John 15:13). A young, married prisoner was set for execution as an example because another prisoner had escaped. Kolbe took his place. As far as I know, this young man wasn't a particularly close friend; Kolbe did what he did because he knew what following Christ means.

John Paul II says that Kolbe is "the patron saint of our difficult century," meaning the twentieth, and I think that's true. A hundred years from now, people will remember the twentieth century as the one with the Holocaust. And I hope they'll remember St. Maximilian Kolbe too.

The most deadly poison of our times is indifference.
(St. Maximilian Kolbe)

AUGUST 15
The Assumption of the Blessed Virgin Mary

(By Sister Mary Ann Heyd, OP)

Having had this opportunity to reflect more deeply about Mary, I am newly aware of her importance in my life and the lives of the whole human race. The gift of my lifelong exposure to Marian devotions and prayers, such as the rosary, the Litany of the Blessed Mother (with forty-six different titles that reflect her relationship with Jesus), and the Memorare prayer written by St. Bernard, is that I'm relearning at an older age the treasure God gave me in sharing Mary with all of us.

At a recent memorial service I attended, the presiding priest, having survived cancer operations and now in remission, related his near-death experience. He spoke eloquently of death as nothing but passing through a doorway. This simple explanation seems to fit Mary's Assumption especially well because of the absence of pain and anxiety at the time of completing her earthly journey.

The basis of all Christian religion is Jesus in whom we share the eternal life celebrated with God after our resurrection. The loved ones we now know will again be with us in heaven. All those who have gone before us are waiting for us on the other side of the heavenly door. Mary's exceptional freedom from original sin and her obedience on earth were rewarded by her glorious Assumption. Just as we admire the justice and generosity in Jesus' care of his Blessed Mother, our hope soars for God's similar reward that his mercy and generosity will provide for us after our life's work is finished. We wait and pray that we will be faithful all the way to that holy day so that we also will share eternal life with God, Mary, and all our family and friends.

I will greatly rejoice in the Lord, my whole being shall exult in my God; for he has clothed me with the garments of salvation, he has covered me with the robe of righteousness, as a bridegroom decks himself with a garland, and as a bride adorns herself with her jewels.
(Isaiah 61:10)

AUGUST 16
Dancing

If I could choose one physical skill to perform perfectly, I'd choose dance. I love it—ballet, ballroom, Irish, rock-n-roll, disco, modern, jazz. You name the dance, I like it. I've spent many an afternoon with the sound on the TV up really loud while I dance along with the people on the video—be they Gene Kelly, African tribespeople, or Mikhail Baryshnikov. I'm not a good dancer, but I am most definitely an enthusiastic one.

That's one reason I was flabbergasted to learn that some Christian denominations prohibit dancing. The idea is that dancing requires moving the body around, and moving the body around is . . . well, it is, by definition, sensual—it involves the senses. And "sensual" in American culture leads right straight to "sexual."

But King David danced his pants off when the ark of the covenant came home. God apparently likes dancing and the sensual aspect of it. To tell the truth, I think it's a natural instinct for humans. After all, you don't make a rule against something unless people are prone to do it.

Do the hustle!

David and all the house of Israel were dancing before the Lord with all their might, with songs and lyres and harps and tambourines and castanets and cymbals.
(2 Samuel 6:5)

AUGUST 17
Back-to-School

In many parts of the country, school doesn't start until after Labor Day, but unlike my childhood days, more and more school systems today are starting classes in late August. There's something about it that *feels* wrong—buying notebook paper and folders is supposed to go along with buying knee socks for cool weather. Going to school in summer clothes somehow just isn't right.

It does show, though, how adaptable we humans are. It's quite remarkable, when you think about it. Starting school in the heat of August is nothing. Since life apparently started in Africa, that means we spread out over the entire earth, adapting to our environment as we went. Human beings were created to live in hot climates, but there are lots of folks who cherish long underwear and long winters. The first people were dark-skinned so they were protected from the sun by melatonin. The people who went north didn't need it and eventually became pale-skinned.

I don't know of any human product that can function in all those extremes of environment. But God's "product," the human race, can. That's just a little peephole into God's amazing power. What kind of power must it take to create a living thing that can survive and thrive in the tundra of Russia *and* beside the palm trees of Tahiti? It's mind-boggling.

So—back to school in August? Piece of cake for a God with that much power.

Therefore we will not fear, though the earth should change, though the mountains shake in the heart of the sea. (Psalm 46:2)

AUGUST 18
Calendars

I can't believe they're already selling calendars for next year! I swear, I really and truly did a double take when I saw the display table at the bookstore yesterday when I went to have tea with a friend. Calendars—in August?

We do a lot of that, we Americans. I could be cynical and talk about how the corporations have done precise scientific studies that show if you put Halloween decorations out on September 12, people will start buying them and will, overall, buy more than if you put the decorations on the shelves October 1. But I won't go the cynical route today.

The other thing this says to me is that I live so much in the future. I plan ahead. I imagine how things are going to be *when* . . . when the kids are grown, when the weather changes, when I lose twenty pounds. There's some good in that, of course; anticipation is one of the joys of being human. I not only enjoy an event, but the time leading up to it.

On the other hand, I can get in the habit of living in the future more than I do the present. The fact is that there's no guarantee I'll be around when the weather changes. There's no guarantee I'll lose twenty pounds. One of the attractions of Eastern religions, I think, is their wisdom about living in the present moment. AA offers the same worldview. I enjoy life best if I live today, today: feeling the humidity in the air, noticing the gorgeous sunset, laughing with a friend, getting a particularly difficult lecture written.

Ram Dass says, "Be here now." AA says, "One day at a time." Either works.

"So do not worry about tomorrow, for tomorrow will bring worries of its own. Today's trouble is enough for today." (Matthew 6:34)

August 19
Diet Soda

I refuse, on principle, to drink diet soda.

I imagine having a conversation with a starving child from a developing nation. I'd offer the child a diet soda, and I suspect she'd love it. Human beings are made to like sweet things. And given her skinny little frame, she could use a few extra calories. In her world, people don't worry about fat and cholesterol. Fat is good because it has more calories, and that's what everybody in her world needs: more calories.

But I imagine her amazement when I tell her how much this diet soda costs. When I translate the sixty-five cents I paid into the currency of her native land, it would probably be shocking. I suspect it's the equivalent of a day's pay. Maybe a week's, in some places. I imagine her looking at me and thinking I must be rich to be able to afford to spend so much money on flavored sugar water.

But then I imagine telling her that what she's drinking has no calories in it. It will give her body absolutely no nutrition—not even the simple carbohydrates of sugar. In other words, I spend money to purchase a treat that has had the calories taken out of it. This little girl, sitting in the chair next to my desk, simply wouldn't understand the concept. Calories are good. Calories are what make people live. She struggles every day to find enough calories to stay alive; finding enough calories to be strong and healthy is a near impossibility. Why would I spend money on something with no calories?

Why indeed?

> *"But woe to you who are rich, for you have received your consolation."* *(Luke 6:24)*

AUGUST 20
Stars

Toward the end of August here in the mid-South, we will get an occasional break from the stifling humidity and be granted a clear night sky. These are special times for me because I have always loved the night sky. I once pastored a rural church, and more than once on the way home late at night, I pulled the car over to the side of the winding country roads to look at the night sky without the light pollution of the city where I lived at the time. One of my dreams is to see the night sky out west before I die, or perhaps in Alaska. From everything I hear, it's a breathtaking experience.

These visions preach to me about a God I didn't—and, truthfully, still don't—learn about in church. Yes, this God is mighty enough to create such a limitless universe, but she is also an artist to whom beauty counts as much as function. Yes, we humans have a special place in her heart, but there is room there, too, for sentient beings on other planets, should they exist. Yes, this God sent Jesus as the savior for the people of this fragile blue-green planet, but perhaps she has given salvation to other beings in different ways. If that is so, then perhaps this God is also open enough to save people of earth who travel toward her on a path not blazed by her son, Jesus. Perhaps this God, who created a far bigger universe than necessary for even the teeming billions of her children on earth, also has a heart equally expansive.

It is true that the night sky overwhelms me with the vastness of creation and my tiny, insignificant place in it. But it also strengthens in me the belief in a God who has her eye on me, pulled over on the side of a country road, car door open, head back, mouth agape, straining for a sight of her amidst the glory of the heavens.

When I look at your heavens, the work of your fingers, the moon and the stars that you have established; what are human beings that you are mindful of them, mortals that you care for them? (Psalm 8:3-4)

AUGUST 21
Anniversaries of Death

Every year on this day—since the year 1983—I remember my mother's mother, the woman I called "Bigmommy." That's the day she died from complications of cancer. It was perhaps a blessing in many ways because she had suffered for years. But I was only twenty-five and at her death felt I had been robbed of a person who loved me unconditionally.

When I was eighteen and wild, I ran off with a young man. I was in love, of course, and he was a musician and had a dream. I got lots of letters from my relatives. From my immediate family, I had letters of recrimination and pleas to return home. But from Bigmommy I had a different kind of letter. She was a bit bewildered, there's no doubt about that, and sad. She didn't like the idea of my estrangement from my immediate family and from her. But she also told me that she understood. She and her husband married when she was only fifteen, and they did so against the wishes of both sets of parents. "We were crazy in love," she wrote.

It only took nine months for me to figure out I didn't want to be a groupie, and I returned to my immediate family, ready to be a well-behaved member of society. But it was Bigmommy's letter I saved. I have it still, and any time I feel that absolutely no one loves me, I get out her letter and read it. In those moments, her words are words from God.

It's been a long time since Bigmommy died, but I still miss her. Especially since my diagnosis with cancer I have missed the opportunity to talk with someone who *understands*. But each year on this day, I remember her, and those memories are good. They are happy. And they are full of love—unconditional love.

"Which one of you, having a hundred sheep and losing one of them, does not leave the ninety-nine in the wilderness and go after the one that is lost until he finds it?" (Luke 15:4)

August 22
Art Museums

Believe it or not, Nashville opened the doors of its fine arts museum in the year 2001. When I first moved here in 1991, I was aghast that the city had no museum. After all, didn't Cincinnati, Louisville, Raleigh? And for a woman who'd spent hours in the many Smithsonian museums, the new Frist Museum's collection was disappointingly small. But that's okay. It's a start.

Long before I took a class in church history, I learned that the major force shaping Western European history was Christian. It's all there to see in any art exhibit that covers the last two thousand years. Until the Renaissance, fine art *was* Christian art. So many great painters put their brushes to canvas in order to portray some aspect of the Christian story. The artisans of the medieval cathedrals, busily creating away in the midst of what some call the "dark ages," were taking chisel to stone and lead to glass in order to create visual representations of Christ and his church for a citizenry that couldn't read.

The art of many ancient civilizations is also religious in nature. Aside from practical creations like pottery, ancient artists seem to have spent the bulk of their gifts on works glorifying the gods they knew. I think of the paintings of ancient Egypt, the carvings of Paleolithic goddesses, and the cave paintings in France of what appear to be religious rituals.

To some Christians, art focused on any religion but their own is nothing but idolatry. But I prefer to take St. Paul's view—that in a world that had not yet heard the preaching of the good news, artists, like others, still sensed the presence of God.

Then Paul stood in front of the Areopagus and said, "Athenians, I see how extremely religious you are in every way." (Acts 17:22)

August 23
Anthropology

The anthropology department at Vanderbilt has, God bless their souls, invited me to teach one course a semester for them, even though anthropology was only my minor in my doctoral work. Combined with my disability payments, those courses allow me to live.

Whatever the course, the nature of anthropology means that my preparations include examples from many cultures. That's what anthropology is—the study of human beings. That means humans across time (archeology) and across cultures. Every course also includes a lecture on "cultural relativism," the jewel of the anthropological mindset. Cultural relativism says that each culture is valid and should not be measured against our own to determine its worth. That's a deterrent to thinking that *we* (whoever *we* happen to be) have everything right, but it's also an outlook that demands we approach morals and ethics from inside each culture. While Americans joke about incest between cousins and outlaw it, there are cultures in which such marriages are preferred.

Cultural relativism is a difficult lesson for my students. It takes practice. And I have to say, when I step out of the shoes of the anthropology teacher, I can't wholeheartedly endorse it. Some cultures sanction rape and female genital mutilation. My Christianity says these things are wrong.

My students often approach me privately in confusion, saying that they now don't know how to decide what's "right." Aren't their morals arbitrary? What if they'd been born into an Amazonian tribe? These are very important questions, and these young people must struggle with them. But when they come and ask what I, personally, think, and when I think they've truly grappled with it, I tell them I must step into my role as minister. Cultural relativism is a marvelous concept, and it's opened many narrow minds. But everyone has to decide what is at the foundation of their belief system. Mine is Christianity. I'm not a very good anthropologist.

Hence, as to the eating of food offered to idols, we know that "no idol in the world really exists," and that "there is no God but one." (1 Corinthians 8:4)

AUGUST 24
Water

It's a fact that every grade-schooler learns, but it still amazes me to know that my body is mostly made of water. My amazement, I think, stems from the ordinariness of it all. Human bodies are amazing and marvelous; I don't have to be a doctor to know that. The fact that they work as well as they generally do floors me on many occasions. But the base of this body is something so simple that I have created it in chemistry class: water.

My scientific wonder turns to understanding, though, when I look at this fact with religious eyes. I ask myself: But isn't that just like God? This is the same God who uses plain, everyday items like bread and wine to feed us with the most miraculous spiritual food that exists. My own tendency is to think that something holy must be made of something rare in order to reflect the honor it deserves. I suppose that's why the cups and plates we use for communion are made of precious metals.

But I think God is sending me a message through bread and wine and water. It is not scarcity that makes something valuable, nor is it complexity. Quite the opposite, apparently: the holy is made of the most common things on the planet. Given the choice of owning a beautiful silver chalice or a quart of water, everyone I know would choose the first. Everyone but God, that is. And given the fact that we human beings are a dime a dozen and about as ordinary as mud, that's a very, very good thing.

Instead, one of the soldiers pierced his side with a spear, and at once blood and water came out. (John 19:34)

AUGUST 25
Four Months Until Christmas

I'm not going to calculate how many shopping days there are until Christmas. I've already seen that done in a couple of feature stories in the newspaper. I've complained before about the way our culture presses us into anticipatory spending.

It's something different that's nagging at me today. It's August and it's deathly hot and humid. I'm so sick of summer that one night I turn the air conditioning down so low that I have to curl up and put blankets on the bed to sleep without shivering.

August 25 has no special significance in the life of the church. It's not celebrated as a holiday by any religion or culture of which I'm aware. And that's just the point: August 25 is about as ordinary a day as you can get.

And yet four months from now, it will be Christmas Day. Four months isn't a very long time; it's a third of a year, it's less than half a pregnancy.

My tendency is to squeeze holiness into certain special days, special objects, and special people. I think of Christmas as one of the most important days of the year. I have Christian friends from the Congo, though, for whom December 25 is just another important church holy day. No tree for them, no gifts, no big meals. They go to church, and that's about it.

I think my friend Muratananga and his family have some wisdom about this. It's not that they aren't caught up in American consumerism—although that's certainly true. It's that they realize that holiness doesn't limit itself to particular days . . . it's spread through each and every day. My tendency is to think that holiness is four months away. Instead, the truth is that I don't have to reach very far at all to touch holiness—just as far as August 25.

This is the day that the Lord has made; let us rejoice and be glad in it. (Psalm 118:24)

August 26
The Shakers

When I was in seminary in Lexington, Kentucky, I took as many opportunities as possible to visit the Shaker settlement at Pleasant Hill, less than an hour away. While it's not an active settlement any more, it has been restored, so I could wander through the buildings, see the way the Shakers lived, and attend the reenactments of the Shaker way of worship.

Although I don't know what it is, the Shakers had something right. I can't say I like the idea of celibacy.

It may have diverted their sexual energy into lively worship and beautiful, bountiful work, but it also meant their eventual disappearance. At this writing there are, I believe, only five remaining Shakers in the world. I also can't say I believe that Mother Ann Lee was the second coming of Christ.

But whenever I've visited a Shaker settlement—and I've now been to three—there has always been a palpable sense of holiness to the place. An afternoon trip to Pleasant Hill brought peace and energy to an exhausted seminarian. The settlement near Nashville has the same sort of feel to it. There is peace—and I mean peace of the soul—at Shaker settlements. It's overwhelming. I don't know anyone who's been to one and not felt it.

My gut tells me that the Shakers had something right. If that wasn't so, how could their settlements provide spiritual comfort to weary visitors a hundred years after they've been vacated by the Shakers themselves? They had something right. I just don't know what it was.

'Tis a gift to be simple, 'tis a gift to be free, 'tis a gift to come down where we ought to be, and when we find ourselves in the place just right, 'twill be in the valley of love and delight. (Shaker hymn)

AUGUST 27
St. Monica

It is said that "The hand that rocks the cradles rules the world," and St. Monica may be the best evidence that this is true. Without her persistent prayer and badgering, her son Augustine might never have become a Christian, and our faith would not have had perhaps its greatest theologian.

St. Monica didn't have a very happy life. Her husband was apparently violent and opposed to Christianity. She persisted in prayer and in what we today might call nagging to the point that even he finally converted. The greater challenge, though, was her eldest son.

St. Monica worked and prayed for *seventeen years* before her son became a Christian. It's hard for me to imagine keeping at anything for seventeen years without success. When it seems to me that God isn't answering my prayers about a parishioner I'm worried about, it usually takes a friend's reminder that "We are called not to be successful but to be faithful" to settle me down. St. Monica was faithful and persistent. Had she not been so, the church that nurtures us today would be a very different place.

It is not possible that the son of so many tears should perish. (An anonymous bishop giving comfort to Monica)

AUGUST 28
St. Augustine

It is remarkable to me that Catholics and Protestants alike claim Augustine as a foundational authority for their theology, but that the resulting interpretations can be very different. We even say his name differently: for Catholics, he is uh-GUST-in, for Protestants, AW-gus-teen. Other than the Biblical writers, I'm aware of no other theologian who holds such pride of place in both camps of our divided church.

I have my difficulties with Augustine. He didn't think much of women, and the belief that the "original sin" was having sex came from him. (Actually, original sin is disobedience, turning away from God.) He never married his mistress, even after converting to Christianity; he preferred, instead, to remain celibate. All well and good for him, but what about her and their son?

Yet I can't help but like the guy. He was so very human. He lived in the fast lane for a long time, then became a Manichaean, a heretic according to the church. He once prayed, "Give me chastity and continence, Lord—but not just yet." And there's little doubt that his mother's persistence had something to do with his conversion to Christianity. Who among us doesn't know the weight of a mother's continuing request?

At his best, Augustine reminds us of the best news among all the good news in Christianity: our redemption, our forgiveness, our adoption by God, is a matter of *grace*. Maybe he understood grace so well because he'd been such a big sinner. In an odd sort of way, it's a good thing he was. Imagine Christianity without the persistent voice of Augustine, reminding us of God's grace.

Hear the other side. (St. Augustine)

AUGUST 29
Photographs and Memories

Were you to visit me at home, you might be struck by the general lack of photographs. There are two exceptions. In my workroom, a 5 x 7 of my grandmother, Bigmommy, watches over me. And the front of my refrigerator is full of photos—one each of all the people in my life I love but don't get to see very often. I know some people find this strange, and I suspect a couple of my family members might be hurt by it, though they've never said anything.

The fact is that when I tried putting photographs out in nice frames, I couldn't whittle them down to a reasonable number. I couldn't have just one, or two, or even three of, say, my middle sister, because then my memories were frozen into the times and places those three photos were taken. I'd need a hundred pictures of her to come even close to all my many complex and varied memories of her. And I just don't have that kind of room. The compromise is the fridge—one recent photo of each person to spark the full set of memories. The rest go in photo albums smudged with fingerprints from the many times I've looked through them.

I know this is weird, and I had to think about it quite a while to figure out why I do it this way. I came to understand because of my frequent rants about people who—especially in the buckle of the Bible belt of a city I live in—take two or three verses of scripture and try to make God into something they want him to be. No one verse of scripture can come close to describing God; heavens—not even all the verses of scripture can do that. So I guess I'm just the same way about the people God has put in my life: I don't want two or three pictures to freeze them into who I want them to be.

So teach us to count our days that we may gain a wise heart. (Psalm 90:12)

AUGUST 30
A Big-A Ballet

That's how my Uncle Vito used to refer to his prodigious stomach. He was Italian, and he liked to make fun of my young pretensions to culture by rubbing his stomach and saying, "Ah, you want the ballet? I'll show you ballet. This is the kind of ballet you want, a big-A ballet."

Today at the YMCA, as I was walking past the windows overlooking the pool on my way to the weight room, I saw a man with a belly as big as my Uncle Vito's. The kids are back in school, so he stood out against the nearly unpopulated background. He was stretched back in a sun chair, his huge belly brown as a nut and glistening with suntan oil. I envied him.

I don't know one single woman with a similar body who would display it poolside with quite the same aplomb. When the weather starts warming up, the comics fill with the standard jokes about women trying on swimsuits in dressing rooms and what an awful experience it is. Most of the women I know who are as obese as that man either don't go to the pool or they wear swimsuits made to "flatter"—i.e, to hide their fat. Which of course they don't, and the women are pretty miserable about it.

I wish I could feel as comfortable with my body as most American men seem to feel with theirs. Of course health considerations are far more important than cosmetic ones. But that aside, I can't seem to get it into my head that God doesn't care that I have a pot belly. Neither do ninety-five percent of the other human beings I encounter. I don't know the major culprit in my trouble with my body image, but I do know I'm not alone in that concern. In this one case, at least, "Why can't a woman be more like a man?"

"Do not look on his appearance or on the height of his stature, because I have rejected him; for the Lord does not see as mortals see; they look on the outward appearance, but the Lord looks on the heart."
(1 Samuel 16:7b)

AUGUST 31
Clocks

I remember the ditty from my childhood: "My grandfather's clock was too large for the shelf, so it stood ninety years on the floor. It was taller by half than the old man himself, yet it weighed not a pennyweight more. It was bought on the morn of the day that he was born and was always his pleasure and pride. But it stopped—short—never to go again when the old man died."

This may be the reason that I know several people who despise grandfather clocks. It is true that each and every one of us has only a certain amount of time allotted on this earth. And it's true that this time is passing, inexorably, whether we like that fact or not. And finally, I suppose it's true that a grandfather clock could be an audible reminder of each second ticking away.

It's one of those glass half-full or half-empty kind of issues, though. No doubt about it—I can see my life as sand falling through an hourglass, digital numbers running backward toward zero, an old-fashioned clock finally running down. But I can also see it as a time-clock at an athletic event that measures the time that passes as marathoners complete their treks or Iditarod racers mush their dogs through the frozen tundra. The idea here is not so much to finish quickly—in that way the athletic metaphor breaks down—but to live those passing moments fully, to the max, at one's best.

I don't know how much time I have on this earth; no one does. But I do know that God wants me to spend that time not neurotically watching its seconds tick away, but jumping in with all the vigor I can muster, to run the race as well as I can.

For "All flesh is like grass and all its glory like the flower of grass. The grass withers, and the flower falls,

> *but the word of the Lord endures forever."*
> *(1 Peter 1:24-25a)*

September 1
The "Right" Version

I wore out my vinyl copy, given to me as a gift, of Beethoven's 7th Symphony. The version I had was George Szell conducting the Cleveland Orchestra. I knew the symphony down to the note, and part of the joy of listening to it was its very familiarity.

So imagine my disappointment when I bought another record by a different conductor and orchestra. They played it way too fast! I probably bought four or five versions over the years, searching for the "right" one, but wasn't satisfied until the Nashville Symphony performed and then recorded a version that was, almost note-for-note, the one I so loved.

I know this is entirely unreasonable of me. Part of the delight of classical music is that different artists can give it different interpretations. That way there's not just one Beethoven's 7th—there are seven, eight, or twenty for all I know.

My stubbornness about my favorite version, though, does help me understand the perspective of some older members of several congregations I know who've faced the decline in popularity of their old favorite hymns and the intrusion of new hymns and—even worse!—new music with guitars and drums.

The growth-oriented pastor part of me wants these people to jump on board these new ways that so draw younger generations; I want them to be willing to give up a body of nineteenth-century hymns or an unintelligible service—despite the beauty involved—that simply doesn't speak to most Americans anymore.

But then there's the part of me that doesn't want to hear any version of Arcangelo Corelli's *Christmas Concerto* but the one performed by Stratos. I need to have more patience with the older members of congregations who know the "right" way to sing church music.

David also commanded the chiefs of the Levites to appoint their kindred as the singers to play on musical instruments, on harps and lyres and cymbals, to raise loud sounds of joy. (1 Chronicles 15:16)

September 2
Runner's High

Years ago, when I first started swimming, I started having a strange problem. When I got out of the pool after a long swim—fifty laps or so—I felt very strange. It worried me so much I went to the doctor about it. She asked me to describe this feeling and as I did, she started to smile. "Have you ever had strong pain medication?" she asked; I said I had and that, in fact, the feelings were similar. "Then you're just experiencing an endorphin rush. That's what the athletes are all out there working for!"

How embarrassing. Just goes to show how nonathletic I am—I was almost forty before I had this experience. And I thought there was something wrong with me!

But after I'd digested all this new information, I had to admit that feeling was part of what kept me going back to the pool. In the high I didn't feel any pain. I felt an incredible sense of well-being, and very often when I got home I just sat, staring off into space, until it wore off. I was an endorphin junkie.

I still get endorphin highs, though I have to work harder for them and they don't come as frequently. I suspect that any leader of the "war against drugs" who's reading this is in a great state of alarm. I shouldn't be talking this way—it might encourage young people not only to go for the athlete's high, but for the pill version.

I can't see it that way. I've had enough surgery that I've felt the buzz of narcotics, and they just aren't the same. That doesn't surprise me. After all, it's drug companies who make morphine and God, endorphins. Apparently, God wants us to have that high. It's not the experience that's bad—it's looking for it from the wrong source.

David danced before the Lord with all his might.
(2 Samuel 6:14a)

SEPTEMBER 3
A Table

When I was the pastor at Central Christian Church in Springfield, Tennessee, the congregation sent four people on a mission trip to Haiti sponsored by my denomination's local leadership. They came back with moving pictures and incredible stories, but the story they kept repeating was about a table.

The group had a nurse practitioner along, so they were able to give some very basic medical care to the desperately poor Haitians they met. She taught others in the group how to do basic things like take blood pressure. And at this church, someone brought the missionaries a table to use for supplies—bandages, vitamins, antibiotic cream, etc. The group worked hard all morning as the line of patients kept getting longer.

Lunchtime came and the table that had held medical supplies was cleaned off and used to prepare

lunch. I think it was peanut butter and jelly sandwiches—nothing special. After lunch, again it held
medical supplies.

At the end of their long day, the missionaries
joined with the Haitians in a worship service. For the
service of communion they used the table that they
had used all day.

When I take communion, I'm used to seeing the
officiant stand behind a gorgeous altar or a beautifully carved wooden table. It would never occur to me
to use an everyday table as the surface on which to
consecrate bread and wine. But the Haitians really
have very good theology. That table, from which they
received the body and blood of Jesus Christ, was the
same table from which they received life-giving sustenance and care for their illness.

That's what communion does—it nourishes us in
body, soul, and spirit. In our ordinary worship lives,
we're left to make that connection from words said by
the clergy. But in Haiti, that truth suddenly took on
a very obvious expression in the presence of a plain,
beat-up, rickety table.

"Can God spread a table in the wilderness?"
(Psalm 78:19b)

SEPTEMBER 4
Why Me?

I'm aware, as a pastor and as a human being, that the question "Why me?" is frequently directed to God. Why me, Lord? Why do I have cancer? Why was my child born with birth defects? Why did I lose my job? Why was my house the one the tornado blew apart? These and a million other instances of the question are all valid ways to start a conversation with God.

But it does amuse me, when I'm able to step back enough to recognize it, that while I'm always ready to ask God "Why me?" when something bad happens, I almost never ask the question when it's something good.

Why me, Lord? Why did I get the gift of a graduate education? Why do I live in a heated, cooled, safe home when so many others don't? Why do I have friends and family who care about me and check up on me when things are tough? Why do I have a reliable car to drive? Why can I go to the supermarket and buy pretty much anything I see there?

If I'm honest with myself, I think I know the reason I never ask God "Why me?" about these situations in my life. Deep down, I believe that I'm the one responsible for all the good things in my life. I have them because I worked hard and so I deserve them. Of course, this is far from the truth. The biggest factor determining that I got all these good-ies is that I had the wisdom to be born in the United States to a middle-class family.

Again, when I'm honest, I have to shake my head when I catch myself at this. The bottom line is that all the good things in my life are there because God has given them to me. I need to ask myself *this* kind of "Why me?" much more often.

[Job said] "I know that you can do all things, and that no purpose of yours can be thwarted." (Job 42:2)

SEPTEMBER 5
Mother Teresa of Calcutta

There's probably not an American alive today who hasn't heard of Mother Teresa—Catholic, Protestant, Anglican, as well as Jew, Muslim, Buddhist, Hindu. We've seen moving TV pictures of the horrible poverty in which she worked, and we've also seen some rather bizarre images that jar us, like the one of Mother Teresa standing next to the tall, beautiful, blond, radiant Princess Diana.

It interests me that there is a small group of very angry people who want to "expose" Mother Teresa. They want to persuade people that her work was self-serving. They ask why all the donations she received haven't been used to build modern hospitals in poverty-ridden Calcutta.

The problem is that these people don't understand the ministry of Mother Teresa. Yes, it is a good thing to take modern medicine to sick people in desperately poor countries. Yet as Jesus reminded us, we will always have the poor with us. No matter how many hospitals we build, there will always be some people who are left to die on the street, utterly alone, without the most basic comforts. Helping these people was Mother Teresa's ministry, and it's a very profound one.

The plain fact is that we all die; the question is under what conditions that death will occur. Mother Teresa can't provide every poor person her order encounters with a nice, soft hospital bed and pain-killing drugs every four hours. But they can take a dying person off the street, give them shelter, water when they're thirsty, food when they can eat, and company in the last hours of their life.

I have no doubt Mother Teresa will, one day, be declared a saint. And so should she be. What if just ten percent of the world's Christians devoted themselves to God's service the way she has? What a different world we'd live in.

"Truly I tell you, whoever does not receive the kingdom of God as a little child will never enter it."
(Mark 10:15)

SEPTEMBER 6
Mr. Spock

Okay, okay, I admit it. The *Star Trek* phenomenon is a little weird. There's a documentary out, called *Trekkies*, that shows a sizeable group of people whose entire lives revolve around something that isn't real. *Trekkies* is full of opportunities to laugh at these people.

But the success of *Star Trek* suggests to me some failures of the American church. Take Mr. Spock. He's a Vulcan and he has pointy ears. The most important thing about him, though, is that he has no emotions. He's entirely logical. Or at least 99.9 percent of the time. On occasion, when affected by some strange plant or the Vulcan seven-year mating cycle, he's *very* emotional. Outrageously, remarkably, uncontrollably emotional.

Trekkies recognize, probably at an unconscious level, that most American mainline churches have been taken captive by rationalism. Of course there are good aspects of that. We want the church to provide modern medicine, to agree that the earth revolves around the sun. But I chafe a bit at the church's lack of enthusiasm for emotion; most expect their members to behave as calm, rational, polite human beings—especially in worship. There are Pentecostal and charismatic churches, of course, but in those services I find myself overwhelmed.

The problem is that I know I'm not 99.9 percent rational. I know it when, against my will, my eyes fill with tears during a hymn, or when taking communion floods me with peace. I know that there's more emotion in me than most mainline church services give expression to. And I guess the reason I like Mr. Spock is I recognize that when emotion finally does break into a rational setting, it can get really out of control.

Could there be a middle ground?

Do not quench the Spirit. Do not despise the words of the prophets . . . hold fast to what is good.
(1 Thessalonians 5:19-21)

SEPTEMBER 7*
Labor Day

(Observed first Monday in September)

If I can completely divorce America's Labor Day from politics (and I can), then I can celebrate it as a day to celebrate rest. I have written before that work, at its best, is an important and fulfilling part of human life. But so is rest.

If I have an addiction, it's work. I have a terrible time allowing myself to spend one entire day doing nothing worthwhile. Sometimes I can put aside preparation for class, my writing of the moment, proposals and plans for future work. Sometimes I can put aside vacuuming, dusting, laundry, dishes, and grocery shopping. But to put aside all these things on the same day, for an *entire* day—well, that's a tough one.

Apparently deep down I believe I'm only a worthwhile person if I'm doing something productive. I know that's not true. Everything in my theology tells me that's wrong. God loves me simply because God chooses to love me, not because of anything I do. But head-knowledge is different from gut-knowledge. And because I don't know these truths at my deepest core, I struggle to give myself an entire sabbath day to rest.

It's truly become a discipline for me, as I imagine it has for many other people, to take an entire day off. After I do, I'm always glad. I find myself refreshed and relaxed and even able to work better.

But there I go again—justifying rest because it improves my work. God, can you do something to get this through to me?

[Jesus] said to them, "Come away to a deserted place all by yourselves and rest a while." (Mark 6:31a)

SEPTEMBER 8
Balancing the Checkbook

I am not a math whiz. I am barely math-competent. I have to write down every addition, subtraction, and multiplication problem that has more than four numbers or symbols involved. As you might imagine, then, balancing my checkbook is not a monthly task I anticipate with glee.

It is a rare event when I can make the statement and my register balance exactly . . . like once-a-year rare. Other months, I just take the bank's word for it and subtract from or add to my bankbook in order to agree with them. I'm not a stupid woman and there's no logical excuse for my hatred of numbers and apparent incompetence.

Which makes it all the more humiliating. Once a month, I have a very vivid reminder that I'm math-impaired. It doesn't make me feel very good about myself. I do have friends who just *don't* balance their checkbooks, but I'm too compulsive for that.

So it's a good thing that being a Christian involves some very simple math. Seven days of creation. Forty days and nights or years in the wilderness. Two denarii. The ten-percent tithe (the easiest fraction problem around). And finally, an equation that would stump the most brilliant mathematician if she weren't a believer: $1 + 1 + 1 = 1$. Father, Son, and

Holy Spirit equals one God and Mother of us all. It's not logical, no. But it's math I can handle.

> *Honest balances and scales are the Lord's.*
> *(Proverbs 16:11a)*

SEPTEMBER 9
St. Peter Claver

A man best known for his missionary work among slaves, St. Peter Claver was also, in an important way, a martyr. He gave his life to the people of Cartagena, Columbia. During the spring season, he traveled to the hovels the slaves lived in, stayed with them, and helped in whatever way he could—with food, medical care, spiritual solace. When autumn set in and many sailors docked to spend the season in Cartagena, St. Peter ministered to *them* too. He was widely admired and respected in town.

Until he became gravely ill. In 1650 he was among the first victims of a virulent epidemic; he was so ill he was given last rites. But he lived four more years. These weren't happy years for him; his illness had left him in constant pain and with debilitating tremors. He was confined to his cell much of the time, and all the people who had received care from him forgot about him. When his last illness did arrive, those same people flocked to his deathbed and carted off anything and everything they could count as relics.

St. Peter Claver is a remarkable example of spending oneself in the service of God. Though he didn't suffer the same kind of martyrdom as being thrown to the lions, he did, like Jesus, find himself abandoned when he was on his "cross."

It's very easy for me today to honor St. Peter Claver. But chances are there is someone in our midst who is expending all her life in service to God, only to be overlooked by all the "good" Christians surrounding her. This day commemorating St. Peter's death is a reminder to me to open my eyes and find the person in my town who is pouring out her life for God. Better to do that now than frantically run to her bedside when she's in her last hours.

I am poured out like water, and all my bones are out of joint; my heart is like wax; it is melted within my breast. (Psalm 22:14)

SEPTEMBER 10
Communion

Beliefs about communion might be the biggest area of disagreement among the many Christian denominations in the United States. The Catholic Church teaches that although the bread and wine continue to taste and feel like bread and wine, they are in fact changed into the body and blood of Christ. At the other end of the spectrum are free churches who believe that the piece of cracker and small cup of grape juice are mere reminders of the Last Supper and the sacrifice Jesus made for us all. In between, Christians believe all sorts of things about what communion is.

I found a great comment about this issue in the letters of Flannery O'Connor, a Catholic, Southern writer whose books I cannot recommend strongly enough to anyone who takes their spirituality seriously. She was at dinner with friends and they were discussing the meaning of communion. One of her friends suggested it was a symbol. Flannery's response, and mine: "If it's just a symbol, then the hell with it."

'Nuff said.

While they were eating, he took a loaf of bread, and after blessing it he broke it, gave it to them, and said, "Take; this is my body." Then he took a cup, and after giving thanks he gave it to them, and all of them drank from it. He said to them, "This is my blood of the covenant, which is poured out for many."
(Mark 14:22-24)

SEPTEMBER 11
World Trade Center Terrorism

As I write these words, the horrible terrorist acts that brought down both towers of the World Trade Center, destroyed a part of the Pentagon, and killed thousands of people is very fresh. It all happened less than a week ago. By the time you read these words, it will probably have faded from history a bit. I know from personal experience that the truths that seem so clear and strong and obvious in the midst of such a disaster can fade over time. So for my readers and for myself, I offer this time capsule.

Don't forget—I say to myself and to you—that there is terrible evil in the world. Most of the time we can ignore it because it's not right in our faces, but it's always there. Don't forget that over the course of human history, we have only "evolved" more and more terrible ways to harm each other. Don't forget what evil lurks in the heart of everyone.

But don't forget how much good people can do. Don't forget the work and self-sacrifice of firefighters and police officers, EMTs and doctors. Don't forget the people who sacrificed themselves so that others could live. Don't forget the depth of compassion you and everyone else was able to feel during those days . . . it's still there, though it may not be on the surface these days. Don't forget the generosity of which the human heart is capable.

Finally, don't forget that one of our first impulses—along with the desire to help—was to go to a church and pray. Something inside of us knows to whom we need to turn when things are bad.

Don't forget.

"No one has greater love than this, to lay down one's life for one's friends." (John 15:13)

SEPTEMBER 12
Toaster Ovens

God's blessings on whoever invented the toaster oven. My apartment is a converted attic, so in the summer, it can get pretty hot. My window air-conditioning units work as hard as they can to keep the temperature livable. Using the big oven tips the delicate balance in the wrong direction. The toaster oven won't produce a gourmet meal, but it will do the basics.

There are days equivalent to a toaster oven. Of course I have to do the basics—breathe, bathe, eat, walk the dog. On a toaster oven day, I do the basics but not much else. That means not working, not cleaning house, not going to the grocery store. Every once in a while, people need a day to do nothing but the basics.

Unfortunately, the world of work doesn't really recognize this. Most employers offer two kinds of time off: sick leave and vacation. If I only have ten days of vacation, then it's awfully hard to justify using one of them to stay home and vegetate. Thus the idea of the "mental health day." That's not official, of course; employers don't want me staying home unless I'm absolutely forced to by a serious illness. But I know that I'll work better and more efficiently if I take off a day to do nothing every once in a while.

God made us into creatures who get tired. Why, who knows? God could have made us as tireless as robots. But that's not what happened. So even if an employer doesn't understand my need for a toaster oven day, God surely does. No, it's not stealing from the company to take a day off when I am not, officially, sick. It's just that most employers don't see things through God's eyes—which are, after all, finally the only eyes that count.

> *By God's will I may come to you with joy and be refreshed in your company. (Romans 15:32)*

SEPTEMBER 13
Motion Sensor Lights

It's dark in my neck of the woods, so I'm very glad that my landlord has installed lights that come on when they detect motion—me coming down the driveway, up the stairs, and across the patio. If it weren't for those lights, I'd have had several falls by now and might have been attacked by a mugger hiding in a dark corner. Those lights have protected me. And the cool thing about these particular lights is that they don't burn all night—just as long as they sense motion and for a little while afterward. Protective but economical—who can argue with that?

Of course, I'm not protected at all times and all places by motion-sensitive lights. But I am, at all times, protected by something far superior: the power of God. I have to remind myself sometimes that angels are watching over me and keeping me safe. While my tendency is to complain when they fail to protect me, what I need to do is thank them again and again for the many disasters they have averted. A few of those I'm aware of—a near-miss car accident, a loss of balance on a hiking trail that could have sent me tumbling down a mountain, a terminal prognosis. In those instances, I knew angels were taking care of me. But there is so much danger in the world, it's very likely that they save me from hurting myself or being hurt by something or someone else every single day—probably several times a day. I don't think about those rescue operations because I was never aware of them.

Any time I move outside my house in the dark, a light comes on to protect me. Any time I move anywhere, in light or darkness, angels take me by the arms and protect me. Protection, but nothing economical about it. Full protection, all the time.

For he will command his angels concerning you to guard you in all your ways. (Psalm 91:11)

SEPTEMBER 14*
My Birthday

This date really is my birthday; I know yours is different. But I hope that my thoughts on this day will be helpful on your own birthday or any other day.

My family has a story about how I came into the world. Parts of that story—a long, arduous labor—are pretty common, while other parts—my father getting lost in a railroad yard on the way to the hospital, bumping my birthing mother over dozens of railroad tracks—are unique. But there's a birth-day story for each of us. Most of us have been lucky enough to have parents or other relatives tell us those stories so we can remember them.

But even if I had no stories about the day of my birth, I would still know several things. First, that I was the product of a remarkable, miraculous natural process God has built into human beings. Next, that my birth was marked and noted in heaven. The record doesn't say, "September 14, 1957: 1.2 million people born on earth today." It says, "September 14, 1957: Karen born today." Each of us, you and I, is a unique creation. There are a lot of us, but our God knows each and every one of us better than we know ourselves.

There's a rather common poster that says, "God danced on the day you were born." Sure, it applies to every person on earth. But it also applies to me, and to you, in all of our individuality.

"Before I formed you in the womb I knew you, and before you were born I consecrated you."
(Jeremiah 1:5a)

SEPTEMBER 15
Vacuuming

My mother hates vacuuming, and over the years she has vociferously reminded the whole family of this fact. Me, I don't mind it.

In fact, I actually like it. I don't mind doing housework as long as I can see visible results. Dusting is the household chore I hate, and I think that's because unless someone's really *looking* for dust, all my hard work doesn't show.

Anyway, crazy as it sounds, I like vacuuming. What I like about it most are the parallel tracks it leaves on the carpet. It's an obvious sign to me (and anyone else who cares about such things) that someone's been cleaning here recently, that someone has worked to make the carpet a nice place to walk and sit on, and that I've actually accomplished something.

I'm sure you've read that poem about footprints in the sand; well, I have an unreasonable distaste for it. I suspect that feeling comes from nothing more than overexposure. People don't know what kind of gifts to get their pastors (especially of the female persuasion), so the number of "footprints" plaques I've gotten over the years is in the double digits.

But vacuuming the way I like it is quite similar to that poem. It's easy to read the tracks on the carpet as a reminder that someone *was* there, whether we were aware of it or not. Footprints in the sand or vacuum cleaner tracks, it's really all the same: Jesus is always with us.

But Daniel laughed and restrained the king from going in. "Look at the floor," he said, "and notice whose footprints these are." (Daniel 14:19)

SEPTEMBER 16
The Dictionary

One sign that I am a true nerd: When I look up a word in the dictionary, I get distracted by the other words around it and end up reading two or three pages of definitions. But dictionaries in a computer database don't work that way; you put the word in a search engine and the program spits out a definition—of that word *and only* that word. Another sign of nerdiness: If that's the way it works, I think it's a shame. I like discovering new words and finding uses for them. My most recent favorite is equipoise, which is a state of equilibrium. If I'd been looking up "eponymous" in a computer dictionary, I never would have learned this other new word.

Everything I believe tells me that God knows *everything*—not the mind-boggling task of knowing everything in an encyclopedia, or knowing everything about how the human body works, but everything about everything. It's hard to imagine that kind of knowledge, though. It's rather paradoxical that with each successive academic degree I've attained, I've only become more aware of how little I know.

I imagine we'll have access to that infinite knowledge in heaven. If being in the presence of God doesn't blow the questions out of my mind, one day I'll know the truth about the Kennedy assassination, Area

51, and the honesty of each and every auto mechanic I've ever met. I'll know the real reason that guy left me and the correct interpretation of Shakespeare's *King Lear*. All I'll have to do is ask the awe-inspiring God who knows everything. Just imagine.

I can't. Just the dictionary is overwhelming for me.

"Where were you when I laid the foundation of the earth? Tell me, if you have understanding." (Job 38:4)

SEPTEMBER 17
Hildegard of Bingen

It wasn't until seminary that I even had a hint that a woman like Hildegard had ever existed in the church. Since I grew up Protestant, I didn't even have the example of the saints, and the women I'd heard about in Sunday School were either sinners (Eve, Jezebel, Mary Magdalene, Sapphira) or the passive Protestant Mary.

Hildegard has never been canonized, but that doesn't affect my admiration one bit. Born of noble blood, she was convent-educated from the age of seven. She became abbess of her community, but that traditional role only begins to describe the contributions she made to the church.

Hildegard was visited by visions, and from them she wrote a three-volume theological treatise that gives us a record of the church's belief at the beginning of the twelfth century. Her talents as an artist are evident because she illuminated her own works. She also wrote several volumes of science, describing animals and plants and the construction of the cosmos; some of this science she focused on the healing properties of herbs. She wrote poetry and music, the latter of which is only now being appreciated as remarkably original and beautiful. Get a CD and listen; it's clear the woman heard the music of the angels. Widely respected as a prophet, Hildegard responded to many requests for help, and also on her own initiative (or, rather, God's instruction), wrote to very important people, including monarchs, giving her advice. At one period she traveled to monasteries and preached; during that time she also preached in public.

Hildegard was a renaissance woman before there was a renaissance. She is an example to me of God's remarkable power; God not only gave her all these gifts but enabled her to use them at a time when most women had very limited roles in society. More than that, most of her work has survived for the edification of modern Christians.

There have probably been many "Hildegards" in the history of the church. Some of them have been canonized, but most probably died in obscurity.

Nevertheless, her example suggests to me that the little I was taught about Christian women as a child only scratches the surface of the contributions they made to the faith.

O orzchis Ecclesia, armis divinis precinta et iacincto ornata tu es caldemia stigmatum loifolum et urbs scientiarum. O, O, tu est etiam erizanta in alto sono et es chortza gemma.
(O measureless Church girded with divine arms and adorned with Jacinth; you are the fragrance of the wounds of nations and the city of sciences. O, O, and you are anointed amid noble sound and you are a sparkling gem.)
(Hildegard of Bingen, in the unique language God used to speak to her.)

SEPTEMBER 18
Bad Mommy!

Last night I spilled some liquid potpourri over many things: the papers I was grading, myself, and Buzz, who was sitting in my lap. I grabbed the startled Buzz, rushed him to the kitchen sink, and used the sprayer to wash off the goop. I didn't want him to lick it off and get sick. I apologized profusely all the while.

Apparently that wasn't enough, because this morning, I found that he'd attacked one of my pillows. It used to have four gold tassels, but this morning only two remained. The other two Buzz had chewed off sometime during the night. I picked up the mess and said under my breath, "Well, I guess he had to show me he was mad at me."

Suddenly I was hit with an insight: Is this how God reacts when I "act out" because of my anger? By now I've gotten to the point that I can usually say, "Lord, I'm really pissed at you." But sometimes I do something foolish—like miss church—unconsciously trying to show God I'm mad.

I thought of all the people I've attended at their deathbeds, and how many of them have felt guilty and afraid because they'd done things to "attack" God. They were petrified that retribution was coming. I've always reassured them of God's grace, but this morning I understood at a deep level that my reassurance was correct.

I felt no anger at Buzz this morning. Sure, I would *prefer* to have a pillow with four tassels. Given how tiny he is, he probably stole at least an hour's worth of sleep to destroy both tassels; they were quite big. I would prefer that he'd spent that time getting the sleep he needed to recover from his trauma. But anger? Not even close. I understood.

Is it possible God could be so forgiving?

For you, O Lord, are good and forgiving, abounding in steadfast love to all who call on you. (Psalm 86:5)

September 19
Jessica Lange

Andrew Greeley, the widely known priest and author, once said, "God is sexier than Jessica Lange." What? God doesn't have a body and so can have no gender, and therefore no sexuality.

Nevertheless, Greeley is right. Many of the church's mystics have experienced God's presence in remarkably erotic ways. Teresa of Avila's famous experience of having her heart pierced by God could be any Freudian's delight. John of the Cross wrote love poems to God.

On the whole, the Catholic Church has a healthier attitude toward sexuality than do most Protestants. The influence of Puritanism has left most American churchgoers certain that sex is awful good but awful evil too.

Nothing could be further from the truth. God created women and men in such a way that we desire each other and take great delight in each others' bodies. All natural theology suggests sex is a very good thing. And while St. Paul was no champion of sex, the writer of the Song of Songs most definitely was.

The fact is that God relates to us through every aspect of our being—our minds, yes, but also our bodies, spirits, feelings, and sexuality. God uses every part of what we are to be in an intimate relationship with us. When we are united with God, our intellects are fulfilled, as are our bodies, feelings, and spirits; and when we are united with God, our sexuality is fulfilled too.

So. God is sexier than Jessica Lange? I'm still not buying it. Tom Selleck, maybe.

Let him kiss me with the kisses of his mouth! For your love is better than wine. (Song of Songs 1:2)

SEPTEMBER 20*
The Autumnal Equinox

When I was a child, I loved summer for the obvious reason. As a young woman, I preferred spring—a time of warmth, new life, flowers, and love, love, love. As a middle-aged woman, though, I like autumn the best.

That's not just because my menopausal body is fairly faint with relief from heat. Autumn is the culmination of the cycle of nature God created. The trees that flowered in the spring offer their ripe fruit and the green shoots that pushed their way to the surface in barely-warm soil turn into fresh corn. Pumpkin vines produce their almost laughably-abundant fruit. Walnuts and acorns pepper the ground.

While spring is a beautiful season, autumn has its own special beauty. It's the beauty of maturity, as the trees recover the life juice they've worked all summer to make from the leaves of scarlet, yellow, and orange that swirl around me. A drive through the Appalachians offers breathtaking sights that words simply cannot exhaust.

Fall is also an honest season—it's most reflective of life. Our lives contain the enthusiasm of spring and the abundance of summer, but they also have their share of naked tree limbs. Autumn doesn't allow me to make simple judgment about things. While I may mourn the loss of greenery, I also know this retreat is an integral part of the cycle of life.

It doesn't surprise me that it took this long for autumn to become my favorite season of the year. After all these years, I can appreciate the gifts of the year's middle age.

May those who sow in tears reap with shouts of joy.
(Psalm 126:5)

SEPTEMBER 21
St. Matthew the Evangelist

Matthew's is the most "Jewish" of all the gospels. It is Matthew who reminds his readers, again and again, that Jesus was the messiah of God's chosen people. He quotes the Old Testament more than any other gospel writer, and offers his readers asides to remind us that some event in the life of Jesus happened "to fulfill all righteousness," or the Law of Judaism. Matthew reminds me that without Judaism there is no Christianity. His version of Jesus' life keeps front and center the fact that Jesus, his family, and his disciples were good, observant Jews.

Matthew's gospel reminds me of the many gifts the world received from this small but ever-present group of people. Judaism gave us the idea of one God. Today we confess this belief off-handedly, but in the environment in which Judaism was born, monotheism was a radical idea. One of the reasons the Romans persecuted Christians was that they considered us atheists: we rejected the existence of all but one God.

Judaism gives us our history; without the Hebrew Bible, or Old Testament, we would know little about our roots. We would live without the ethics produced by the Jewish faith, the understanding that it is God who created this world, and the very good news that

God wants us to rest one day out of seven. More than anything else, we would not be able to understand who this Jesus was; we would not know that he was the culmination of thousands of years of God's relationship with the chosen people.

Thanks, Matthew, for reminding me that my Lord was a Jew.

"Do not think that I have come to abolish the law or the prophets; I have come not to abolish but to fulfill."
(Matthew 5:17)

September 22
Addictions

Though we don't like to admit it, we freedom-loving Americans, we are slaves. Part of the reason we have trouble recognizing our slavery is that these days we like to call it something else. What do we call it when someone drinks so much that he damages his liver, loses his job, and drives away his family and friends? What do we call it when someone smokes so much she has a very good chance of dying from lung cancer? What do we call it when someone sticks a needle in his veins for that brief high, despite the costs, both fiscal and physical?

Well, we call it addiction, that's what we call it. And if we want to get broader about it, we call it disease. But anyone who's ever tried to quit smoking or drinking knows that it really is slavery, whatever the words we use to describe it.

Too often our twenty-first-century minds rush right over the idea of slavery—it doesn't apply to us, we think—because we abolished it ages ago. But if I allow myself to realize that I am enslaved to something—not just substances but work, relationships, material things, even my own righteousness—then it is very good news indeed that it is God, not me, who has the power to free the enslaved.

That God will free us there is no doubt. The millions of people who have been helped by the twelve-step programs can testify that it would not have been possible except for their surrender to a "higher power." Even good old St. Paul, who advised literal slaves to remain slaves since the end of the world was coming so soon, understood that slavery, in and of itself, is a terrible thing, and that God rescues every Christian from it.

For you did not receive a spirit of slavery to fall back into fear, but you have received a spirit of adoption.
(Romans 8:15)

SEPTEMBER 23
Slow Learners

When I was in seminary, I met a man named "Troy." He was one of the sweetest, most gentle, kindest men I've ever known. He'd been a carpenter before he came to school; more than that—and I swear I'm not making this up—his wife's name was Mary. Perfect minister material, right? There was only one problem: Troy was a bit of a slow learner.

Now, I don't mean here that Troy just wasn't very intellectual. He tried to be—he read all the theologians he was supposed to. You never saw him without a book. Plain and simple, he just wasn't very smart. He finally failed enough classes that the faculty had to throw him out.

Troy had to leave his field placement too. It was a tiny little church, off somewhere in rural Kentucky. I guess he told them he'd be leaving on a Sunday, because Monday morning, the whole governing board of the congregation showed up in the dean's office. They were plain country people, and elderly, all of them. They begged the dean not to kick Troy out. "He has his problems, we know," they said. "But that's just exactly the point. When he's with us we don't see Troy, we see Christ. He's the best pastor we've ever had."

This was quite a lesson for a seminarian who was starting to get ideas about going on for a Ph.D. and making a living as a professor. I liked thinking of myself as an intellectual; I took pride in it. But what Troy taught me is that my intellectualism can get in the way of my ministry. It's too easy for other people—and me—to assume I'm the one responsible for anything good that comes out of my work.

It took Troy two more years to finish twelve more credits, but finally he did it. And today, he's a pastor . . . one of the best, I imagine, his congregation has ever had.

For God's foolishness is wiser than human wisdom,
and God's weakness is stronger than human strength.
(1 Corinthians 1:25)

SEPTEMBER 24
Perfume

I was standing in line at the library the other day when I got a whiff of someone's perfume. It was White Shoulders—I knew it in a second. That's what my grandmother wore, and just one tiny whiff of it flooded me with memories of her.

Scientists say our memory is closely tied to our sense of smell, and my experience says they're right.

The smell of roasting marshmallows makes me remember Girl Scouts; and the fragrance of cinnamon puts me right back in the fuzzy comfort of my mother's kitchen.

Most of the time it's hard for me to remember that I'm an animal. I am a mammal, though one whose species has lost the expert sense of smell of my fellow mammals. It's remarkable to me that our extremely sophisticated scientific community hasn't been able to build a machine that can smell as well as a dog—which is why some canines have jobs as drug- and bomb-sniffers.

My friends say I'm disgusting for saying this, but every person I've ever known has a unique fragrance. Sometimes I can tell someone's been in an elevator because their smell is there. Every house I've known well—my own or a friends'—has its own smell too. Every time I smell a boxwood, I'm thrown back to my Uncle Ralph and Aunt Vivian's house.

It's a gift, really, one that comes from God. It's not just the pleasure of smelling nice fragrances like perfume or incense. It's the connection to my past, one that doesn't just make me remember but also makes me experience times, places, and people that have otherwise disappeared.

The mandrakes give forth fragrance, and over our doors are all choice fruits, new as well as old, which I

have laid up for you, O my beloved.
(Song of Songs 7:13)

SEPTEMBER 25
Pagans

Here in Nashville, we've got a full-scale model of the Parthenon. It was built for the state's centennial celebration in the nineteenth century and now sits in the middle of a lovely park. Inside the Parthenon is a forty-two-foot-tall statue of the goddess Athena.

Each summer, a group of pagans from all over the country makes a pilgrimage to Nashville. During the day they have athletic contests, set up booths to sell trinkets, play music, and basically have a good time. At night the group carries a smaller version of Athena in a procession. They go into the Parthenon and there they have a worship service. They offer prayers and pour out libations of wine in front of the statue. There are indeed twenty-first-century Americans who worship the goddess Athena, along with other gods and goddesses.

I heard about "pagans" in Sunday School as a child. They were the most messed up people in the world, according to my teachers. And the word "pagan," over the centuries, has come to mean, for people in the church, "anyone who's not a Christian."

But a better definition of pagan is someone who worships an idol. I have to admit that I participate in a form of paganism that thrives among many Christians. I worship the idol of consumerism. The god of consumerism says, "If you have lots of things, you'll be happy." This is a very sneaky god who hides behind some very subtle images. Think of that commercial we see every Christmas: a bunch of people holding candles and singing about teaching the world to sing and giving everybody a Coke. The underlying message is that if we drink Coke, there will be peace on earth. Right.

I have a little index card taped to the visor in my car. Every time I go to the mall and put the visor up when I park, I see this message: "Are you going to buy something to make yourself feel better?" If the answer is yes, then I'm as much of a pagan as the folks who party at the Parthenon every summer.

Put to death, therefore, whatever in you is earthly: fornication, impurity, passion, evil desire, and greed (which is idolatry). (Colossians 3:5)

SEPTEMBER 26
Nudes

My friend Heather's mother, Diane, is an artist and also an art teacher. She teaches part-time in a couple of private elementary schools. Heather tells me that Diane has to carefully screen the books she takes to her classes, because the schools have decided the children shouldn't see nudes.

In the South, we've got two words to describe the state of wearing no clothes. One is "nude," the other, "nekkid." Being nekkid is being nude and up to no good. Diane's books don't contain pictures of nekkid people; they do have a few nudes.

Of course children should not be exposed to pornography, but Botticelli's "The Birth of Venus" is a long way from that. Michaelangelo's "David" is one of the most beautiful sculptures in all of Western civilization. Are we to withhold some of the world's best art from our children until they're twenty-one? Or maybe eighteen. Should art museums be rated R?

Children are curious about their bodies and those of others, and if it occurs in the right atmosphere, exposure to nudity doesn't damage them one bit. In fact, it can be quite good for them. Learning when nudity is proper and when it isn't protects them from sexual predators, who sometimes target very young children. The human body is also one of God's exquisite creations.

I have a button that expresses it quite well: If God approved of nudity, then we'd be born without clothes.

[Job] said, "Naked I came from my mother's womb, and naked shall I return there; the Lord gave, and the Lord has taken away; blessed be the name of the Lord."
(Job 1:21)

SEPTEMBER 27
Grades

Well, the first papers of the semester went back to students today, and some of them were none too happy. Vanderbilt is a pretty good school, so my students probably went to good high schools and made good grades. They're not used to making Cs.

I've learned that I have to explain to students, in very plain language, just exactly what a grade is: "This grade doesn't mean you're a 'C' person. It means you did 'C' work on this paper. The grade is about your work. It doesn't say a thing about your value or worth as a person."

Actually, I empathize with them, because I tend to measure myself the same way—by my accomplishments. If I were to write a best-selling novel, then I would be an A+ human being. If I lived my whole life and never did anything spectacular, I'd be a C human being. If I did something *really* bad, like use the wrong fork at dinner, I'd be an F.

But I'm messed up when I start thinking this way. God doesn't work the way schools do, nor the way our culture does. God isn't impressed by 4.0 GPAs or multi-billion-dollar fortunes. In fact, God doesn't ask me to be successful; that's something I impose on myself. What God asks is simply that I be faithful. So when I think about it, I realize that God is an easier taskmaster than am I. If God were teaching my class, it wouldn't just be that grades don't determine a person's value. If God taught my class, there wouldn't be grades at all.

For my yoke easy, and my burden is light.
(Matthew 11:30)

SEPTEMBER 28
Rx: Prayer

I attended a lecture by a physician who had collected all sorts of scientific information about prayer and church-going. Study after study showed that people who pray have lower blood pressure, live longer, and recover more quickly from illness. People who go to church regularly are happier in their marriages and get sick less frequently than those who don't. This doctor acted like he'd discovered penicillin: The next great drug is prayer! Just prescribe your patients two Our Fathers, one Hail Mary, a bedtime prayer each night, and you'll get miraculous results!

Trouble was the good doctor missed some other studies, ones that have been around longer, from the world of psychology. These studies examined the differences between "intrinsic" and "extrinsic" religion. Extrinsic religion means going to church because it does good things for you: building business contacts, accruing respect in the community, or lowering your blood pressure. People who have intrinsic religion go to church because that's who they are. They go more for the going of it than for any particular benefit it gives them.

These studies show that religion has positive physical effects only in people for whom it is intrinsic. In other words, if people go to church just to get the goodies available there, it's not going to do them any good.

That shouldn't be a surprise. Jesus taught that doing the right things for the wrong reasons won't do us any good. We're not to pray in public to get others' approval. We aren't meant to make a big show of how much we give to the church.

So as much as I like the recent scientific studies that show the power of prayer, I can't get too very excited about them. Christians who pray have known its power for centuries. People who pray just to get physical benefits from it never will.

For I tell you, unless your righteousness exceeds that of the scribes and Pharisees, you will never enter the kingdom of heaven. (Matthew 5:20)

SEPTEMBER 29
Women's Intuition

My grandmother had it, my mom has it, and so do my sisters and I. It's just a little creepy. I'll find myself suddenly thinking about someone whom I haven't seen or talked to in ages. It'll happen several times a day, several days in a row. Sometimes that person calls me—out of the blue—with big news. More often I end up calling them, and it's almost always the case that they're going through something difficult.

I'm not saying I have ESP. I'm not saying my family has a long line of women with a heightened sixth sense. But what I am saying is that most women have remarkable intuitive powers. I call it "the gut."

Sometimes a woman just knows something is so, whether or not there's evidence to support it. Unfortunately, we've been trained to reject that intuition.

We live in a rational world and our educational system is oriented toward hard science. Take a psychology class and you'll find at least ten different ways to explain away gut-level knowledge. We're told we're superstitious to believe in such things.

My gut isn't always right about a particular event, but it has never failed to tell me what my next step should be, or how I should make a decision I'm facing. I've discovered that the smartest thing I can do, when I'm facing a difficult situation, is get quiet and listen to what my gut is telling me. My gut can't choose the right stocks, but it can always tell me the right answer for decisions in my personal life.

I know some people who think believing in intuition goes against Christianity. I don't have that kind of problem with it. God made us the way God made us, and if there's something inside us that knows in a way that's not rational, then it can't be bad. In fact, it could well be that God has put it in us to give us a kind of receiver for messages from God. God talks to those of us who don't have mystical visions—through our feelings. Of course God talks to us through the church, the Bible, tradition, and our rational minds. But it's silly to reject another, additional, avenue of communication just because our scientific world hasn't yet figured out how to measure it.

> *Naomi said to Ruth, her daughter-in-law, "It is better, my daughter, that you go out with his young women, otherwise you might be bothered in another field." (Ruth 2:22)*

SEPTEMBER 30
To Be Seventeen Again . . .

I look back at pictures of myself at seventeen and see a beautiful girl, surrounded by friends and plenty of dates. Although I was never homecoming queen, I was popular enough in high school.

Yet at the time I constantly played a song called *Seventeen* by Janis Ian. It's a searingly honest account of being an unpopular, ugly-duckling seventeen-year-old. Obviously there was a part of me back then that identified with the lyrics. My memories of high school are mostly positive, but today when I listen to *Seventeen* I can remember long nights of adolescent tears and intense feelings of insecurity.

I recently bought a copy of Ian's CD because I have caught myself thinking, on occasion, of how wonderful it would be to be seventeen again. I suspect that's come up partly because my friends' children are reaching that age, and also I guess because middle age has definitely snuggled into my body and made it home. It's all too easy to idealize my high school years, something I find my friends prone to doing too.

Although churches can become places where people put on their Sunday best faces as well as clothes, that's an ironic opposition to the reality of our faith. Christianity, at its best, doesn't look away from suffering—whether it's the suffering of a teenaged girl or a crucified savior—and doesn't minimize it. That's one reason it has spoken to perhaps billions of people in the last two thousand years.

The next time I catch myself thinking that seventeen is a great age, I'll have Janis Ian to remind me otherwise.

We have a little sister, and she has no breasts. What shall we do for our sister, on the day when she is spoken for? (Song of Songs 8:8)

October 1
St. Thérèse of Lisieux

The Carmelite order seems to have produced more than its fair share of saints, and St. Thérèse is the most recent. She entered religious life while still a young girl and died at the age of twenty-four. Plagued by a frail constitution and many illnesses, Thérèse nevertheless insisted on performing the most menial tasks, like her Carmelite sisters.

When someone so young has so much spiritual wisdom, it's pretty hard to argue that she has a remarkable relationship with God. It's easy to understand how an eighty-four-year-old woman, for instance, may be spiritually wise, but someone who's twenty? It is partly because of Thérèse's youth that we can see God's hand at work in her life.

Social commentators like to say the United States is a youth-oriented culture. In many ways this is true. But we don't, as a culture, assign any particular wisdom to young people. Quite the opposite, in fact; it's pretty difficult for someone to command authority until they're about thirty.

But Thérèse never reached thirty, and she didn't need to. Her relationship with God was so close that she had the wisdom of an old woman within a girlish personality.

It wasn't until I pastored in Springfield, Tennessee, that I spent much time with teenagers. In that church, I ran the youth group, and got to know twenty or so young people pretty well. While they were immature in many ways, I often marveled at the depth of their devotion to God and the intensity of their idealism. It was the youth themselves who more or less oriented themselves around a yearly mission trip. They enjoyed lots of activities all through the year, but the entire time, they were preparing for a week of service to people less fortunate than themselves.

So many churches bemoan the loss of their youth as they move from childhood to adolescence. Is there any chance that the fault lies not with them, but with us—the adults who can't believe that someone so young can have any wisdom about God? I imagine St. Thérèse responding with a sly smile when I ask that question, especially since she's now the third woman Doctor of the Church . . . and probably one of its youngest.

The church has a heart and that heart is afire with love. (St. Thérèse of Lisieux)

OCTOBER 2
Guardian Angels

In my first ministerial position, I taught an adult education class that met on Wednesday nights. We covered a wide range of topics, but one particular session stands out in my mind many years later.

The topic of discussion was angels. As I heard my rationally-oriented Disciples of Christ students laugh off such a childish idea, I decided to play Angel's Advocate and made a strong argument that they do exist. Quite frankly, at the time I actually agreed with them; I thought it was simply my role to prod them to further thought and discussion. We ended the class with a general consensus that we were too modern to believe in angels anymore, and the group thinking that their young, new minister was rather naïve.

But something incredible happened over the next week. One by one, *eight* people in that class crept into my office to tell me that while they weren't comfortable sharing it with their fellow classmates, they had each had an experience with an angel. I heard eight compelling stories from people who lived in and enjoyed the modern, scientific world. That's one reason they'd kept their stories a secret; they thought they would be objects of derision if they shared them. By the end of the week, these folks had converted their minister.

Several years later, the United States had an explosion of interest in angels, and the reading population devoured book after book of stories about them. I'd been gone from the Winchester congregation a long time by then, but each new angel book that came out reminded me of that class and those eight people. I suspect that my own guardian angel used them to open my mind enough to see and believe in what is truly there. I like a saying I once saw posted on a religion professor's door: "I'll see it when I believe it."

"Take care that you do not despise one of these little ones; for, I tell you, in heaven their angels continually see the face of my Father in heaven." (Matthew 18:10)

OCTOBER 3
Organizing

Since my illness means I don't have the stamina for a full-time ministry job, I live on disability and supplement it with various part-time jobs. One of those is organizing. I never thought of it as a "skill," but it's something that comes naturally to me, and apparently some people have so little of it that they're willing to pay to borrow someone else's. A happy coincidence on both sides.

I was working with my latest client in her office, and we were sorting the massive clutter into different piles: stuff to go in files, stuff to throw out, stuff to sell, stuff to go in scrapbooks, etc. She looked up and said brightly, "You know, this makes me feel like a goddess!"

I laughed and asked why. "Well, you know, the first thing God did in creation was separate stuff. You know, dark from light, earth from sky, land from water. I guess dividing things up is the first stage in creating something out of chaos."

I think she's right, even though it never occurred to me to think of God as the Great Organizer.

And God said, "Let there be lights in the dome of the sky to separate the day from the night; and let them be for signs and for seasons and for days and years."
(Genesis 1:14)

OCTOBER 4
St. Francis of Assisi

I was the church secretary once for a parish named after St. Francis. It was called that, I think, because it was set on seven acres of old farm land in a densely-populated suburban area. The church itself was built to look like a barn, and it wasn't unusual to look out the clear windows behind the altar during communion and see deer.

But it always struck me as ironic that this church was named after St. Francis because it was in the wealthiest neighborhood in a large metropolitan area. I entered pledge payments into the computer every Monday, so I knew that even if a particular person was tithing, his yearly contribution of $600,000 meant he was quite comfortable. He wasn't the only one.

I'm afraid the good people of this parish loved St. Francis' association with nature, but they hadn't a clue that his ministry was, on the whole, focused on poverty. Unlike other orders of his time, in which individual monks may have owned nothing but the communities as a whole were quite wealthy, Francis organized his friars so that they actually owned nothing. With nothing but the rough brown robes on their backs, Francis' brothers wandered the countryside preaching and begging for food.

It's not surprising, then, that the Franciscans came to have a special ministry to the poor. While choosing poverty is different from involuntarily suffering from it, Franciscans still have some of the same experiences as the very poor—in this country and all over the world.

I hear the televangelists preaching the "prosperity gospel" these days and wonder what Francis would think. I wonder, too, what he would think about a parish named after him that had a budget of six figures and gave only two percent of it to outreach.

"Take no gold, or silver, or copper in your belts, no bag for your journey, or two tunics, or sandals, or a staff; for laborers deserve their food." (Matthew 10:9-10)

OCTOBER 5
When They Grow Up

I accompanied Carol to the closing night of Hume-Fogg High School's production of *Cinderella* last night. Her son Greg was the stage manager. I'd seen him perform as an actor before, but last night he didn't appear until the very end of the evening, when he came out from behind the curtain to give flowers and thanks to the teachers who'd worked on the play. When Greg spoke, his voice was deep and confident; since I'd last seen him, he'd grown a goatee. I said to Carol, "He's not a boy anymore. He's a man."

She knew that, of course. I'm not a parent, so I don't have the privilege of participating in the day-to-day aspects of rearing children into adulthood. Even so, Greg was ten when I first met him—a little boy.

I was full of mixed emotions. I was stunned that seemingly overnight he'd become an articulate adult who was confident speaking in front of a crowd. I was proud of his abilities. I was sad that he wouldn't be around much longer; very soon he'll be gone to college and then on to a life of his own. I'll miss him.

This mixture of emotions is called ambivalence, and it's a state that's peculiarly uncomfortable for human beings. I like to be happy *or* sad; being both at the same time makes me squirm. Yet watching

Greg grow up and away can be nothing but an ambivalent experience.

I usually think of God as regarding me with pride and love as I grow toward the fullness of who I was created to be. It never occurred to me that God might feel some sadness, too, for my loss of childhood innocence and my mistaken belief that I can take care of myself and don't need anyone else. But since I know that God loves me more than even my parents do, I must allow that it could be so.

Rejoice, young man, while you are young, and let your heart cheer you in the days of your youth. Follow the inclination of your heart and the desire of your eyes.
(Ecclesiastes 11:9a)

OCTOBER 6
Neighborhood Associations

I live in Green Hills, one of two upscale neighborhoods in Nashville. It's not that I can really afford to live here; it's just that I found a converted attic apartment that rents for half of what real apartments do. I enjoy the perks of living in a wealthy neighborhood; the people are generally quiet, the police respond quickly, and the clerks in the stores treat me very well.

There's a small group of townhouse condominiums right across the street from me, and I often take Buzz there during our short walks. The residents I've encountered—once they saw that I carried poop bags to clean up after Buzz—have been pleasant.

Until yesterday, anyway. I was confronted by the president of the neighborhood association, who told me that I was on private property and it didn't matter how close I live or that I clean up after my fifteen-pound dog—I was not to trespass again.

I'm not good at comebacks in the moment, so I just turned around and walked away. But what I wanted to say to him was this: "Listen, buddy, this is supposed to be a neighborhood. I'm a night owl, and I'm often out in your parking lot at two in the morning. Twice I've scared away people who were trying to break into cars. Sure, you've got the law on your side, but I am a child of God—a God who tells me that *everyone* is my neighbor."

I suspect that even if I'd made my little speech it wouldn't have mattered, and the fact is, the man was technically in the right. But I do wonder—if he went to church this morning and heard a homily on the Good Samaritan, would he even make the connection? And more important, if *he* didn't, how many times have I missed what should be obvious connections between what I believe and what I do?

But wanting to justify himself, he asked Jesus, "And who is my neighbor?" (Luke 10:29)

OCTOBER 7
Writing in the Margins

I grew up in a family with very high regard for reading. Not only were books excellent for teaching you things and entertaining you, but they also were objects worthy of respect. Part of that respect meant not writing in them.

Then I went to college and noticed, to my disbelief, that my professors' copies of the books we were reading had writing all over the margins. I took up the practice and have never stopped. That means that my library has very few books in pristine condition— a disappointment for book collectors of the future. But what I *do* have is a record of my thoughts, opinions, and reactions to passages I was reading at the moment. Writing in the margins helped me engage the books at a deeper level. It doesn't mean I have little respect for books; on the contrary, it means I have a great deal of respect for what's in them.

I think God likes us to write in the margins of our lives too. Whatever church we were raised in or attend in our adult years, there's a body of knowledge that's passed along from Christian to Christian and generation to generation. Doctrine says, "This is what we believe." It's important to be the recipient of doctrine, but it's also important to write in the margins by acting it out in our lives. What our church teaches us about our faith doesn't mean a whole lot if we don't appropriate it for ourselves, and one way of doing that is "writing in the margins"—whether literally, in the books we read, or figuratively, in the events of our lives. It turns a passive, one-way lesson into an active three-way conversation between the believer, the church, and God.

But there are also many other things that Jesus did; if every one of them were written down, I suppose that the world itself could not contain the books that would be written. (John 21:25)

OCTOBER 8
Crying With Relief

I just finished wiping my eyes and blowing my nose after reading an e-mail from my sister. Her daughter has been having a difficult time lately, and my sister was writing to tell me the problem has suddenly been resolved. It was about the best news I could possibly have.

I don't understand why we cry when we're happy. I've read several theories by psychologists and none of them convince me. I do know that cry-when-you're-happy tears are chemically different from cry-when-you're-sad tears, but other than that, I am puzzled.

I am amazed that I've lived forty-four years with this body and soul and they still hold mysteries for me. Sometimes when I see a science program on the human body or take one of my rare forays into medical literature, I am overwhelmed by the complexity of one single human person. How in the world does God keep so many of us running generally quite well most of the time?

It doesn't make sense to me that I cry when I'm happy. It doesn't make sense to me, either, that there are things like depression, child abuse, and cancer in this world. But I know that God does understand these things and that one day—should I still have the curiosity when faced with the blinding glory of God—the answers will all be there.

For now we see in a mirror, dimly, but then we will see face to face. Now I know only in part; then I will know fully, even as I have been fully known.
(1 Corinthians 13:12)

OCTOBER 9
Standing Up for Myself

I was at home yesterday working on choosing books for my spring class when my landlord called (yep, the same one). I had actually canceled class for the day and cleared my calendar so I could spend the entire day focused on this one onerous but necessary chore. My landlord, it turned out, was downstairs. He had a contractor with him and they wanted to come up and get in the attic to look at some things. That meant I had to move the couch, coffee table, a pedestal, a magazine basket, and three large candlesticks to clear the way to the attic door. Since I live in most of the attic and since the place is so small, the access door is on my level and takes up so much room that I simply cannot arrange furniture around it.

I screwed up my courage and took my landlord aside. I told him what I was doing at home and said, "You know, it's really hard for me to say it's not a good time when you're right outside with someone already here. It'd really be helpful if you could give me some notice in the future."

My military-wife mother, God bless her soul, insisted on proper behavior from her daughters, and that kind of behavior did not include giving people in authority what for. But I've allowed myself to do it because I really and truly do think that God not only allows it, but likes it.

I think of Moses, faced with God's command that he go to Pharaoh and demand freedom for his people. Moses tried to beg off—"Me? You want me? I stutter, you know. You don't really want me."—but God insisted. Of course Moses spoke on behalf of his people, but it's also true that "his people" included himself. As long as I do it reasonably, I think God is quite pleased when I stand up for myself and demand to be treated as a child of God.

Finally, be strong in the Lord and in the strength of his power. (Ephesians 6:10)

OCTOBER 10
Acting Religious

When I was growing up, my grandmother had a lot of rules when we went to visit her. We couldn't play cards, couldn't chew gum, couldn't dance. My mother told us Grandma had these rules because of her religion.

Our culture has a pretty good idea of what it means to "act religious." We don't have mail on Sundays because years ago people went on a campaign to get rid of it—it just wasn't right to get mail on Sunday, the holy day. Even today, many stores are closed on Sunday. In some states, you can't buy any kind of alcohol on Sunday; in Tennessee, you can't get liquor, but you can get beer "if you go to see the preacher first"—in other words, after noon.

All this seems pretty minor until I realize that there are more serious consequences to acting religious. Some women stay in abusive marriages because their ministers tell them their duty is to stay, no matter what. The Bible, after all, tells wives to be submissive to their husbands. Some children have parents who beat them terribly, reciting Bible verses all the while.

Jesus ran into people who believed in acting religious; in his day, they were called Pharisees. They complained that he let his disciples work on the sabbath, by stripping grain off of plants in order to eat. Jesus told them they had it backward—the sabbath, or religion, was meant for human beings, not human beings for the sabbath.

I try to remember that when I find myself conforming to some rule about how a religious person "should" act. Of course I'm not talking about sin or anything serious like that. I mean rules like my grandmother's. I think that could she have heard him, Jesus would have said to her, "Annie, Christianity was made for you, not you for Christianity. C'mon. Let's have a dance. I'll lead!"

One sabbath he was going through the grainfields; and
as they made their way his disciples began to pluck
heads of grain. (Mark 2:23)

OCTOBER 11
Superstar Athletes

Some of the best-paid people in our country today are sports stars. That wasn't always the case, and sports have taken on an importance they didn't have thirty years ago. Everybody is supposed to be good at some kind of sport. Seems to me like the fun has gone out of it. The point should be to have a good time and get some exercise, but now winning is so important that kids who aren't first string hardly ever get to play, and adults press themselves so hard that we have a relatively new medical specialty called sports medicine.

I have several problems with the amount of attention and money we give athletes today, but probably the biggest one is that the bar by which we measure ourselves has been raised. The fact is that the superstar athletes who get so much praise make up less than one percent of the population. But today even children feel pressured to excel in sports; little league parents have gotten a bad name for taking their children's games as seriously as death and taxes.

That's why I find relief in Jesus' story about the mustard seed. I don't mean the usual interpretation—that if we have faith the size of a mustard seed, we could move mountains. I mean the fact that Jesus used a very ordinary, very mundane, very un-extraordinary example to explain the kingdom of God.

Mustard trees aren't really even trees. They're bushes at best. Jesus didn't use the top one percent of anything to describe the kingdom; if he had, he might have chosen the cedars of Lebanon. Apparently the kingdom of God is not measured by what we think of as the best, the biggest, the brightest.

That's a mighty comfort for a middle-aged woman who is probably in the bottom one percent of athletic talents. I can live in this world if what I have to measure up to is very ordinary, very mundane, and very un-extraordinary.

"[The kingdom of God] is like a mustard seed, which, when sown upon the ground, is the smallest of all the seeds on earth." (Mark 4:31)

OCTOBER 12*
Columbus Day

(Observed the second Monday of October)

I long for the days when the celebration of Columbus Day was free of ambivalence. "In fourteen-hundred-and-ninety-two, Columbus sailed the ocean blue." His ships were the Nina, the Pinta, and the Santa Maria. After he discovered America, then our ancestors came and settled here to create the great country called the United States.

It's not that simple anymore. Historians have robbed us of Columbus' primacy. He wasn't even close to being the first to discover America; even if we forget the Vikings, the fact is that the native people who lived here when he arrived had found the place thousands of years before. And the European settlement of the American continent meant the literal genocide of those native people.

I approach Columbus Day differently today than I did as a child. When I pray on this day, I certainly thank God for the existence of this country—a country I love dearly and which is the only place in the world I'd choose to live—and the circumstances that brought Columbus here and opened the route for my ancestors to immigrate. But I also ask God to protect me from the kind of arrogance that allows me to think that people of white European heritage are the only ones who count.

Columbus Day isn't a day for flag-waving for me anymore—I leave that for the Fourth of July. This day is a time when I try to allow God to teach me that every single human being belongs to the same family and has the same status. In a world that tempts me to narcissism—individual, cultural, and racial—that's a deeply valuable lesson. Because if things had gone just a little bit differently, my forebears might be the ones who almost disappeared from the face of this land, instead of the ones whose descendants cover it.

Seek the Lord, all you humble of the land, who do his commands; seek righteousness, seek humility; perhaps you may be hidden on the day of the Lord's wrath.
(Zephaniah 2:3)

OCTOBER 13
If I Were God

I have to admit that our creator puzzles me much of the time. Almost every day I encounter some situation I just can't understand. "Why does God allow this to happen?" I ask.

If I were God, I'd do it differently. I'd fix the world so there wouldn't be any hunger or natural disasters. If I were God there wouldn't be wars or famines. If I were God, there would be no unhappy marriages and so no divorce at all; there would be no troubled children. If I were God there wouldn't be miraculous healings because no one would get sick in the first place. If I were God, no one would ever die.

If I were God, Jesus would never have died on the cross.

Yikes. Jesus would never have died on the cross, because that was a terrible thing. Right? But it was a very good thing too.

My love of Gregorian chant introduced me to a felicitous phrase: *O felix culpa*, or "O fortunate fault." It's terrible that I have the fault—my sinfulness—that means Jesus died on the cross. And yet how fortunate too. Not just fortunate because now I get saved from my sin, but fortunate because out of that death on the cross came something good that had never before existed: the resurrection.

I continue to question God almost every day: "What are you doing, Lord? Are you sure about this one?" But when I think about what the human race would have missed had God been like Karen, then I have to finally assume that as frequently as it might appear otherwise to me, God's plan is the right one.

O the depth of the riches and wisdom and knowledge of God! How unsearchable are his judgments and how inscrutable his ways! (Romans 11:33)

OCTOBER 14
Anti-Semitism

I hate the fact that so many good Christian people are prejudiced against Jews. Most of us know we're not supposed to be, so we avoid the word "kike" and say that some of our best friends. . . . But the prejudice is still there, on a subtle level.

Volney is a psychoanalyst and he's not Jewish. But his patients assume he is, and when they have to discuss their bills with him, they start talking about the kind of attitude "you people" have about money. I couldn't find one of my favorite hymns, "The God of Abraham Praise," in my denomination's new hymnal. The first line of the hymn, and so the title, had been changed to, "Praise to the Living God." Why take out that reference to Abraham?

I've heard people say that the Jews run all the banks, all the stores, the entertainment media, the news media. I have to say that for a people who are only one percent of the world population, the Jews must be very busy to do all that.

It is true, though, that there *is* a group of people who are one percent of the U.S. population, who do, in fact, have proportionately more of the money, more of the political power, more of the control over commerce. It's been proven statistically. But we rarely hear people make nasty remarks about Episcopalians.

I sometimes run into Christians who think Jesus wasn't Jewish. He was Christian, they say. Of course he wasn't—Christianity didn't exist until he had died and been resurrected. Jesus was also an observant Jew; he went to synagogue and the temple.

I can't condemn all those good Christian people who are prejudiced against Jews. Their religious leaders haven't taught them any better. As a member of the clergy, I've got to take my place among the group of people who are supposed to tell the children of God about their brothers and sisters the Jews, but don't. So to my colleagues and to myself, I issue a challenge: C'mon, guys and gals—let's get with the program.

For if you have been cut from what is by nature a wild olive tree and grafted, contrary to nature, into a cultivated olive tree, how much more will these natural branches be grafted back into their own olive tree.
(Romans 11:24)

OCTOBER 15
St. Teresa of Avila

St. Teresa was this Protestant girl's introduction to Catholic spirituality, and she was the perfect guide into what were for me uncharted waters. She taught me that it was not only okay but absolutely necessary to be honest with God.

I'm sure if I'd asked any of the ministers I had growing up, he'd have told me that honesty was the way to approach God. But the spontaneous prayers I heard in church on Sundays were definitely not. These public prayers were variations of, "O God, you're really great and we're worms. We don't deserve anything good and we're sorry that we complain so much. Teach us to act right and be satisfied with your will."

This was not Teresa's way. She was excruciatingly honest with God about what she was feeling. In the midst of one trial she once prayed, "No wonder you don't have many friends. Look at the way you treat the ones you do have."

Teresa talked to God as if this were someone she knew, and knew quite well. She could be as gushing and rapturous as a schoolgirl in her praise, but she could be quite sharp-tongued in her disappointments. It's not that she didn't want to align herself with God's will; that was, in fact, her highest goal. But Teresa knew very well that living according to God's will isn't always pleasant, and she went ahead and complained when it wasn't.

That's all the more remarkable because the piety of the time was one that encouraged rejoicing in trials and tribulations. The idea was that if things were tough, it meant the devil was attacking you, and therefore you had a good relationship with God. Difficult times meant a maturing of the soul, and were something to be welcomed.

Teresa knew of this piety and expressed it herself. But she also knew that a real relationship is one that includes all of our feelings, whether they're feelings we're "supposed" to have or not.

Teresa bucked the status quo in many ways, and the church was changed because of her. She is one of the three women Doctors of the church. But the most radical idea she conveyed to this young soul was that it is okay to be mad at God . . . and say so.

> *Life is a night passed in a bad inn.*
> *(St. Teresa of Avila)*

OCTOBER 16
Bureaucracy

Argh! I just spent forty-five minutes on the phone with the medical center where I receive my cancer treatments. My nurse of five years took another job, and when the new nurse gave me my treatment for the first time, she coded it wrong on the billing sheet. The difference in charges is about $200, so the mixup is definitely worth correcting. So far I've talked to three levels of billing people, and it's still not resolved. At this point, they're going to "get back to" me.

There's nothing like bureaucracy to make you feel like a number instead of an individual. If I got my treatment in an idealized setting where they could care for a reasonable number of patients and know them all, this wouldn't be a problem. They would know me, I would know them, and all it would take to fix a problem would be one phone call. But there are ever-growing numbers of people who need the medical care provided by the Vanderbilt-Ingram Cancer Center. It's no surprise to anyone that more and more institutions become bureaucratic every day.

What scares me is that the church can be a bureaucracy. All the studies I've read say that after a church reaches an active membership of two hundred or so, a pastor can't keep up with everybody. Lots of congregations are bigger than two hundred people, and I've seen only a few that have recognized this dynamic and taken steps to fix it—like training lay people to be pastoral caregivers.

It's easy to feel, in the bowels of a bureaucracy, that this is just the way things are, that I shouldn't expect any better. But that's definitely not true when it comes to my faith life. One of the revolutionary aspects of Christianity is that God relates to us not only as a people but also as individuals.

I guess I'll just have to live with bureaucracy in this life; it's not going away. But it comforts me to know that when I enter the next life, no one will have to consult a computer or a code to know who I am.

"So do not be afraid; you are of more value than many sparrows." (Matthew 10:31)

October 17
Too Tired to Eat

I am a very disciplined person, but my most common failure at discipline is in trying to live a life consistent with my stamina and energy. When I was in chemotherapy I learned a great deal about doing this because I simply had no choice—I was physically incapable of doing more than two or three things a day. I'm much recovered since then, but I still don't have the stamina of most women my age. That doesn't really matter; every woman has her own level of energy and many of us exceed it day after day.

Yesterday was one of those days for me. I'd taken on too much: a session of organizing a client; a meeting with a student that turned into a counseling session; teaching class; holding office hours; errands; laundry; and having a friend to dinner. When I sat down at the table I had no appetite. This is quite unusual for me; my usual struggle is with eating more calories than my body burns. But once in a while I exhaust myself so thoroughly that my body stops functioning in some of the most basic ways. I learned my lesson yesterday. I got a good night's sleep and have simplified my calendar for the next couple of weeks. But I also know that sooner or later I'll lapse into working too much again.

There are a hundred reasons for my tendency to workaholism, and I won't bore you with them here. The point is that if I pay attention to my body, it will give me signals that I'm doing something that's bad for me. If I come to the end of a day when I've had only a bowl of cereal and a package of snack crackers and am not hungry, then something's gone awry. My body is fearfully and wonderfully made; not only does it work remarkably well, it also has ways of telling me that I'm hurting myself. I continue to learn to give it the respect and attention it deserves as a creation of God.

For many were coming and going, and they had no leisure even to eat. (Mark 6:31b)

OCTOBER 18
St. Luke the Evangelist

I have a feeling St. Luke loved women. His gospel has more stories featuring women than the other three, and he often holds those women up as examples of the way to follow Christ.

I'm not saying the other evangelists didn't like women. I might be a little suspicious of St. Paul's true feelings about the fairer sex, but he, like all the other writers of the New Testament, lived in a culture that simply didn't give as much importance to women as it did to men.

Luke is different. My friend Paul once told me his fantasy about the way Luke got so much information, especially about Jesus' early life, that Matthew, Mark, and John apparently didn't have. Luke was, he reminded me, a physician, and it's not at all unusual for women to confide in their doctors. Because of the nature of the relationship, a certain level of trust must exist, and when I reflect on my own experience, I know that I've discussed many things with my doctors that I would never have told other men.

So what if Luke sat down with Jesus' mother and, having gained her confidence, teased out of her some stories about her son's early life? There is absolutely no evidence to support such a theory—as I said, Paul called it a fantasy. But perhaps it seems possible because in the life of Jesus as Luke portrays it, there are many women—and many with strikingly important roles to play.

> *His mother treasured all these things in her heart.*
> *(Luke 2:51b)*

OCTOBER 19
Making Excuses

Unlike most colleges, Vanderbilt doesn't really have a "fall break." The school shuts down the week of Thanksgiving, but that's a mighty long ways into the semester. So they've started giving students a Monday and Tuesday off. That's coming up next week, and as my Friday class approaches, I'm getting a remarkable number of e-mails from my students.

Several of them have family emergencies and have to leave before class on Friday afternoon. One said the only flight he could get left right as class would be getting over—of all the luck! Another tells me she's feeling a bit queasy so don't be surprised if she doesn't show.

Do they really think they're fooling me? Who wants to stick around for a two o'clock class on Friday afternoon when you've only got four days off? I don't really mind that they're going to miss class—it's not as if it's a life or death matter—but I am bemused they think I'm that stupid.

Then I remember how very often I've made excuses for myself to God. Sometimes I was wholly convinced these excuses were reasonable, other times I knew I was . . . um, just on the edge of . . . well, a lie. Was I *this* transparent?

No doubt about it, since God knows everything and I'm nothing but a skeptical teacher. That realization makes me want to blush. And then I ask myself: If I, a cantankerous middle-aged professor set in my ways, can give my students this much grace, isn't it likely that God can give more?

You mean I really didn't have to make all those excuses?

Even before a word is on my tongue, O Lord, you know it completely. (Psalm 139:4)

OCTOBER 20
Good Taste

When my middle sister and her husband got married, their "colors" were purple and teal. Neither of them is a pastel kind of a person, so this made a lot of sense to me. I cooperated by putting a purple cover on the book out of which I read the wedding ceremony.

The wedding was at his mother's house and a lot of people came, so there was no formal sitting-in-rows stage of the event. It was basically one big reception, with a wedding ceremony in the middle of it. Before the wedding itself, I was wandering around the room, meeting people and nibbling on crudités. I heard a woman commenting on the décor to a friend, clearly unaware that I had a pretty close relationship to the bride: "Purple and teal. Now that's what I call good taste." Her voice was dripping with sarcasm.

I look at my big flower pot of pansies—they're purple and yellow and red and white. I look at pictures of the Grand Canyon and Hawaii's Haleakala Volcano Crater and their vibrant hues of oranges and reds. I watch an aquarium full of tropical fish sporting color combinations that one rarely sees at weddings.

God, it seems to me, doesn't have good taste. At least not bourgeois middle-class American taste. While northeastern forests, for example, may put on tasteful combinations of earth tones, tropical forests burst forth in exuberant colors. I think God likes it all, from pinstripe gray to sequined red.

And to tell you the truth, teal and purple actually look quite lovely together.

For the beauty of each hour of the day and of the night, hill and vale, and tree and flower, sun and moon, and stars of light. (Folliot S. Pierpoint)

OCTOBER 21
Maids

A friend and her husband are in the midst of arguing about whether to hire a maid. They both travel for their jobs, and she says the last thing she wants to do when she gets home on the weekend is clean house. I don't blame her.

I've been on both sides of the mop. I've worked as a janitor, and I've hired a maid. Well, "maid" is a little strong—I paid a young woman in my youth group to come and do the basics every couple of weeks: vacuum, dust, and scrub the bathroom. I don't know many people who *like* to clean, but it's one of those things that simply must be done. It seems an honorable occupation to me as long as the cleaning person is fairly compensated.

Nevertheless, hiring a maid has a slightly questionable moral tinge for some people. It's as if there's some kind of shame in not being able to manage one's own dirt. I had to get over that too. My prayer time, of all things, fixed this issue for me. I was confessing my sins to God, and all of a sudden I realized that when I've got my theology straight, I'm certain there's no way I can handle my own spiritual dirt. The whole point of our faith is that we make a big mess of things and can't put it right all by ourselves. I suppose it would be possible to think of God as a maid who sweeps that mess away.

And if God is like a maid, then isn't it okay to hire one? I know I was always glad to have the work, and my teenaged maid seemed to appreciate the money too.

Wash me thoroughly from my iniquity, and cleanse me from my sin. (Psalm 51:2)

OCTOBER 22
Revenge

When my family was moving from Indianapolis to my father's next assignment in Hawaii, we stopped in East Tennessee for two weeks to visit his family. I stayed with my cousin; she was two years older than I, and in my freshman eyes, extremely cool. Since there was nothing better to do, I went to school with her each day, and in those two weeks met some of her friends. I developed an immediate, huge crush on "Fred." We flirted quite a bit and on the Friday night before my family was due to leave, Fred and I were going on a date. I was so excited I could hardly stand it. But Fred never showed up. I was heartbroken.

Four years later, I was a freshman at college in the same east Tennessee town. Guess who was in my sociology class? But I had changed quite a bit—I'd grown eight inches, lost enough weight to have a model's figure, switched to contacts, and gotten my acne under control. Fred not only didn't recognize me, he didn't even remember me when I gave him my name. Long story short—I flirted with him, led him on, got him all in a lather, and then stood him up.

Someone once said that "revenge is a dish best served cold," and I know what they meant. For about two hours I gloated, thinking of how humiliated Fred was—because we were expected at a party as a couple. But then I started imagining what he was feeling, and that was the end of my glee. Having been stood up myself, I knew how awful it felt. My revenge wasn't sweet, but cold.

There's a reason, I guess, that God says, "Vengeance is mine." It's not just that avenging myself is a bad way to treat another person—turns out it's also quite unpleasant for me.

"Vengeance is mine, I will repay." (Romans 12:19)

October 23
Osama bin Laden

As I write, America's hurt and rage are focused on a man named Osama bin Laden. He is, we're told, the mastermind behind a broad terrorist network that has infiltrated every corner of the world. Our leaders tell us he's the one who planned the devastation of the World Trade Centers. If all this is true—and time will tell—then Osama bin Laden is an evil man.

I am puzzled when I look at pictures of bin Laden. Quite truthfully, I'd love to personally be the one to catch him. It's the first time in my life I've ever really wanted to kill someone. My puzzlement comes from my God's directive to love Osama bin Laden. I don't get it. I can love my enemies in the world of work, the church, the political arena. It means stretching my spiritual muscles, but when I stop and consider the fact that they are human, too, no matter how angry they make me, I can love them at some level and pray for their well-being. But Osama bin Laden? Am I supposed to pray for Osama bin Laden?

Yes, I think so. Jesus, after all, forgave even the people who were unjustly putting him to death. So God loves Osama bin Laden—though that love must contain a lot of anger about what he's done—and I'm supposed to pray for him. Today is the day I discover that when the rubber hits the road, I'm still a baby

Christian. I can't love bin Laden, I cannot wish him well. I want some day to be able to truly feel that way, but right now I'm just not there, and it's stupid for me to pretend I am. Maybe someday.

"But I say to you, Love your enemies and pray for those who persecute you." (Matthew 5:44)

OCTOBER 24
Memorizing

I have a terrible memory—always have. I loathed tests in school because I had to memorize dates and names; I did it, but then all that information just drained away. Further, while I can give you an off-the-cuff, thirty-minute lecture on the publican and the Pharisee, I cannot tell you what chapter, verse, or even gospel the story's in without looking it up.

So I'm fascinated by people who grew up in churches that focused on memorizing Bible verses. In seminary, I saw a video of a Biblical scholar who had memorized the entire gospel of Mark and presented it as if it were a story. My friend Sharyn Dowd, the New Testament scholar, can probably answer any, "Where in the Bible does it say . . ." question thrown at her.

I've always felt embarrassed by my memory problems, but for a long time didn't think it was a big problem. After all, I knew how to *find* the information even if I couldn't remember it. But then I heard stories from men who were prisoners during the Vietnam War. Since I was an Army brat, these men weren't strange faces on TV—they lived a few doors down from me. I remember one, in particular, who survived seven years as a POW. He had lived chained to a bed, sometimes for years at a stretch. More than one POW was broken mentally by similar experiences, but this man was whole. He credited his survival to his ability to remember and repeat Bible verses and poetry he had memorized in his childhood.

That man's story had a very powerful impact on me. So now, even with my terrible memory, I work very hard to memorize some important Bible verses and snatches of poetry. I never know when memorization just might·save my life.

For the memory of me is sweeter than honey.
(Sirach 24:20a)

OCTOBER 25
Running Into People

There's a problem with running into someone when you're out and about. For some reason, we seem to think that when it happens, we're supposed to respond with nothing but our brightest and cheeriest selves. Church people are especially prone to this syndrome. A typical conversation in the grocery store with one of my parishioners: "Well, Al. How are you?" "I'm great, just great." "How's Lisa, how are the boys?" "Great, just fine. Everybody's doing great."

A couple of days later, Al might be in my office telling me that his father has been dying for the last three weeks. Things are far from "great," but he—and I, and most of us, I think—felt obligated to respond with pleasantries.

Wouldn't our world be different if we were a little more honest with other people when we ran into them? I did that when I was in treatment for cancer. I was simply too tired to pull up a bright, cheery attitude, so I was honest. "Things are kind of rough right now." What I discovered was that my honesty often gave the other person permission to be honest too. In those days I had some of the most caring, intimate talks I'd ever had, with people I ran into at the video store or gas station.

Of course it didn't always go that way. Some people really didn't want to hear it; "How are you?" was another way to say "Hi." When I gave those people my honest answer, they would murmur something like, "Sorry to hear that," and speed off. And that's okay. Nobody's obligated to listen to my troubles.

But when I hear people complain about how impersonal the world has become, I wonder about being more honest when we run into each other. So what if it leads to a few tears in the produce aisle? I think the world would be a much warmer place.

Say to wisdom, "You are my sister," and call insight your intimate friend. (Proverbs 7:4)

OCTOBER 26
Dogs' Noses

There must be a new dog in the neighborhood, because Buzz has been going nuts on our walks. We cover a very limited territory, given the length of his legs, but something has most definitely changed. Buzz stands and sniffs at a pile of leaves until I drag him away. He tracks the movement of the intruder, nose to the asphalt, in a series of loops, backtracks, and stops.

I envy Buzz's ability to track someone who's most definitely been there, but who leaves nothing visible as evidence. I wish I had a nose for God the way Buzz has a nose for other dogs. I know in my deepest self that God is present in my life every single minute of every single hour, but often it's very hard to see the evidence of that presence.

Sometimes I think God is doing one thing in my life and it turns out, in the end, that I had it completely backward. Fr. Kenney worked with me for three years to teach me St. Ignatius' techniques for discerning God's work in my life, and other spiritual directors have tried their hand with me since. But I must be a very slow learner.

Just about the only time I can confidently say, "Look! That's God!" is years later. With a decade or so of hindsight, I can often see the ways and places God was working with me.

Unlike Buzz's intruder, God definitely leaves visible tracks in my life. It's just that I can't see them until time has passed. I can't see—or smell—the God who's working right under my nose.

This is evidence of the righteous judgment of God, and is intended to make you worthy of the kingdom of God, for which you are also suffering. (2 Thessalonians 1:5)

October 27
Molly Roses

Heather and her partner Brooks had to have his cat Molly put to sleep. She had a thyroid problem and then turned out to be allergic to the medication. She scratched off the fur and top layer of skin on her face because the itching was so bad.

Brooks had dug a grave for Molly in the backyard before they went to the vet, so they brought her home and buried her right away. They put a stone on top of her grave, and a small little tray of rocks nearby. The grave is purposely under a rose bush. In the spring, when the fertilized roses bloom beautifully, they will call them "Molly roses."

I like to think that my life will be fertilizer for something beautiful. Not my body so much, although I suppose there could be "Karen roses" too. But I hope that my presence in this world will, long after I'm gone, contribute just a bit to making something beautiful and good. I guess only geniuses and great artists are certain they'll leave that kind of legacy. Plain folks like me just have to trust that if God makes Molly roses out of the tortured remains of a beloved pet, then God can make something good out of what I leave behind too.

Wisdom is as good as an inheritance.
(Ecclesiastes 7:11a)

OCTOBER 28
Cafeteria Believers

American Catholics have been accused of being "cafeteria" believers, taking what they like about the faith and leaving what they don't. Lots of Protestant thinkers accuse their splintered flock of the same thing. I think that's an unfair call, and I also think Jesus would have great sympathy with American Christians today.

Back in Jesus' time, there were plenty of people around to tell you what made a "good" believer. That's not how Jesus operated, though. When Jesus met the Samaritan woman, he didn't criticize her faith life. He simply showed her, in plain language, that he knew what her life was like. That straightforward approach allowed the Samaritan woman to understand that the focus of her faith was to be Christ himself.

When she went off to tell people about Jesus, she got some of the details wrong. She didn't fully understand who Jesus was. But according to scripture, because of her the entire town came to believe. Not bad for a sinner who was doing all the "wrong" things according to the religious experts. That's pretty good news for us today; even if we're not sure we are good believers, even if we think we don't follow the rules one hundred percent, we are still able to accomplish remarkable things simply by telling people about our experience with Jesus.

Are American Christians cafeteria believers? I think that's God's judgment to make. But I can say for certain that Jesus understands us thoroughly, accepts us completely, and sends us out into the world with the simple job of telling the stories of our own faith journeys. We don't have to be expert Christians to make a difference.

Jesus said to her, "Woman, believe me, the hour is coming when you will worship the Father neither on this mountain nor in Jerusalem." (John 4:21)

OCTOBER 29
Supermarket Tabloids

My skepticism thermometer starts rising any time I see the word "secret" combined with something concerning religion. It's fascinating, there's no doubt about that, or the tabloids wouldn't put those headlines on their front pages so often. Inside, we're told, we'll be told the secret truth about God, or heaven, or angels, or . . . whatever.

Oddly enough, there's a technical, theological word for the belief that we will be saved by secret knowledge known only to a few: gnosticism. The gnostics who get all the attention from religious scholars lived back in the first century, but gnostics exist today too. Any time somebody starts telling us that 1) we don't know the truth about God, 2) only a few people do, and 3) discovering it is the only way to be saved, we ought to get skeptical.

The Christian faith teaches us that salvation doesn't come from knowledge. It's not a bad thing to have knowledge; it's a good thing to be educated. It's especially good to be educated about our faith, the Bible, and the church's tradition. But that knowledge isn't what saves us; what saves us is Jesus Christ.

A person who is completely uneducated can be one of God's children and have the same hope for heaven as someone with a Ph.D. and a professorship in religion. And if knowledge doesn't affect God's attitude toward us, then secret knowledge certainly doesn't.

Draw near to me, hear this! From the beginning I have not spoken in secret, from the time it came to be I have been there. And now the Lord God has sent me and his spirit. (Isaiah 48:16)

OCTOBER 30
Enthusiasm

I suffer sometimes from an excess of enthusiasm. I ran into Volney a while back and he asked whether I was enjoying the class I'm teaching. "Oh, yeah!" I said, very enthusiastically and rather loudly. He looked surprised for a moment and smiled.

Every world has its own ethos and code of behavior. Right now I live in the world of academia. Real scholars are supposed to be measured, serious, professional, and a little bit jaded. To be overly enthusiastic suggests naiveté and lack of experience. It's very common for me to hear my senior colleagues complain that they're tired of teaching. I think they take a bit of pride in saying so; it means they've been doing it a long time, that they've completely mastered whatever subjects they're teaching, that there's nothing that could surprise them or make a particular class enjoyable.

It's a bit that way in the church too. We ministers who've been at it for a while glance at each other with understanding when we encounter a fresh, young, enthusiastic pastor. "Ah, youth and inexperience," we silently telegraph each other: "Remember when we were so clueless about the church that we could be that enthusiastic and idealistic?"

I think about the woman who anointed Jesus' head or feet (depending on which gospel you're reading) with nard and wept while she was doing so. The others at the table were obviously very uncomfortable, because this woman was going way overboard. Her behavior was extreme. But Jesus praised her, and one of the lessons of the story is this: There's no such thing as "too much" when the subject is Jesus. (Thanks to Sharyn Dowd for this interpretation of the story.)

Enthusiasm, at least when the subject is God, is admirable. I think God likes it all the way around too. No, it's not cool; it's not sophisticated to be enthusiastic. But it is fun.

But Jesus said, "Let her alone; why do you trouble her? She has performed a good service for me." (Mark 14:6)

OCTOBER 31
Halloween

There are some Christians these days who are very upset about Halloween. They say it's a pagan holiday and of the devil. They don't want their children being taught about witches and ghosts in school. No black cats. No scary pumpkins. No costumes or trick-or-treating.

To such sisters and brothers, I say, "Relax." Yes, Halloween was originally a pagan holiday. In the fertility religion that predated Christianity in the Celtic world, Halloween was the night between the old and new years, and the time when the veil between those worlds was thinnest. People really believed in evil spirits, and they dressed up in costumes as disguises. Halloween was also a time for especially powerful magic.

Of course, many of the traditions we treasure about Christmas have pagan roots too. The date, for one. No one knows exactly when Jesus was born. It's just that when the church began its missionary drive, it often superimposed Christian holidays on pagan ones. That way, people who were used to celebrating on a particular day could continue to do so as Christians. Before it was Christmas, December 25 was "The Feast of the Unconquered Sun." That's s-U-n. Yule logs, Christmas trees, and garlands all have pagan roots.

But the source of something doesn't determine its meaning today. Except for the very small group of modern witches, or Wiccans, Halloween has become a holiday with no religious associations. It's healthy for children, especially, to have one night a year to confront their deepest fears by dressing as them: ghosts, pirates, monsters. It's a time for kids to get lots of candy, adults to pretend they're someone else for a night, and in general for everybody to have some fun. The Jesus who provided wine for a wedding at Cana liked parties. I imagine if he were around today, in the flesh, he'd celebrate Halloween too.

He will rejoice over you with gladness, he will renew you in his love; he will exult over you with loud singing as on a day of festival. (Zephaniah 3:17b-18a)

NOVEMBER 1
All Saints' Day

I really like it when the church does things to make its holy days as fun and interesting to children as the secular holidays they so enjoy. It helps to counter children's common belief (and, I regret, frequent experience) that church is boring.

I loved All Saints' Day at an Episcopal church I once attended. The children dressed in costume—as saints—and joined the procession at the start of the service. Then when it came time for the homily, the priest talked to the entire congregation about the saints the children represented. That meant we had children in our congregation who knew who St. Justin Martyr was.

Too often congregations pass over the needs of the littlest ones in our midst. As a pastor, I know how easy it is to pitch everything to adult ears; as an adult myself, it's what comes most naturally. But many times we miss opportunities to get our children invested in the church. Then we wonder why they stop attending as soon as they're allowed to make the decision for themselves, and don't usually return until they have children of their own.

The rich history of Christian saints has much to teach every believer of every age. Even if a particular congregation doesn't target children on this wonderful day of remembrance, parents can at home. Then maybe we adults can learn, too, who St. Justin Martyr was!

O blest communion, company divine, we live and struggle, they in glory shine; yet all are one in thee, for all are thine. Alleluia, alleluia. (William W. How)

NOVEMBER 2
All Souls' Day

On All Saints' Day we recognize our forebears in the faith who were such extraordinary examples of piety that the entire church remembers them. All Souls' is a day of remembrance too—of the "saints" we've encountered in our lives and who have gone on to heaven. All Christians are called to be saints; St. Paul uses the word as a synonym for "believer" in his letters to the early church.

The matter of saints is a touchy one for Protestants, but I see no reason it should be. Nor do I understand why Catholics can't confer sainthood—not official canonization but recognition of a life lived especially close to God—on people in their own lives. Almost everyone I know has loved someone whose life was a vivid illustration of what can happen to ordinary people when they encounter an extraordinary God.

The influence of such everyday saints shouldn't be underestimated. Although I have learned much about God from, say, St. Teresa of Avila, it was my grandmother who taught me—at a gut level—what it means to be unconditionally loved.

The death of such saints creates a hole in the families they leave behind, and a hole in their congregations too. All Souls' Day is a good time to remember these saints, pray to God for their well-being, celebrate their legacies, and heal a bit from their loss.

Therefore, since we are surrounded by so great a cloud of witnesses, let us also lay aside every weight and the sin that clings so closely, and let us run with perseverance the race that is set before us. (Hebrews 12:1)

NOVEMBER 3
St. Martin de Porres

One of my favorite contemporary artists is Robert Lentz. His work, sold through a company called "Bridge Building Images," portrays saintly figures in the church's history in the style of Orthodox icons. Long before it was politically correct, Lentz was painting icons of saints whose skins weren't lily white.

St. Martin was one such saint. It's no surprise he is the patron of social justice, because he worked extensively with the poor, helped establish an orphanage and other charities, and ministered to slaves who'd been brought from Africa to the New World. I put myself in the place of those slaves and imagine the horrors of captivity and the ocean crossing. I imagine they would have welcomed the smallest expression of love and kindness from anyone. But what a comfort it must have been to find themselves cared for by someone who looked like them. In a world that had to be frighteningly strange, St. Martin provided a comforting bit of familiarity to hundreds of tortured souls.

Black Americans, over the centuries, have been offered too few role models by a church controlled largely by whites. That is changing, thank God, partly because of the work of Robert Lentz. But St. Martin isn't just a saint for black Americans. He's a saint for all of us—a reminder of the fact that God loves every human being of every race, and also that God often chooses to work through people our society looks down on. Since I am not one of the wealthiest and most powerful people in our country, that's very good news to me.

In eager obedience to the Master's exhortations, St. Martin cultivated an ardent love for his brothers, a love grounded in purest faith and humility. He loved people, because he sincerely regarded them as children of God and his own brothers. (Pope John XXIII)

NOVEMBER 4
The Cable Guy

When I called to have cable installed, I was told that the cable man would come sometime on Thursday. Did they have any idea what time that might be? No. Even just the broadest guess—closer to 8 a.m. or 5 p.m.? No. So I ended up sitting home all day long, waiting for the guy to come and release me from what felt like a prison. At 3:45 he finally arrived and delivered me from suspense so intense it made me cranky.

Such days teach me about what it was like to live among the earliest Christians. Paul makes it very clear that he expected Jesus to return very, very soon—as in "any day now." So did all Christians. That's why it didn't much matter, they thought, if they were single or enslaved or in a job they hated. Maybe even this afternoon, Jesus was going to return, and then there would be no more male or female, slave or free, Greek or Jew.

But then Jesus kept *not* arriving. Two thousand years later, only a small portion of the world's Christians wait for the second coming in suspense so heightened that it might match that of Paul and his companions.

I don't know whether that's good or bad. I do know how frustrating it can be to wait and wait and wait for someone. I know, too, how it can wear to have an expected event continue *not* occurring. But I wonder if those of us who don't wait with bated breath for Jesus' return aren't missing something.

I've never had an experience of suspense connected to God that comes close to matching the suspense I felt about the cable guy. Given what will arrive along with Jesus' return, and what I will enter when I die—the kingdom—it seems a shame to deprive myself of a sense of anticipation. That's half the fun, isn't it?

There is no longer Jew or Greek, there is no longer slave or free, there is no longer male and female; for all of you are one in Christ Jesus. (Galatians 3:28)

NOVEMBER 5
Answering Machines

"Hello, Auntie Karen. I just wanted to call and talk to you and tell you I love you." These words changed my entire day.

It was a very ordinary day—rushing from here to there, teaching, running errands, all that sort of thing. My head was full of practical details and a few leftover curses at bad Nashville drivers when I checked the answering machine as a matter of course and on the way to the computer.

When I heard the voice of my niece, everything switched gears. The little annoyances of everyday life dropped away and my heart opened and melted. In the space of twenty seconds I went from harried worker to loving and beloved aunt.

I've never thought of answering machines as angels before, but maybe they are—very small, inferior angels, of course, but angels of a sort. My answering machine is most definitely a messenger. Of course it records summons to more work ("I'll be waiting for your return call."), little shots of nastiness ("Today's column proves once again that you're a mindless, bleeding-heart liberal."), and the most quotidian aspects of my life ("Your pictures are ready.") But my answering machine also captures the voices of people I love and who love me. Most of the time those messages are lovely but no surprise; once in a while, like yesterday, a message can stop me in my tracks and remind me of the really important things in life.

And suddenly there was with the angel a multitude of the heavenly host, praising God and saying, "Glory to God in the highest heaven, and on earth peace among those whom he favors!" (Luke 2:13-14)

November 6
The Opera Singer

My friend Jackie sang in an opera company for a while before she attended seminary, where we met. Since graduation she got married, had two children, and pastored two churches. Jackie is a wonderful minister with a delightful sense of humor and comforting sensibility about God and all things pertaining. She told me recently that she sings only occasionally now, and I was sorry to hear that.

Before I met Jackie, I'd never heard anyone sing like that. As we bustled about the chancel preparing for a worship service, she warmed up with the organist. Absolutely casual, Jackie fiddled with her shirtsleeves and paced around while one of the most remarkable sounds I'd ever heard came out of her. I sat in the congregation several times when Jackie sang. When she lets go with that voice—no need for a microphone, no matter the size of the sanctuary— it's like being hit by a rolling tidal wave of God's power. Her voice has evoked in me deep sorrow during Holy Week, soaring hope in the Easter season, and stunned amazement at Christmas time. While she takes care of her voice, Jackie is also extremely modest and matter-of-fact about it. There is absolutely no diva in her.

My friend can minister in many ways: in the pulpit, at the altar, beside a sickbed, and with her voice. She teaches me about holding lightly the gifts God has given us. In Jackie I see someone who understands the talent God has put inside of her, accepts it, nurtures it, and uses it—and also someone who knows that this voice full of spiritual power is a gift from God. Jackie is one of my role models; while she has never sought to teach me anything, I am learning from her the best way to approach the gifts God has given me.

I will be glad and exult in you; I will sing praise to
your name, O Most High. (Psalm 9:2)

NOVEMBER 7
Watching Football With Him

I have discovered one of the many differences between men and women. (Fair warning: outrageous generalizations ahead.) While women feel that they have spent time with their friends only if they've had the opportunity to talk about things that matter, men can find friendship in simply doing the same thing together. No conversation necessary.

I'm afraid I was once rather dismissive of a man's desire to have me sitting there on the couch watching football with him. It was clear I wasn't interested, there was no way to hold a conversation of any depth, and after all—what difference did it make whether I was there on the couch or upstairs? All the difference in the world, it turns out. For men, simply being there together constitutes quality time.

Again, for many years I thought men just didn't know how to have friends. But then I realized that the bulk of my relationship with God is much like watching football with a guy. I'm not paying direct attention to God; we're not having a conversation of any depth; and yet, there is absolutely no doubt that God's continuing presence is part of what increases our intimacy.

Of course, I relate to God in the "woman's" way too. There are times when I am completely focused on the holy, and sometimes I even want to fuss about the nature of our relationship: "You don't pay enough attention to me!"

So it appears that the guy way of being close has value and meaning, too, even though it's not what I normally think of as intimacy. Apparently, it can even teach me—supposedly the intimacy expert in a man/woman relationship—something about God.

Where can I go from your spirit? Or where can I flee from your presence? (Psalm 139:7)

NOVEMBER 8
Nodding Off

I hurt myself in the gym the other day and have been taking some strong pain medication. I didn't realize just how powerful it was until I was talking to a friend and actually fell asleep in the middle of the conversation! She hollered into the phone and then suggested—rather pithily—that I ought to call her when I was awake. I was so embarrassed.

Usually the only person I fall asleep on is God. It doesn't happen as often as it used to, but every once in a while, I'll settle down for prayer and startle awake to discover two hours have passed. Not a good thing when you've got places to be and things to do.

Not to mention how rude it is. God is right there, at full attention, any time I want to talk. It certainly doesn't go the other way around. I'm not bad at listening during prayer, but as for other times. . . .

I remember the grace I felt back when I first started praying seriously and was seeing Fr. Kenney. Ashamed, I confessed that I had fallen asleep during prayer. He didn't blink an eye. "If you're that tired," he said, "then God wants you to sleep. Start getting enough rest and you won't have that problem."

I had expected a stern lecture on mindfulness or the discipline necessary for prayer, and I got permission to nap. God spoke to me through Fr. Kenney that day, with a word of grace and deep understanding. Now if I can just get my friend to be as forgiving.

I will both lie down and sleep in peace; for you alone,
O Lord, make me lie down in safety. (Psalm 4:8)

NOVEMBER 9
The Vet

I remember very well the time in junior high when we had Career Day and I went to the room where they were going to be talking about being a veterinarian. I was stopped at the door and told I couldn't come in, "because girls can't be veterinarians." That was from an adult!

So I'm a bit smug these days when I take Buzz to the vet. There's a mysterious Dr. Greene who owns the place, but we always end up seeing the younger vets, and they're both women.

I love to watch them work with Buzz. They are gentle and kind, all the way from the way they touch him to the tone of their voices. He hates getting shots and things like that, but Buzz loves the vets themselves. He knows they care about him.

I have learned since Career Day how difficult it is to get into veterinary school—man or woman—and just how difficult and lengthy the training is. So I thank God for the spiritual heirs of St. Francis who are so kind to my four-legged best friend.

All things bright and beautiful, all creatures great and small, all things wise and wonderful, the Lord God made them all. (Cecil F. Alexander)

NOVEMBER 10
Group Projects

When I announced to my class that the oral presentations at the end of the semester were going to be group projects, I heard a few groans. I know how they feel. I always hated group projects, because even as a high school student I was so compulsive that I ended up doing my work and that of the students who were slackers. It always outraged me that they got the same grade I did, when I did "all" the work.

I use group projects, though, because although those dynamics are still a problem, I've now lived long enough to discover that life is a group project. What's important is not so much the end result as what happens between people in the getting there. God created us as social beings, and except for a few wild hermits, most human beings seek out the company of others like themselves. It's really in the lifelong process of being in relationship with other people that I become the person I'm meant to be. That's something I can't do by myself.

And if I have to give more sometimes, so it goes. That's life, quite realistically. I've also lived long enough to know that there are times when *I* will be the one who can't contribute my fair share, and someone else will pick up the slack. Isn't that part of what the doctrine of the saints is all about? On a large or small scale, sometimes I'm the worker bee and sometimes I'm the slacker. And since God is the one providing the limitless resources, I always come out ahead in the end.

And at this sound the crowd gathered and was bewildered, because each one heard them speaking in the native language of each. (Acts 2:6)

November 11
Veterans Day

Not long after the period when the books of the New Testament were written, the fledgling Christian church started struggling with the issue of military service. Could Christians be soldiers? The initial, general feeling was no—Jesus had clearly advocated turning the other cheek.

But as the years wore on and Jesus didn't return to establish the kingdom of God and ultimate peace, the church discovered that war was sometimes necessary to bring about justice. Soldiering then became an honorable profession—one that perhaps reached its height in the Crusades.

I've heard of veterans who love war, but I've never met one. At best, the men and women I know tell me that they formed strong bonds with other soldiers during combat. But those bonds aren't worth the pain and horror of war. The vets I know have stories they could tell that would leave civilians ashen.

But despite the awfulness of war, time after time in the history of the United States, people in the prime of life have volunteered their lives as soldiers. They have offered themselves as potential sacrificial victims.

All veterans, whatever their service history, deserve our thanks and respect on this day. Military service at the very least took time out of their lives as ordinary citizens and thrust them into a subculture that's hardly Club Med. Many veterans sacrificed much more: limbs, healthy psyches, relationships, careers.

War is a horrible evil but one that is sometimes necessary. It's easy for peace-loving Christians to look down on those who serve in the military, but even the most pacifist among us must face the fact that those of us who are never soldiers have had that privilege only because of the ones who were. I hope the church is always ambivalent about war; that's the stance that's least likely to get us involved in one. But we should never be ambivalent about veterans. In giving their lives—potentially or in fact—they teach us something about that amazing man, Jesus of Nazareth.

When Jesus heard [the centurion], he was amazed and said to those who followed him, "Truly I tell you, in no one in Israel have I found such faith." (Matthew 8:10)

NOVEMBER 12
Bikers

My dear friend Harry Tueting is a biker. He rides a Harley-Davidson motorcycle—one of the big ones. Harry's a big guy and when he dresses in black, doesn't shave for a couple of days, and puts on a helmet, he is one scary looking man.

If you are my age or older, then you remember a group of people called "Hell's Angels." They were a bunch of people who rode motorcycles, dressed in black leather, lived rough, beat people up, and terrorized whole towns.

At least that's what we were told they were like. Maybe they were, but I now have to wonder. Harry is a kind, generous, and gentle man. He is one of God's children, there's no doubt in my mind. He once considered going to seminary. He worked for the Boy Scouts for years. Now he owns a musical instrument store. He employs several people, pays his taxes, and . . . rides a motorcycle.

I love it when Harry comes to town on his bike and takes me for a ride. I love the way it feels to be on a motorcycle, with the wind rushing past. It's as if you're going so fast that your problems can't catch up with you. But if I happen to wear black, and when I wear my helmet, then when I get off that Harley, the people in the restaurant we're going to look at me as if I'm going to snatch their children away. If you asked them what I did for a living, I'll bet a month's pay that not a one of them would say, "She's a pastor."

Every time I see a biker now, I of course think of Harry. And I also get the frequent reminder I need not to judge people, whether they're bikers or anyone else I don't understand.

"Do not judge by appearances, but judge with right judgment." (John 7:24)

NOVEMBER 13
Getting Lost

I confess that I have a terrible sense of direction. Many of my friends would laugh and say I give myself too much credit. When I'm driving, I couldn't tell you which way was north or west if my life depended on it. When I leave a building, I almost always turn the wrong direction to get to my car. And when I'm hiking . . . well, the only thing that saves me is up and down.

This means there are many times that I've made a wrong turn somewhere and headed down the wrong road. It usually takes me a while to figure out I've messed up. When I start seeing dairy cows I realize I'm probably not headed into downtown Nashville. When I finally figure it out, I find someplace to turn around and speed along to make up for lost time.

One of the best things I learned in seminary was that the Greek word we translate as "repentance" means, quite literally, turning around. To repent, then, would be like me taking a wrong turn, figuring out I'd done so, turning around, and heading back in the right direction.

I like this so much because it's so concrete. In many ways I'm a simple person. Don't give me all this multi-syllabic theological mishmash about repentance. Tell me that I have a terrible sense of direction in my spiritual life. And remind me that God's arranged things so I can turn around when I realize I'm lost.

I have gone astray like a lost sheep; seek out your ser-vant, for I do not forget your commandments.
(Psalm 119:176)

NOVEMBER 14
Never Say Never

I met my friend Greg when we were both students at Vanderbilt. I was working on my doctorate, he on his Master of Divinity degree. We belong to the same denomination, so we got to know each other and became friends.

I remember very well sitting in my apartment with Greg and another friend. He was telling us that he was not going to become an ordained minister. He used words like "no way," "absolutely not," "forget it." I don't even remember what the particular reasons were; I just remember the vehemence.

About three years later, I preached at Greg's ordination service. He didn't wake up one day and decide, "Hey! I've been wrong! God really does want me to be a minister!" He changed, little bit by little bit, over three years. And he fought all the way. But because Greg really does love God, he tried as hard as he could to follow the call he was hearing; eventually, that call led him to the ordained ministry.

I've learned the hard way to never say never. Part of me thinks that God has a marvelous sense of humor and takes this as a challenge: "Oh, yeah? Just wait." I cannot think of one single thing about which I have said "never" that has not come to pass.

We certainly have free will. It's part of the package that comes with being human. But God can also be mighty persuasive. I might even say God can be a nag.

Greg could have said no to God, and could have continued to say no to this very day. But I guess he got tired of fighting it and finally said, "All right, all right! I'll do it your way." I think he'd tell you today that he made the right decision.

Never say never.

He prayed to the Lord and said, "O Lord! Is not this what I said while I was still in my own country? That is why I fled to Tarshish at the beginning; for I knew that you are a gracious God and merciful, slow to anger, and abounding in steadfast love, and ready to relent from punishing." (Jonah 4:2)

NOVEMBER 15
Generics

I am a fiend for generics. I especially like generic medications. As a cancer patient, I take a lot of pills, and the way my health plan works, each prescription costs me $15 if I get the name brand and $3 if I get the generic. As far as I'm concerned, it's a no-brainer.

I asked a pharmacist once whether there are people who insist on the brand-name drug and she said yes. Some folks swear the brand name works better, even though on a chemical level there is absolutely no difference between it and the generic.

Now, it's true that not all generics are equal in all situations. I'll never again, for example, buy generic cotton swabs. It's horrible to have the cotton tip come off in your ear. And as for generic nose tissues—well, why not save myself some time and use sandpaper?

I can't help but think about generics and name brands when people ask me whether all religions aren't the same—which they do rather frequently, since I teach about them. The way I see it is this: God is God, no matter the label we attach. There is only one God; there's not a Christian God, a Jewish God, and an Islamic God. At the most basic level, then, all religions are the same—it's the same God.

But it's also true that not all religions are equally as good. I imagine trying to make that argument to a resident of early Palestine. Could I honestly say that the worship of Moloch, who demanded the sacrifice of the worshiper's eldest child, was just as good as the worship of Yahweh, who in the story of Abraham and Isaac taught that such sacrifice was not right? Absolutely not.

I'm not making any statements here about salvation—as always, I leave it up to God to decide who's saved and who isn't. But I get uncomfortable when people take discussions of different religions to either extreme.

[God] said, "Do not lay your hand on the boy or do anything to him; for now I know that you fear God, since you have not withheld your son, your only son, from me." (Genesis 22:12)

NOVEMBER 16
The Martyrs of El Salvador

Unbeknownst to most Americans, in the 1980s Jesuit faculty members at the University of Central America were playing a leading role in trying to resolve the long civil war in El Salvador. Their work came to fruition in February 1992 when a cease-fire was declared. But that victory came at a tremendous cost.

On November 16, 1989, troops from the El Salvadoran army came onto the grounds of the university in San Salvador and gunned down six Jesuit priests: Ignacio Ellacurio, Joaquin Lopez u Lopez, Amando Lopez, Ignacio Martin-Baro, Segundo Montes, and Juan Ramon Moreno. They also killed the men's housekeeper, Julia Elba Ramos, and her fifteen-year-old daughter, Celina Mariset Ramos.

These murders were horrible enough in themselves. But they gained a gruesome element when several of the victims were found with their brains scooped out. The Jesuits ascribed to liberation theology, which suggests that God has "a preferential option for the poor" and works to align the institution and power of the church with the interests of the poor. It was this theology that the murderers wanted to destroy when they emptied the skulls of these men.

The martyrs of El Salvador should be remembered in their own right, for the work they did, the loss of their lives, and the cause for which they died. But they are also sober reminders to us that sometimes being a Christian means questioning the status quo—using our God-given intellects to think our way through to divine justice. There are many places in our world in which the poor are despised and persecuted, and liberation theology is not the only way of thinking that can lead a believer to an understanding of God's will for such people. But it definitely takes thinking outside the box—the box of "the way things are," the box of the powerful and wealthy, and the box even of self-preservation.

Too often these days, American Christians can slide into complacency. It's almost unthinkable to us that we could be called upon to die for our faith in this day and age. But 1989 was not so very long ago, and surely no one would suggest that these are the last of the church's martyrs. I know I am called to live and think in such a way that my actions reflect Christ so thoroughly that people will want to kill me. It's a sobering thought.

These martyrs do not want revenge, nor are they interested that justice be brought about for them. What they want is peace and justice for El Salvador through the best means left to achieve them. (Jon Sobrino, S.J.)

NOVEMBER 17
A Woman's Man

I heard from my friend Michael Duncan today. I came to know Michael when I was in seminary. I was a young, inexperienced ministerial candidate and he was a pastor working on his Doctor of Ministry degree, with years of experience under his belt.

Michael is the pastor of a Baptist church in a small Kentucky town, where he has been for twenty-two years. He is a loving caregiver, thoughtful theologian, bold preacher, and deep thinker. And Michael is also "a woman's man."

Michael loves women. His wife Donna is first on his list, but he likes our gender overall. He brags on Donna all the time, and to hear him tell it, she's the more talented of the two. He apprenticed himself to an ordained woman Southern Baptist New Testament professor despite his denomination's official pronouncements about the roles women should play. He learned all he could from her while telling everyone how great she was. Michael isn't intimidated or threatened by smart, competent women—in fact, he seems to like us! Despite the fact that he is my senior in the faith in every way, he has always treated me kindly and as a colleague. He even tells me that he learns from me.

Every woman knows that not all men are like that. If we're lucky, we find one to share our lives with. Sometimes, though, we have a run of bad luck and meet man after man who isn't able to be affirming of women.

Michael helps me get a grasp on Jesus. There is no doubt that our Lord loves women utterly and completely. He had women friends and charged women with important commissions, like spreading the gospel. Unfortunately, even the men of the church can sometimes be dismissive of women. Michael reminds me that those men are the ones who are wrong, and that the only man whose opinion I'll give weight to is a woman's man.

Greet Andronicus and Junia, my relatives who were in prison with me; they are prominent among the apostles, and they were in Christ before I was.
(Romans 16:7)

NOVEMBER 18
The Impossible Dream

My friend Paul is a very talented man. He's extremely intelligent, well-educated, an engaging teacher, and an artist. He is also a songwriter.

There's a saying in Nashville that you're never more than ten feet away from a song demo, and that's not much of an exaggeration. There are probably thousands of people in this town who are excellent musicians and songwriters and are trying to get their break. Sometimes it seems like an impossible dream.

That dream feels all the more impossible for Paul because he comes from a family that wasn't at all supportive of his songwriting. As far as they were concerned, there was only one job in the world worth having: being a minister, like his father. For Paul's father, only hymns and classical music were legitimate.

People to whom God has given artistic talent of any kind often have a rough go of things. It's hard to support oneself as a musician, writer, painter, or dancer, and it's hard to be taken seriously. It's always easier to develop our talents if our parents have given us their blessing. All children, whatever their gifts, need to know that their parents are behind them one hundred percent in developing those gifts, even if they're not the sort that easily lead to wealth and security. No, that's wrong—*especially* if they're not that sort of gift.

Unfortunately, not everybody gets that kind of reassurance or blessing from their parents. It's a horrible shame, but it's true. That's why it's good that it is the very parent who has put those gifts within us—

God—who has the only trustworthy measure of them.

Paul keeps writing songs, despite the odds. He sometimes feels he's dreaming an impossible dream, but he keeps at it because he knows he has the blessing of the one who put his talent in him.

I have not hidden your saving help within my heart, I have spoken of your faithfulness and your salvation; I have not concealed your steadfast love and your faithfulness from the great congregation. (Psalm 40:10)

NOVEMBER 19
Foreign Films

Kevin needed a DVD player, so he came over and together we watched Czek director Jan Svankmajer's *Faust*. It was an extremely compelling movie—I'm still thinking about it days later—but boy, was it weird. It was full of very surreal things that I know are highly symbolic, but I know I'm only understanding about ten percent of them.

That's one reason I like to watch movies like this with Kevin. He's not the film school type who would give me a half-hour lecture on what the movie means. He's willing to say he hasn't a clue. That frees me to be clueless as well, and so I can be open to something strange and new. If I had to be "smart" about it, I couldn't bear to watch such things.

I wonder why I can't give myself the same grace when it comes to God. Maybe it's because I'm a minister and we're taught to have answers when people ask us questions about God. After all, that's my job, isn't it? To explain the ways of God?

Actually, no. Whether clergy or lay, my job is to seek God on the unique path laid out for me, and to assist others, when I can, on their journeys. That doesn't require having the answers.

That's very good, because answers I don't have. Being completely clueless about a movie gives me permission to say those three words that you hardly ever hear come out of a pastor's mouth, when asked about God: "I don't know."

Claiming to be wise, they became fools. (Romans 1:22)

NOVEMBER 20
A Good Man

My friend Tim is a remarkable man. He's a major brain—he not only has a Master of Divinity degree, but he's done most of the work for a master of arts, and is in the process of getting a doctorate of psychology. He's a great therapist. He's also musically talented. Tim has a lovely voice and plays the guitar beautifully. And funny? He's one of the few people in my world who can make me laugh out loud.

Problem is that Tim doesn't see himself this way. His head is so full of his shortcomings that there's little room for the good stuff. Most of the time when I try to give him a picture of himself that's different from his own, he'll have none of it. I wish he could see himself through my eyes. Or God's eyes.

There are secret rooms and corridors inside Tim's soul that I can't see and probably never will. But I'm certain God knows Tim through and through, and I also know that God sees the good in him.

Along with Tim, I also find myself struggling with what pop psychology calls self-esteem. I think most of us do. It's very hard for me to remember that God has created me and called it good. No, actually; after creating Adam and Eve, God said not "good," but "very good."

God saw everything that he had made, and indeed, it was very good. And there was evening and there was morning, the sixth day. (Genesis 1:31)

NOVEMBER 21
Anthrax

As I write, the American public is becoming more and more concerned about anthrax. Several people have died, and right now it looks as if contamination has reached further than was originally thought. I know people who are so frightened they are thinking of leaving the country, and others who don't give it a second thought.

By the time this book is published, you'll be able to look back on the early response to anthrax and say either, "Oh, if only we'd known it wasn't going to be such a huge, horrible problem" or, "Back then we had only the slightest hint of how bad it was going to get." Right now, though, there's no way to know what will happen and like many people, I'm afraid.

It's scary to think that I could die soon from biological or chemical weapons. I can't take the perspective of people who say serenely, "Oh, God won't let it get too bad." Why would God stop this horror but not the plague or influenza?

The reason I can live with all this and lead a relatively normal life is that nothing has really changed since September 11, 2001. I mean nothing as far as my mortality goes. I could die today, next week, or next month from any number of causes. It's just that

I'm able to ignore this fact most of the time because the news media isn't constantly pushing it in my face.

Finally, all I can do is take sensible precautions and put myself in God's hands. I don't want to die, but the fact is that sooner or later I will, whether it's from anthrax, cancer, a car accident, or old age. My hope is in God's goodness and a home in heaven. Of course I want to stick around this beautiful world as long as possible, but when I get so scared I can't function, I need to remind myself that the next world is going to be better.

Shall I ransom them from the power of Sheol? Shall I redeem them from Death? O Death, where are your plagues? O Sheol, where is your destruction? Compassion is hidden from my eyes. (Hosea 13:14)

NOVEMBER 22
Nightmares

Nightmares stink. There's nothing quite like waking up in the middle of the night, terrified and sweaty, to make a girl's day.

But everything I know about psychology tells me nightmares serve a purpose and are, in fact, important. Whether we are conscious of it or not, we have fears lurking inside of us, and they've got to pop out once in a while. Trying to ignore them is just exactly the wrong thing to do—that only pushes them further into the unconscious and makes them better fodder for nightmares.

I don't really even need psychology to help me deal with nightmares. Again and again, people in the Bible received dreams that we could easily call nightmares. If Joseph's dream about the seven-year famine wasn't a nightmare, I don't know what is.

Of course, my dreams aren't prophetic—not for the whole country, anyway. They are, on the other hand, prophetic for my life. Nightmares are sort of like bulletin boards that give me warnings: "You are afraid of people you love getting hurt. Deal with it." "You are afraid of dying. Deal with it." Dealing with it means, first, not ignoring the fear, and then of course taking it to God. Praying about a nightmare concerning someone I love getting hurt doesn't make me any happier about the prospect, but for some reason, it does allow me to put the whole matter in God's hands. Once I do that, my nightmares go away and I can sleep again.

It's good to have a mechanism that forces me to deal with things that are bothering me. As little as I like having nightmares, I've got to admit that—once again and as always—God was pretty smart for building them in. Otherwise I'd be tempted to keep my fears to myself and think I was the one who had to deal with them. Nightmares almost force me to hand them over to God. And that's just fine.

When I say, "My bed will comfort me, my couch will ease my complaint," then you scare me with dreams and terrify me with visions. (Job 7:13-14)

NOVEMBER 23
X-Rays

I'm seeing a new internist and so had to cart my x-rays to him from Vanderbilt. I've had more x-rays in the last seven years than I care to count, and there's absolutely no reason for my new doc to order more.

Since I had that huge folder at home for an evening, I took out a few films and looked at them. I'm astounded by x-rays. They show the faint outline of my body, but what stands out are my bones. Who knew there were so many bones in this body I call home?

As a pastor, I've been with lots of people when the x-rays go up on the light board. Sometimes the patients are children, and I am once again amazed by the sturdy skeleton inside such fragile, tender bodies.

There is no doubt that I am a mortal creature, created by God and destined for the earth from which

I came. Sometimes—especially when I'm ill—it's all too easy to start focusing on my fragility. One thing cancer has taught me is that I have inner resources I could never have imagined. I've done things I never thought possible back in the beginning. So while I am, indeed, frail in some ways, I also have a strong, hard skeleton—both physically and emotionally—that God has put inside of me to keep me standing when I think I can do no more than turn to jelly. I am stronger than I think I am, and seeing my bones reminds me of that.

He said to me, "Mortal, can these bones live?" I answered, "O Lord God, you know." (Ezekiel 37:3)

NOVEMBER 24
Burned Toast

I cremated the toast again. I soon found myself in a position that's all too familiar: bent over the kitchen trash can with a butter knife, scraping off the burned part. But this time was different. Somehow I lost my grip on the toast and it went tumbling into the trash.

I probably stood there a full thirty seconds trying to decide what to do. My uncertainty may sound odd, but there's a reason for it. My parents were wonderful about educating me and my sisters about poverty and hunger in the world. We learned that many children didn't have enough to eat and that we were very lucky to have whatever was set before us. Wasting food was a no-no, for very good reasons. There are families in the third world that could exist quite well on the amount of food their American counterparts throw away.

On the other hand . . . it's two pieces of toast. It doesn't matter how well I scrape them; they're never going to taste like two slices rightly done. With a determination better suited to climbing mountains, I threw out the other piece of burned toast and made two new, unburned ones.

As I was eating my toast, I realized something: This is okay! I am worth two pieces of bread. Yes, it's terrible that poor people don't have enough food. But the point of social justice is not to bring everyone down to poverty but to raise the poor to a state in which they, too, have a little extra. I realized that God would not at all be angry at or ashamed of me for throwing out some burned toast.

How many other hardships do I impose on myself, when it's not God who requires them, but my own neurosis? This is worth a lot of reflection—it could well be that there's more grace and abundance in my life than I ever knew!

Come, ye thankful people come, raise the song of har-
vest home; all is safely gathered in, ere the winter
storms begin; God, our maker, does provide for our
wants to be supplied. Come to God's own temple, come,
raise the song of harvest home. (Henry Alford)

NOVEMBER 25*
Thanksgiving

(Observed fourth Thursday of November)

Turkey and pumpkin pie, family and football: Thanksgiving is an American holiday full of traditions. In my own family, tradition dictates that, among other things, there must be fresh cranberry relish, even though none of us except my mother actually *likes* fresh cranberry relish. Every family has their own traditions that—logical or not—absolutely must be observed, or it's not Thanksgiving.

There is good reason to observe the day of Thanksgiving. We have been put on a bounteous earth and showered with abundance. The cornucopia is an apt symbol not only for Thanksgiving Day, but for all the days of our lives.

We are blessed 365 days of the year, not just one. Though the table may not groan as loudly, though the number of family members gathered around it may not be as large, each and every meal is an opportunity to thank God for all the many blessings of our lives—culinary and otherwise. If we open our eyes and refuse to take the good things in our lives for granted, then we can say the same as Elizabeth.

"Blessed is she who believed that there would be a fulfillment of what was spoken to her by the Lord."
(Luke 1:45)

NOVEMBER 26
Flying

Carol flies all the time—twice a week, in fact. That's how she commutes. She doesn't think a thing about it; it's as normal to her as getting in the car and driving to work is to me.

I envy her the frequency of her flights, because human beings seem to be put together in such a way that when we do things often enough, we lose our nervousness about them. I have to confess that although I'm a big girl now, I still get anxious before I fly.

On the other hand, I don't envy Carol's matter-of-factness about flying. I suppose I'm a romantic, but I think it's one of the greatest marvels in human history that we have figured out how to fly. Since earliest times, human beings have wanted to fly; we've recorded it in our art and myths. And apparently dreams of flying turn up in every human culture.

There's that moment when a plane first lifts off the ground. My insides scream two things: "Aiyeee! This is very bad. Human beings can't fly." And the other: "I'm flying! I'm flying!"

It's quite remarkable, when you think about it— that we could identify so closely with another species that we can long to share its experiences. It's easy to forget in an urban world, but God created us *within* nature, as one part of the puzzle that is the earth. It doesn't matter that we're able to fly because of technology. What had to exist before the invention of the airplane was the desire to fly, to be like our neighbors the birds.

Wild animals and all cattle, creeping things and flying birds! (Psalm 148:10)

NOVEMBER 27
Going Home

Every year the news people do a story about the fact that more people travel over the Thanksgiving

weekend than any other time. I'm sure the days surrounding Christmas come in at number two.

There are probably one hundred theories out
there about why we want to go home—wherever that
is—for the holidays. The one I hear the most is that
since we've become such a mobile culture, family
members live far away from each other and want to
gather on special occasions. But longing to go home
was a part of human nature long before the huge continent of North America gave us so much room to
spread out.

The Jews longed to go home to Israel, and more
specifically, to Jerusalem. Every time they were
thrown out, they struggled to get back. Jesus
returned to Nazareth, hoping for a level of acceptance
by his hometown that he simply didn't get. Paul had
several homes—all the churches he planted—and he
traveled constantly to visit them as often as possible.

St. Augustine had it right when he said our hearts
are restless except in God. As much as I may want to
get home for the holidays, that desire doesn't come
close to the deep longing I feel for my real home—
the kingdom of God. It's good to know that one day
I'll be at that home and planes, trains, and automo-
biles can go by the wayside. It definitely won't be
humble—but there's no place like home.

Those who go out weeping, bearing the seed for sowing, shall come home with shouts of joy, carrying their sheaves. (Psalm 126:6)

NOVEMBER 28
Tender Souls

My niece, at the ripe old age of six, is often troubled because of the fact that people on the other side of the world are suffering. At the moment, her attention is on the people of Afghanistan for obvious reasons. She cries about the war, and while she's afraid for herself, it also makes her feel terrible that other people are going through such horrors.

She can even be empathic toward insects. She recently wrote a book entitled "The Lonely Butterfly." Luckily, by the end of the book, the lonely one has found a mate, and they live happily ever after. My niece could not leave that butterfly alone.

While I cherish my niece's care and concern for all living things, I ache for her, too, because I know there is much suffering in the world and if she continues worrying for others, she will hurt a lot during her life. I can't wish her tender soul to be toughened, though; it's one of the most charming things about her.

It's all too easy to focus on the selfish, self-centered people of the world. But then I talk to a child, and I am reminded of the bottomless compassion of God. I don't understand why some theologians maintain that we cannot affect God's feelings. Why else would Jesus have been sent to earth? Whatever the theological implications, I am quite certain that God was moved by compassion for our predicament, even though we had only ourselves to blame for it. God, it seems to me, must be tenderhearted. How much anguish do we cause for our creator, then, when we do things that create suffering for ourselves and others?

Finally, all of you, have unity of spirit, sympathy, love for one another, a tender heart, and a humble mind.
(1 Peter 3:8)

NOVEMBER 29
Dorothy Day

Dorothy Day herself would want me to be clear about the fact that she was not and never will be declared a saint. When someone once suggested to her that she might be canonized some day, she responded, "Don't call me a saint. I don't want to be dismissed so easily."

Day was a complex woman. Despite the fact that she thought sainthood would remove the power of her radical message, there are other reasons she probably won't be canonized. She was a woman who sinned, and sinned big. Of course, the only reason we know that is because she wrote about it herself.

Whatever Dorothy Day's shortcomings—and she would be the first to insist they were legion—she is still one of the most important Christian figures of the twentieth century. Along with Peter Maurin, she started the Catholic Worker movement. Among its many accomplishments were *The Catholic Worker* newspaper, a network of urban and rural houses of hospitality for the poor, and a radically strong witness for pacifism and civil rights.

Perhaps not since St. Francis have the poor had such a passionate advocate. Dorothy Day is a reminder of what can be accomplished by an ordinary, sinful Christian who is suffused by the grace, power, and forgiveness of God.

We let them stay forever. They live with us, they die with us, and we give them a Christian burial. We pray for them after they are dead. Once they are taken in, they become members of the family. Or rather they always were members of the family. They are our brothers and sisters in Christ. (Dorothy Day)

November 30
Computers

I am old enough to have been in on the second generation of computers, the ones that were made available to people and organizations outside the government. When I started working for a data management nonprofit in the late '70s, punch cards were just being phased out. There were no personal computers; instead, users dialed up over phone lines to access a central computer. The computers themselves, as opposed to the terminals, occupied entire rooms. And the terminal I worked on had no monitor. I would type words onto paper and thereby to the computer, and the computer would respond by typing words back to me.

I am ancient indeed. Computers have increased in power exponentially during the last thirty years. By the time this book is published, the computer I'm using to write it will be obsolete. It's hard to overestimate the things computers will be able to do in just ten years.

And yet whatever those 2011 computers are like, they won't even come close to the complexity of the human brain. No matter how powerful they are, they won't be able to match the billions of cells in one human brain. Although computers can work more quickly than we can, they are incapable of coming up with the simplest original thought. They are wonderful tools and will undoubtedly be even more useful in the future, but I'm afraid that people who say computers will one day surpass the human mind are overly enthusiastic.

We human beings have created a wonderful thing in computers. But it is hubris to think that we are better creators than is our God.

Yet you have made them a little lower than God, and crowned them with glory and honor. (Psalm 8:5)

DECEMBER 1*
First Sunday of Advent

Here it is: the beginning of the Christian year. On this day, the church begins once again the marvelous year-long story of the way God has acted in human life through the birth of Jesus, the Christ. It *is* the "greatest story ever told," no doubt about it.

Yet one of the paradoxes of Advent is that the Christian story is also one of the most ordinary. The cosmic revolution began with something quite everyday and not at all unusual: a pregnancy.

Because much of the church's history has been written by men, pregnancy has been given short shrift as a metaphor for the Christian story and life. In a book of meditations for women, it makes sense to explore some of the facets of pregnancy during Advent and see what they can teach us about God.

One of the ironies of doing such a thing is that I am not a mother. I've never given birth. I can never know the realities of pregnancy the way most of you, my readers, do. Nevertheless, because I so honor the miracle of human birth, I have spent a lot of time listening to mothers talk about pregnancy. I hope that I will be able to accurately reflect that experience.

I start, then, with the first day of Advent—as I said, the first day of the Christian year. It is the day, in church, that we begin anticipating the arrival of Jesus. It's the birth for which the world waited for millions of years. For many people, it's the most special day of the Christian year. Once they've picked up the wrapping paper and stowed the leftovers, they start looking ahead to the next Christmas.

Other babies are long-anticipated too. Many mothers remember their first longings for a child appearing when they were still children themselves. A six-year-old wants a baby in a different way than a twenty-five-year-old does, but both of them yearn for someone they hope will one day come into their lives. That hope may exist for two, three, even four decades before it's fulfilled. Any woman who has longed for a baby understands the depth of hope and anticipation in which the world existed before the birth of Jesus.

Now Sarai, Abram's wife, bore him no children.
(Genesis 16:1a)

DECEMBER 2
When?

My friend "Clarissa" is one of the most organized people in the world. You know how at job interviews they ask, "Where do you hope to be in five years?" Clarissa has her life planned for the next *thirty*.

She was clicking right along on schedule. She'd finished college and graduate school in record time, found the perfect man and married him, and then one morning, about seven years too soon according to The Plan, Clarissa discovered she was pregnant. It devastated her. So much for the plan to establish herself in her career and be ready financially first. But when her daughter arrived, Clarissa scribbled on the birth announcement, "She came at exactly the right time."

Of course it's sensible and responsible to plan pregnancies, and some women are lucky enough to get pregnant when they want to—no sooner, no later. It doesn't always work that way, though. Nevertheless, many mothers who have "surprise" pregnancies later swear that the timing was just right.

Jesus came at exactly the right time—right for Mary, right for Joseph, right for the Jews, right for all of creation. Why that time was the right one we cannot know, but that God had a plan there can be no doubt. When I find myself griping about some "bad timing," I remind myself that in God's world, everything happens just when it should.

But when the fullness of time had come, God sent his Son, born of a woman, born under the law, in order to redeem those who were under the law, so that we might receive adoption as children. (Galatians 4:4-5)

December 3
Trying

Sex between a loving husband and wife is a wonderful thing anytime it happens. But sex when they are trying to make a baby can be one of the most moving experiences there is. Every baby deserves to be born into a home that has wanted it, longed for it, planned for it. It is a mark of God's grace that even unplanned babies are wanted too.

But there's a difference in sex when you're "trying." These days we're so sophisticated about ovulation and the best times to get pregnant, the act of making love carries with it an awesome, earth-shaking undertone: "We may be creating a human life at this very moment." Along with the desire to give pleasure and receive it, there is the hope that these loving caresses will bring about new life.

Ancient, cranky, celibate theologians thought sex without the goal of pregnancy was sinful; married couples have always known this is nonsense, and we are lucky to live in a time when the church recognizes it too. God created sex not only for reproduction, but also to bond husband and wife to each other. Its pleasure is good in God's eyes.

Still, that one instance of intercourse among hundreds over the course of a marriage has a special glow about it. Women like to think back and remember "which time" it was that created their children.

It's rather sobering to realize that God created us with all the intentionality, all the love, and all the pleasure (though obviously not *physical* pleasure) with which we create babies. The Bible assures us that God knew us in the womb; Christianity has always maintained that each and every individual is unique, beloved, and important to God. A couple making a baby can, if they reflect on this sacred act, turn the joy of their experience around and realize that God felt all this and more in the act of creating them.

I am my beloved's, and his desire is for me.
(Song of Songs 7:10)

DECEMBER 4
The Pregnancy Test

Remember the *"I Love Lucy"* episode when Lucy found out she was pregnant and had a terrible time getting Ricky to sit still long enough to tell him about it? Like all those episodes, it was hilarious, but also became quite moving near the end when Ricky realizes it is his own wife who has requested that he sing a song about having a baby.

Things have changed since then, and the rabbits must be happy about it. Today it's not nearly as complicated to know whether you're pregnant, and you don't even have to go to the doctor. A trip to the drug store, a little urine, a little time, and voilà.

When the news comes from the doctor's office or when the test turns up positive, a woman is flooded with feelings. Usually the first thing she wants to do is tell her husband. It's a remarkable event in the life of a couple, repeatable only a very few times.

This is the time that the church hears the message of John the Baptist: "He is coming. We've been waiting for ages, but now he's coming. The time is here." The coming of Jesus was preceded by much powerful and hidden work on the part of God, and it is on this day that all the preparations that have been so carefully made come to fruition. Today, we Christians walk out of the bathroom and into the arms of a loving husband, saying, "We're going to have a baby."

But God said to Abraham, "Do not be distressed because of the boy and because of your slave woman; whatever Sarah says to you, do as she tells you, for it is through Isaac that offspring shall be named for you." (Genesis 21:12)

DECEMBER 5
The Due Date

Every pregnant woman knows the first question people will ask when they discover she's going to have a baby: "When are you due?" And most pregnant women know, down to the exact date. It's not, "Oh, probably late August." It's, "August 28." The doctor is the one who calculates the due date, but it's the pregnant woman who gives it such importance.

This makes sense to me. Having a baby is a major event, and it's always nice to know when major events are going to occur. "When?" is a very human question.

The church tells us that "in the fullness of time" God sent Jesus to be born among us. Jesus had a due date, too, one that had universal importance. I don't know why Jesus was born around the year 1 instead of 632 BCE or 1412 CE. But God knows, and apparently it wasn't just a matter of picking any old time. All of eternity revolves around the birth of this particular child, and God knew what had to happen beforehand and what would happen later. Jesus came at exactly the right time.

Human babies aren't that precise. Due dates can vary up to a couple of weeks. But whatever the actual day of their birth, they, too, come at exactly the right time.

And the Lord remembered her. In due time Hannah conceived and bore a son. She named him Samuel, for she said, "I have asked him of the Lord."
(1 Samuel 1:19b-20)

DECEMBER 6
St. Nicholas

So popular is St. Nicholas and so well his story known, it's difficult to find a fresh way to think about him. Most everyone knows the story that he was a bishop in Turkey, and that he threw gold coins down the chimney of a destitute nobleman so the man's three daughters could have money for a dowry. Even more people know that Santa Claus is a fattened-up version of St. Nicholas.

What many people don't know is that St. Nicholas is the origin of the symbol commonly used for pawnshops—three gold balls. Originally, Nicholas was portrayed in art with three gold balls representing the three sacks of coins he threw down the chimney. That symbol was taken up by bankers and moneylenders, and pawnshops are really the final vestige of Nicholas' symbol.

Most people I know feel that pawnshops are a little unsavory. Because in the past stolen property was fenced through pawnshops, they got a reputation for living on the shady side of the law. But today, pawnshop owners cooperate with the police and often inform them of particularly obvious thefts, like a church's candlesticks or communion silver.

So even the seedy side of town, where pawnshops are wont to set up, has signs of God's presence and power. This should be no surprise; Jesus hung out in some pretty seedy places himself. St. Nicholas followed his Lord's lead and visited his entire diocese during a famine, providing them with bread—bread, some say, that he made miraculously. I suspect he would like it a great deal to know that his symbol is still to be seen—and seen in the particular parts of town it is.

We call upon your mercy, O Lord. Through the intercession of St. Nicholas, keep us safe amid all dangers so that we may go forward without hindrance on the road of salvation.
(Shonnie Scarola)

DECEMBER 7
Morning Sickness

Did Mary have morning sickness?

I don't know. I know some women, like my youngest sister, have such terrible morning sickness that they're miserable for the first months of their pregnancy. Then there are others, like my other sister, who sail through early pregnancy without so much as a burp.

I am constantly amazed by the fact that women keep getting pregnant even though it makes them want to throw up. I'm one of those people who hates throwing up; I've imbibed to the point of vomiting exactly once in my life. So I find it remarkable that most female human beings not only look forward to a physical state that will make them feel ill, but even do it more than once, knowing how awful it can be.

Of course morning sickness is a walk in the park compared to labor—so I've been told. Central Park, maybe, but a park nonetheless. Every pregnant woman I see reminds me that there are human beings who walk this earth willing to suffer for the welfare of others. More than that, they seem to suffer gladly!

Maybe this is how God suffers over us. I have no doubt that I, for instance, break God's heart on a regular basis. I don't think this is rare; on the contrary, it's normal. But God keeps loving me, keeps giving me the free will that allows me to do the things that hurt God. More remarkably, God continues making more human beings, knowing that they will each be the cause of suffering for their divine parent.

Of course this is the profound message of the cross—that God was willing to suffer and die for us. Problem is there aren't many people getting crucified these days as a way to remind us of God's great love. I guess pregnant women will have to do.

[Jesus said] "Jerusalem, Jerusalem, the city that kills the prophets and stones those who are sent to it! How often have I desired to gather your children together as a hen gathers her brood under her wings, and you were not willing!" (Matthew 23:37)

DECEMBER 8*
Second Sunday of Advent
The Immaculate Conception
(By Sr. Mary Ann Heyd, OP)

Each year our church celebrates the solemn feast of the Immaculate Conception of the Blessed Virgin Mary. Special readings chosen for the day's liturgy provide the background for three profound mysteries connected with Mary's holiness. From Genesis 3:9-15 we hear of Eve as "the mother of the living," who surrendered her own title by choosing to disobey God's command. This Old Testament story prepares the redemptive plan of God to create a new Eve who would be the mother of Jesus as well as mother of the whole human race. The second reading, Paul's letter to the church at Ephesus 1:3-6,11-12, reminds us that neither Mary's life nor ours is unimportant in God's plan. The predestination of God tells us we were chosen before the world began. Luke's gospel, the third reading, continues to reveal God's plan of salvation with Gabriel's announcement to Mary in Nazareth of Galilee, that she was chosen to be the mother of the savior. Mary said, "I am the maidservant of the Lord. Let it be done to me as you say."

The gift of faith makes it possible for us to believe that God loves each one of us so much that God's

Son suffered and died on the cross for us. The plan for God to become human became a reality when Mary agreed to be mother of our savior. The intimate relationship of mother and child, and in this context, God-born-of-woman, prompted the gift of preservation from original sin, or Mary's Immaculate Conception in the womb of Anne, her mother. Predestination allows us to believe that Mary was chosen by God before she was born because she would choose to obey God's will and be "mother of the living" that the first Eve refused.

Mary's unique gift of freedom from sin inspires me with hope that I and all others who desire eternal life with God will surely one day attain it. We believe that Mary the mother of Jesus shares heaven now and with her son. Jesus gave us his mother to be our model and our counselor through our days of trial and temptation here on earth. Mary's fullness of grace is meant to encourage us, knowing that we have such a relationship connecting us as children of God with her, "mother of the living."

[God] destined us for adoption as his children through Jesus Christ, according to the good pleasure of his will.
(Ephesians 1:5)

DECEMBER 9
Tests

Blood tests, ultrasound, amniocentesis. I guess on the whole these are good things, but I do wonder sometimes. Even the youngest, healthiest women I know go through a lot of anxiety as they await the results of all the tests modern medicine has devised to tell parents about the health of their growing child. Sometimes the results are devastating, and the parents are faced with unthinkable decisions.

But I guess parents are just getting plenty of practice for the future. Every mother I know says she never stops worrying about her children—no matter how old they are or how well they seem to be doing. So many find within themselves a depth of love they didn't know existed before they had children. And along with love comes concern.

We know that God loves us and is also greatly concerned for our welfare. God has a huge advantage over us—the ability to live outside of time and so know how things are going to turn out. But even if there's going to be a happy ending, no mother likes to see her child go through a struggle, through pain, through suffering. And God's concern for us has no end . . . it will always be there.

"Before I formed you in the womb I knew you, and before you were born I consecrated you; I appointed you a prophet to the nations." (Jeremiah 1:5)

DECEMBER 10
Thomas Merton

I attended seminary in Lexington, Kentucky, and the Abbey of Gethsemane was not so very far away. During my time in Kentucky, I visited the monastery many times, sat in the loft for the daily office, and walked the silent grounds. Under that ground, marked by a simple cross identical to all the others, lies the body of Fr. Louis: Thomas Merton. It is a very powerful experience to read the man's writings and then walk the same paths he did.

Merton is best known for his *Seven Storey Mountain*, the tale of his slow conversion to Christianity and discernment of a call to monastic life. He wrote innumerable other works, though—from prayers to academic pieces to essays to poetry, including love poetry.

Much hay is made over the fact that late in his life Merton fell in love with a young nurse who tended him after surgery. They exchanged some furtive telephone conversations and anguished letters, and the poetry he wrote for her is indescribably beautiful.

Unfortunately, it's only available in a limited edition of less than 200 copies—each of which, as you might imagine, is quite expensive. Somebody doesn't want those poems widely available.

But Merton's love for M. was truly an instance of the great love he felt for all humankind. He wrote powerfully about standing on a street corner in Louisville and being overwhelmed with a sense of the fragility and value of human life, and a depth of love that would enable him, in later years, to correspond with Buddhist masters as brothers.

In the end, Merton's relationship with M. confirmed for him the fact that his vocation was to religious life. And she apparently does not regret the relationship because she attends conferences on Merton held at Bellarmine College. Loving and being loved deepened the man's relationship with God and his spiritual writings.

I like Merton's story. It reminds me that love is always a good and godly thing.

There is in all visible things an invisible fecundity, a dimmed light, a meek namelessness, a hidden wholeness. This mysterious unity and integrity is Wisdom, the mother of all. (Thomas Merton)

DECEMBER 11
Maternity Clothes

My plastic surgeon was pregnant during the period she was seeing me for reconstructive surgery. It wasn't until I met her that I learned there are, indeed, beautiful and flattering maternity clothes out there.

Every woman has her own approach to dressing her expanding body. My surgeon wore designer clothes; my sister opted for leggings and oversized shirts. But I have never known a woman to wear her maternity clothes any longer than she had to.

I know that's because maternity clothes are shapeless and floppy, but I like the whole idea for another reason. The time of a woman's pregnancy is very special—I would go so far as to call it holy—and so it makes sense to me that there would be special, set-apart clothing to go along with it.

Most religions have some special garments set aside for people who are participating in an "extra holy" part of life. Indigenous tribesmen wear masks during fertility rituals; Buddhist monks don saffron robes; to say Mass, priests wear an alb, stole, and chasuble. This unique clothing conveys a visual reminder to all the believers: here is someone serving God in a very focused way.

So why shouldn't women have maternity clothes that might be worn only a few months? They, too, are serving God in a very focused way.

The priest who is exalted above his fellows, on whose head the anointing oil has been poured and who has been consecrated to wear the vestments, shall not dishevel his hair, nor tear his vestments.
(Leviticus 21:10)

DECEMBER 12
The OB

Seems like all the women I know in Nashville use the same two or three obstetricians. I think word gets around about who the good ones are.

And a pregnant woman definitely wants the best obstetrician she can find. Even during a normal pregnancy, her body will go through radical changes. If there are complications, things become even more involved. So it makes sense that a woman wouldn't want to put her body and her baby in the hands of just any old physician.

Since the beginning of time, women have consulted experts on childbearing when they are pregnant. That expert might be a board-licensed, world-famous OB, or she might be the old woman in the village who knows what kinds of tea will relieve nausea but won't hurt the fetus. There seems to be an understanding that pregnancy and birth is not something a woman can or should do by herself. Not even OBs or midwives try to go it alone when they have their children.

Just so it is with our spiritual life. Christians are, by nature, members of a community. One Christian is no Christian. Each of us and all of us need someone to help us on our lifelong journeys to God. That someone might be the priest or pastor, a spiritual director, or a friend from Bible study. None of us has all the pieces of the puzzle of Christian life, and we need the wisdom and experience of others who have their own unique relationship with God to fill in our gaps.

In pregnancy and in the spiritual life, even the experts need an expert to lean on. Whether a woman is growing a baby or a soul, she needs wise companions to help her flourish.

And because the midwives feared God, he gave them families. (Exodus 1:21)

DECEMBER 13
Pregnant Bodies

Remember when a very pregnant Demi Moore posed nude on the cover of *Vanity Fair*? The photographer had her hands and arms arranged strategically so all her "private" female parts were covered. What wasn't covered was her huge belly. And she was beautiful.

I remember stories my mother told me when I was growing up, about how women used to have to quit work when they got pregnant—or at least when they started showing. A secretary in my father's office created a huge scandal when she made it to six months before being discovered—she wore big, bulky sweaters and the men in charge apparently had their minds on other things. But there was most definitely a time when it was unseemly for a pregnant woman to appear in public, much less in the nude.

Times have changed and that's a very good thing. The pregnant female body is beautiful. Funny that "primitive" people knew that; they left behind innumerable little "Venuses"—palm-sized statues of pregnant women. And these Venuses don't look like de Milo. They have no facial features, and the enlarged breasts, stomach, hips, and thighs of pregnancy are even more exaggerated than normal. Scholars think these are evidence of fertility religions in which women's ability to give birth was a mysterious thing, much to be revered.

God made the female body and made it beautiful—in all stages of life, and all stages of pregnancy. The curves and swells of women's bodies somehow look just right next to the planes and angles of men's. That should be no surprise, given the artist. And while Demi Moore is a beautiful woman, what's even more beautiful is the gravid pear shape of any ordinary woman who is creating a child in her body.

> *[Joseph] went to be registered with Mary, to whom he*
> *was engaged and who was expecting a child.*
> *(Luke 2:5)*

DECEMBER 14
St. John of the Cross

Although Teresa of Avila's rather feminine writings resonate with me more than those of St. John, he's a favorite of mine nonetheless. That's partly because it appears that Teresa and John were best friends.

When Teresa was in the earliest stages of reforming the Carmelites, she discovered John. Though he was very humble and spoke of himself as "half a monk," Teresa was able to see through all that and perceive a man who had a passionate relationship with God. She depended on John to apply the same energy to male Carmelites as she did to the women. And so he did.

I like to imagine St. Teresa and St. John sitting around drinking tea, swapping war stories of life on the road, encouraging each other when things got tough, and laughing uproariously at the general indignities of life, such as the time Teresa was bucked off a donkey.

There's something very special that happens when men and women work together in the service of God. There is a wholeness, a completeness, a balance to their ministry and lives that is often missing when people have soul friends only of the same gender. One of the ways women and men can partner in God's service is to marry; that becomes their vocation. But women and men can also be friends, colleagues, and coworkers. There is always some sexual energy when a man and a woman work closely together. When they choose to keep their relationship platonic, that energy gets funneled into their work.

And the results are striking. The Carmelites have produced some of the greatest spiritual masters in all of Christian history. Either St. Teresa or St. John could have done a decent job alone, but together, they did something magnificent.

We want to penetrate more deeply into Christ, who,
like a rich mine, has so many treasures that we can
never finish discovering them all.
(St. John of the Cross)

DECEMBER 15*
Third Sunday of Advent: Quickening

I love this old-fashioned word. It refers to the time in pregnancy when the baby develops enough that the mother can feel it moving inside her. When pregnant friends have taken my hand and put it on their bellies, I have been astounded to feel the child kicking away. It becomes obvious to everyone involved: There's a child in there!

This is an especially joyous time for a couple that has had difficulty conceiving. After so much longing for a child, after so many disappointments when the blood flowed, after so much fear that it never would happen, quickening is a miraculous moment.

All of us, whether we've been pregnant or not, have had the experience of something quickening inside us. It might be the plot for a novel, a solution to a difficult management problem, a sudden epiphany about how to arrange the garden, or the realization of love for a man growing in the heart.

God, of course, is the source of all these different kinds of quickening, and we can even experience quickening in relation to God. I've talked to people who've turned from God and the church for many years and one day found something stirring inside of them that eventually took them back. I've met others who have embarked on a discipline of regular prayer and discovered a small, quiet, but nonetheless unmistakable feeling of God's presence in them.

Do men have the experience of quickening? Probably—but I doubt that they think of it in terms of pregnancy. We women, even those who have never had babies, have the delightful opportunity to imagine God growing something precious and alive in us. On that level, every woman has been pregnant, and will be many more times.

And you hath he quickened, who were dead in trespasses and sins. (Ephesians 2:1, KJV)

DECEMBER 16
Choosing a Name

I always find it interesting to read reports about the baby names that are most popular at the moment. There are some oldies-but-goodies that always seem to make the list—Elizabeth, Mary,

Michael, David—but then there are a bunch of others that most definitely reflect the popular culture of the time the person was born. Many of the Alexises running around now owe their names to the TV show *Dynasty*. Right now, among the crowd I run with, it seems fashionable to give children a first name that is usually a last name: Robinson, Diver, Harrington, and Coulter.

Most parents spend a lot of time figuring out what to name the baby. The process has changed a bit in the last few decades because so many women know the sex of the child long before it's born. But still, many of the mothers I know change their minds several times during their pregnancy.

This rather light and fun process turns dark when we look at naming traditions in another culture: Haiti. Missionary friends who've been there tell me that mothers don't name their children until their first birthdays, because so many of them die before then. That's a horror most of us in the United States simply can't imagine, and I'm glad to know the church is doing much good in Haiti through mission work. Maybe some day, Haitian mothers will feel it's okay to name their babies the day they're born.

This tragic situation tells us that part of being human is having a name. God made sure to give the first people names—Adam, which means "made of earth," and Eve, "life." The animals got names, too, at the beginning of creation, but just one name for each species. Humans are the only ones who each get a different name. Naming a child is a beautiful part of welcoming him or her into the human community— a community blessed by God.

Some take pride in chariots, and some in horses, but our pride is in the name of the Lord our God.
(Psalm 20:7)

DECEMBER 17
The Nursery

One of the exciting parts of pregnancy is preparing a nursery for the child who is coming. There's a lot of specialized equipment necessary for newborn babies, and that definitely has to be brought in. But more important—and more fun—is doing the decorating.

The process of decorating the nursery is partly the same as it is for any other room in a home: creating a visually pleasing, pleasant space to spend time. But there's more to it than just that for many mothers. They are creating a little nest for their children-to-be, and they want that nest to be the best. I've heard tales from my parents' generation of putting babies to sleep in dresser drawers, but that doesn't seem to happen much anymore. Most women who have the financial resources want the nursery to be the best room in the house, and "best" for a particular purpose: taking care of a child.

That's why it's ironic that Jesus' first nursery was a stable and his first crib a manger. Certainly if they'd been at home, Mary and Joseph wouldn't have housed their baby in such a place. I'm sure Mary had the first-century equivalent of today's nurseries. But Jesus' first nursery was curiously prophetic about the life he would lead.

The messiah, so the Jews had long believed, would be a majestic king, a military leader who would throw off Roman occupation and emancipate his people, then rule them. A king would live in a magnificent home, with all the luxuries of the time at his fingertips.

But this isn't the kind of messiah Jesus turned out to be. His kingdom, he told his followers, was not "of this world." He certainly didn't live in splendor. Instead, during his ministry he lived on the road, sleeping where he could and being fed by friendly strangers or the women who financially supported him and the disciples.

Jesus' first nursery, then, was in fact quite apt for the person who was occupying it. If they'd had the vision of hindsight that we do, the shepherds and wise men would have known that the nursery in which they found this baby was no accident—it was an indicator of what was to come.

And she gave birth to her firstborn son and wrapped him in bands of cloth, and laid him in a manger, because there was no place for them in the inn.
(Luke 2:7)

DECEMBER 18
The Expectant Father

I feel sorry for expectant fathers sometimes. They have contributed to the creation of the growing fetus, are taking care of their wives during pregnancy, and will, in the future, provide sustenance and nurture for the whole family. Fathers have a huge role in the life of a child, but during the pregnancy, at least, they tend to be ignored.

That may be one reason for the existence of a psychiatric condition called *couvade*. In *couvade*, the expectant father has the same symptoms his wife is having as she moves through pregnancy: morning sickness, an aching back, and, at the time of delivery, labor pains. There are tribal cultures in which the expectant father is taken off to a birthing hut when his wife is. His empathy with his wife is so deep that he feels the same things she does.

That's why Joseph's role in the Christmas story is a very moving one. He knew this child growing inside Mary was not his biological child. Nevertheless, he married his prenuptually-pregnant wife and took care of her and the baby as devotedly as if Jesus were his son.

And in fact, Jesus *was* the son of Joseph. Of course he was, first and foremost, the son of God. That's made clear from the opening lines of Matthew's gospel through the last verses of the book of Revelation. But Joseph, so tradition tells us, functioned in every way as Jesus' father . . . with the small exception of a contributory sperm. Jesus could not have become the man he did if he'd had an abusive, uncaring, or absent human father. Despite the fact that he definitely was God's son, he was also a human baby, boy, and man. And human babies need human fathers. Joseph fulfilled that role. We don't know the details of how he did that, but we do know the results—which were quite spectacular.

Today's fathers can have as important a role in their children's lives as did Joseph. After all, while their sons and daughters are "theirs," they are also—first and foremost—children of God. Every father is a caretaker of God's child.

When Joseph awoke from sleep, he did as the angel of
the Lord commanded him; he took her as his wife.
(Matthew 1:24)

December 19
False Labor

Once a woman has had her first child, she can often tell when labor truly starts. She may have contractions and other symptoms earlier on, but she knows this isn't "it" because she's experienced "it" before. First-time mothers, on the other hand, aren't so lucky.

Many new mothers have the experience of false labor. They have contractions and feel the pains that presage full labor. They usually rush to the hospital, only to be observed for a while and then released. Some mothers are embarrassed by false labor, while others are merely made impatient.

That's one reason I am always skeptical of religious writers and speakers who tell us the "last days" are upon us. They want us to believe that Christ is about to return, so we can make our preparations. They point out the early symptoms of the second coming as portrayed in the New Testament: wars and rumors of wars, earthquakes, scary political alliances, and perhaps most important of all, the fact that Israel has once again become a nation.

This causes a great deal of fear and consternation among good Christian people. But we should take comfort in knowing that people have been warning that Christ's return is near since very soon after Jesus' resurrection. Even more comforting is the fact that all the hundreds of doomsayers have cited the same "symptoms." It is clear that Jesus has not yet returned, so this means those hundreds of prognosticators were and probably are wrong.

Jesus told us that *no one*—not even he—could know the time when he would return. That's a pretty good authority, so we should stop spending brainpower and emotional energy on trying to figure it out. The best answer is to trust God to take care of it all.

I could be wrong, of course. What's happening today could, indeed, be the signs Jesus and Paul warned us about. If they are, then *maranatha*—come, Lord Jesus. Chances are, though, it's nothing more than false labor.

"And you will hear of wars and rumors of wars; see that you are not alarmed; for this must take place, but the end is not yet." (Matthew 24:6)

DECEMBER 20
Baby Showers

Baby showers are a nice tradition, whether they're the old corny kind attended only by women and accompanied by silly games, or the newer type, which may have both women and men in attendance and generally don't have a lot of games. It's a time when a woman nearing birth can be celebrated by her friends and family, and also receive some of the many supplies she'll soon need to take care of a tiny human being.

It's hard to imagine bringing a baby home from the hospital without lots of diapers, cute little clothes, several important pieces of furniture—a crib, changing table, and my personal favorite, the Diaper Genie—and a recent invention, the sound monitor. It's hard to imagine how women got along without all these conveniences in times gone by.

Mary didn't have a baby shower . . . at least the Bible doesn't say she did. Yet her husband provided everything she needed: food, water, entertainment, and assistance during the birth itself. Since he was a carpenter, he probably made Jesus' crib.

Whenever we are birthing something—whether it's a child, a work of art, or yearly employee evaluations—we need to remember that if God's hand is in this work, it *will* come to fruition. We will be given what we need to welcome this new creation into the world and take care of it.

Then Joseph got up, took the child and his mother, and went to the land of Israel. (Matthew 2:21)

DECEMBER 21*
Winter Solstice

It's the shortest day of the year, and long before this day, the number of daylight hours have become depressingly few. No more sunset at 9 p.m. This day holds the greatest number of hours of darkness.

Human beings always seem to have been afraid of the dark. One of the threats to unbelievers in the New Testament is that they will be thrown into "the outer darkness." All sorts of things happen in the dark—everything from all-too-familiar acts of violence to attacks by demons, witches, and goblins. It is at night that we usually sleep, and during this part of our daily rhythm, we are most vulnerable to being surprised by something nasty. "Darkness," in fact, has come to be a symbol for evil in English.

All these are the reasons ancient pagans lit huge fires on the night of the winter solstice. Not only were they performing sympathetic magic (fire = sun), they were also using fire to protect themselves from all the scary aspects of the night. The Yule log is one of the remnants of this pagan observance.

There's another side to this day too. Once it has passed, then the worst is over. From this point on, the days will only lengthen. We like to tell ourselves, "It's always darkest before the dawn," and in some sense that's true. The predawn darkness is only seconds away from succumbing to the first rays of dawn, and the longest night holds within it the seeds of lengthening days.

In those periods of our lives that we feel the least hope, we would do well to take comfort from this bit of natural theology that is the winter solstice. The light *is* coming into the darkness, even though we sometimes feel it never will. God has put a reminder of this basic hope into the very motion of the planets.

Have regard for your covenant, for the dark places of the land are full of the haunts of violence.
(Psalm 74:20)

December 22*
Fourth Sunday of Advent: Lamaze

Natural childbirth classes used to be the province of hippies and people on the fringes of society in the world of alternative medicine. But like so many other once-questioned health practices, Lamaze has entered the mainstream and is now almost a "must" for expectant parents of a certain socio-economic class. It has become so commonplace, in fact, that it has become a rich source of humor—especially on TV and in the movies. Think *Father of the Bride 2* or *Mad About You*.

There is no magic in Lamaze. Rather than treating birth as a medical illness, it merely points out that birth is, quite the contrary, one of the most common and normal events in a couple's life. Classes involve the father in the birth (unheard of when I came into the world), and also offer the now-famous breathing techniques. The idea is that this special breathing will lessen the pain of birth and also protect the baby from contamination by pain medications that suppress respiration. The downside to this trend is that many women feel they are failures if they ask for help with pain. At its best, Lamaze is a way of preparing the couple for the difficult passage to come.

Going to church is a kind of spiritual Lamaze. Learning about the kind of God we worship during the liturgy of the word, and being fed by God's tremendous power in the liturgy of the eucharist, prepares us for spiritual trials in our future. Unlike a pregnant woman, we don't know when these trials will occur, but we do share with her the absolute certainty that the trial—whatever it may look like—will appear, sooner or later. Depriving ourselves of the spiritual benefits of regular church attendance is very much like a pregnant woman depriving herself of the benefits of Lamaze.

These things I have spoken unto you, that in me ye might have peace. In the world ye shall have tribulation: but be of good cheer; I have overcome the world.
(John 16:33, KJV)

DECEMBER 23
Labor

Sooner or later, it happens. Early or late, it happens. Unless it's cut off by surgical intervention, labor will occur. It is the last stage of pregnancy.

Plain and simple, labor hurts. A proportionally large baby is coming through a respectively small aperture in a woman's body. It's bound to hurt. And it's hard work that goes on for a long time, especially in a first birth. A woman who's been through a twenty-hour labor, with or without the benefit of an epidural, has endured one of the most strenuous experiences a human being can have. And yet mother after mother says the same thing: It's worth it. At the end of this arduous process comes a baby.

Life is a lot like labor. There are many good things that happen in our lives, but very often we have to go through long, arduous, painful trials to get to the point that we can receive them. Why it has to be this way I do not know, but that it is this way I can heartily testify. Once in a while something worthwhile simply drops into our laps, but most of the time it is preceded by great struggle and pain.

Life is painful, and there are no epidurals. Or rather, the epidurals that are available—alcohol, drugs, other addictions—are destructive to us and whatever good thing is trying to be born in our lives.

Our task in life is to follow the example of the laboring woman: sweat, pant, moan, take whatever healthy relief is offered, and just get through it. On the other side of these trials there is something wonderful. And in life as in labor, the end results are worth the pain.

For a long time I have held my peace, I have kept still and restrained myself; now I will cry out like a woman in labor, I will gasp and pant.
(Isaiah 42:14)

DECEMBER 24 AND 25
Christmas Eve and Christmas

Once upon a time, there was a very old soul. He was such an old soul that nobody around could remember a time when he *wasn't* there. I call this person a "soul" because the next character in our story is an angel, and that's how angels refer to human beings—as souls.

Anyway, one day this very old soul was sitting next to the window, very peacefully, watching what was going on outside. And an angel came to him. This angel's name wasn't Gabriel, but Uriel, which means, "Fire of God." Uriel, along with Gabriel, is one of the archangels, who are sort of the head angels, and very important. So we know this very old soul was probably kind of a spiritual big shot to have an archangel come to him.

The very old soul saw the angel standing in front of him and asked her to take a seat. But Uriel just shook her head. "Can't," she said. "I'm afraid it's time to go."

The very old soul, hoping against hope, asked, very politely, "Go where?" Uriel smiled. "You know where. It's time to leave." The very old soul sighed. "You know, if it's all the same to you, I'd like to stay. I like it here." "So does everyone," said Uriel. "Most souls want to stay. But that's life—there's a beginning and there's an end."

"But I'm just a little worried," said the very old soul. "Could you please tell me about it?" Again Uriel shook her head. "I can't." "Why not? You've been there, haven't you?" said the very old soul. Uriel answered, "Of course. All the time. It's not that it's against the rules or anything. It's just that I couldn't describe it to you in any way that would make sense to you."

"All right," said the very old soul. He really was a very cooperative soul. "But you know, I'm a little afraid." "That's natural," said Uriel. "I would be afraid, too, if I were going to a place that's so different."

Then the very old soul got very serious. "Will there be pain?" he asked. Uriel nodded her head. "I'm afraid so. It will hurt. But it won't last too long. I promise." So the very old soul thought for a few moments and nodded his head. Uriel reached over and took him by the hand.

Suddenly, the very old soul was in terrible pain. He couldn't breathe, there were awful sounds going on around him, and he hurt. Boy, did he hurt. There was a horrible feeling of pressure, of a heavy weight pushing in on him. He could just barely feel Uriel with him.

Now, the interesting thing was that he found himself in a long tunnel. And at the very end of the tunnel, there was a light. It was hard to explain, but somehow he knew there was something good waiting there for him at the end of the tunnel. As much as he hated to leave, he also wanted to get to this good thing, whatever it was. As he traveled down the tunnel, he saw a figure in the light, waiting for him. He got very excited and called out to Uriel, as loudly as he could: "Is that him? Is that the Father?"

And he could hear Uriel very faintly. She said, "Yes, that's him. And you'll meet the mother next. And then some shepherds." Her voice trailed off, and the very old soul couldn't hear her any more, and anyway, he lost his very last memory of the place he'd left behind. One more hard sensation of pressure, and there he was, out in the world, a newborn baby boy, cold and screaming, and knowing nothing but the fact that his mother's body was very warm when she held him close and he could hear her heart beating.

Jesus of Nazareth, the son of God, the son of Mary, made a decision and agreed to leave heaven for thirty-some years. This Jesus, the Christ, had been present at the very beginning, with God and the Holy Spirit, before there was a creation. In fact, it was the Christ who created the world he would later go to, millions or even billions of years later. He watched with the others and cried when the world fell, when all that beauty turned bad. He saw the suffering human souls endured. He saw hunger, pain, loneliness, sorrow and poverty, and illness and murder and drugs and children being hurt. And even though he saw all that, and even though he knew how much it hurt to live in a world like ours, he decided to come here and do it himself. He agreed to give up all the perfect joys of heaven to come and live here, to endure a painful birth and die a terrible death.

And he did it so we could have the same experience that very old soul did—except the other way around. While Jesus left heaven to come here, we leave here and get to go to heaven. This tunnel with the light at the end of it used to go just one way—into this life, all the good and all the bad, and at the end of it, death. But Jesus, God himself, opened that tunnel so it goes both ways now.

He became what we are, so that we might become what he is. (St. Athanasius)

DECEMBER 26
St. Stephen

Christianity is a rough faith in many ways. Here we are, just one day past Christmas, a day full of joy, and the calendar suggests that we remember St. Stephen, the first martyr. Can't we have just a few days of completely happy thoughts?

That's the problem with Christianity, though. Every celebration has within it a hint of the greatest sorrow. And every tragedy holds the seeds of joy.

I learned a lovely custom from some people in the church I pastored in Springfield. On Christmas they put a special present for each member of the family under the tree. Most years, the gifts are wrapped in purple paper. When everybody opens their purple gifts, they find something rather astonishing: an empty box.

This is wonderful theology. On the morning of Christ's birth, this family faces a reminder of the other great joy of our faith—the empty tomb, a sign that the baby who was born today will be resurrected.

Of course, the boxes are wrapped in purple—the color of Lent. There's a lot of suffering and agony to get through between Christmas and Easter. But quite realistically, this is the way life is: a few moments of soaring, unspeakable joy, interspersed with the travails of everyday life. Sometimes those travails are not so mundane, like crucifixion or martyrdom.

St. Stephen was able to give his life so freely because he believed so thoroughly in the Good News. That gospel is this: Jesus Christ, the son of God, was born as a human being, lived, died, and was resurrected, and therefore has adopted all of us as brothers and sisters so that after our travails, we, too, can go to paradise.

Then [Stephen] knelt down and cried out in a loud voice, "Lord, do not hold this sin against them." When he had said this, he died. (Acts 7:60)

DECEMBER 27
St. John the Evangelist

While the gospels of Matthew, Mark, and Luke are called the "synoptic gospels" (*syn-optic*, seeing with the same eye) because of their similarities, John's story of the life of Jesus stands apart. There is absolutely no doubt he is describing the same man and events, but he tells his story in a very different way.

John's gospel doesn't begin with the story of Jesus' birth. In fact, it goes back to a time before time: "In the beginning was the Word, and the Word was with God, and the Word was God." John is telling us that Jesus was not created; he is God, uncreated, who existed before there was a creation. In fact, it was *through* the Word—Jesus—that all of creation was made, John tells us.

John records the real events in Jesus' life, as do the other gospel writers. But he also takes us behind the scenes, as it were, to help us understand the meaning of those events, and that meaning is always that this very human man is also God. Paradoxically,

John uses symbols from everyday life—bread, water, light, shepherd, door—to demonstrate the divine nature of his savior.

It shouldn't be a surprise, then, that John's gospel is thought to be the latest, written sometime between the year 90 and 95 A.D. It is clearly the product of a mind that has had a great deal of time to mull over the meanings of all the things that happened in Jesus' life, and the meaning of the God-man himself. It would be hard to understand the life of Christ at this depth without years and years of thought and reflection.

Each of the gospels gives us a slightly different view of the person we know as Jesus of Nazareth. But it is in John, perhaps, that the meaning of that person is clearest.

This is the disciple who is testifying to these things and has written them, and we know that his testimony is true. (John 21:24)

DECEMBER 28
Holy Innocents

It's hard to imagine a more horrible tale. King Herod, the ruler of the Jews at the time Jesus was born, heard from the three wise men the news of Christ's birth. He was frustrated, though, in finding that child because the wise men—warned in a dream, we are told by Matthew—made their way home by a different route and avoided Herod with his demand to know where to find the baby. Fearful that this messiah would be a threat to his throne, Herod ordered the slaughter of all the children in and around Bethlehem who were two years old and younger. All this murder was for naught, because Joseph, having been warned in a dream, had moved his wife and son to Egypt for a while.

It is a terrible, awful fact that innocent children often suffer when evil has the upper hand. It is difficult enough to contemplate the martyrdom of adults, but children . . . their slaughter is almost unbearable to consider.

The killing of the Holy Innocents presaged the great drama of the end of Jesus' life. Here was an adult man who—like no other—was sinless. Nevertheless, he was killed. Yet his death was not meaningless; because of his resurrection, Christ's death changed the ways of the fallen world he so dearly loved, and death lost its ultimate victory over every human being who followed him. That includes children.

It is a tragic, bitter experience for a parent to lose a child; it may be the most difficult thing a human being can go through. The loss felt by today's parents was multiplied at the hands of King Herod. While it can never be a happy event, today's parents who lose their children to death do have the ultimate consolation—the knowledge that the little ones they first brought to life are alive once again, in the company of all the Holy Innocents and the Lord who was once a child like them.

When Herod saw that he had been tricked by the wise men, he was infuriated, and he sent and killed all the children in and around Bethlehem who were two years old or under, according to the time that he had learned from the wise men. (Matthew 2:16)

DECEMBER 29
Taking the Baby Home

My middle sister and her husband used to live a rather bohemian lifestyle. They got home from work, relaxed, and together cooked the gourmet food they both so love. They'd eat around 10 p.m. Not surprisingly, they got up as late as possible during the week and on weekends often slept past noon.

Then came their son, desperately wanted and breathlessly awaited. But no more 10 p.m. meals for his parents. No more sleeping in. My nephew changed their lives in a way that nothing else ever had.

Every new parent knows this reality. A new baby has no consideration for his parents; when he wants to eat, he wants to eat. When he's wet, he wants to be changed. When he's lonely, he wants to be held. It doesn't matter if Mommy and Daddy are eating, watching TV, or sleeping. And most remarkable of all, parents don't seem to resent these radical changes.

Welcoming Christ into our lives creates changes just as dramatic as those accomplished by a new baby. For some, those changes may not seem so obvious or disruptive. But our faith tells us that anyone who is in Christ is a new creation, and all new creations necessarily create drastic change in everyday life. There are people who will testify that choosing to follow Christ saved them from a life of drug abuse, prostitution, or crime. All Christians are saved from the horrors of a sinful life; it just may take a few years for some of us to see the difference that Christ makes. Anyone who thinks they have not been changed by their faith should try living without it for a while. The results are not pretty.

Each year at Christmas time we welcome the child Jesus into our homes and hearts once again. If this new arrival doesn't change our lives dramatically, then perhaps we may not have truly brought the baby into the house.

So if anyone is in Christ, there is a new creation:
everything old has passed away; see, everything has
become new! (2 Corinthians 5:17)

DECEMBER 30
Birth Announcements

Birth announcements come in all shapes and sizes. The ones that tickle me are those that have a calling card with the baby's name attached to an announcement by the parents, usually with a ribbon. The idea that a two-week-old child already has a full complement of social stationery makes me chuckle.

But no matter. Birth announcements are important, whatever form they take. There is something within us that wants and needs to let everyone know that this new human being has arrived in the world.

That's one reason I'm a bit mystified by Christians who are reluctant to speak about their faith to people who are not believers. Now, I'm not saying that all Christians have to go door to door asking people, "Sister, are you saved?" It's just that sometimes the matter of faith comes up naturally—say, a coworker struggling with the death of a parent—and it would be very easy and appropriate to say something like, "I don't think I could ever have gotten through my mother's death without my faith." The nonbeliever is then free to respond to that invitation to discussion or to ignore it. Evangelism has gotten a bad name because there are some Christians, God bless them, who think Christ has to be sold with a gusto normally reserved for used cars.

Telling people about our faith in Christ is like a verbal birth announcement. We have been given new life, and it makes sense that we would want to share this remarkable gift with people we know. In fact, to neglect to do so is to deprive these people of their own new lives.

Maybe it would be easier for us if we had formal announcements. The big card could say, "The Almighty God—Father, Son, and Holy Spirit, one God and Mother of us all—announces the adoption of a sister for Jesus Christ, and invites you to celebrate this blessed event by considering adoption yourself." Then we could just attach a little card with our own names—using pretty pink ribbons, of course.

To you is born this day in the city of David a Savior, who is the Messiah, the Lord. (Luke 2:11)

December 31
New Year's Eve

The new year is always a little bittersweet for me. It's natural for me to remember back to January 1 and all the hopes and dreams I had for the year that has just passed. Some of those hopes have been fulfilled, others dashed. Even more, things have happened—both good and bad—that I could not have imagined 365 days ago.

It's a fine exercise in nostalgia to think back over the year that is ending on this day. I can remember things I'm proud of as well as things I hope to do better in the coming year. But the fact that I am a Christian means that while I acknowledge and give honor to the time that has already passed, my emphasis is always on the future.

The Christian faith is an historical one. There was a specific day in history on which a baby named Jesus was born, and another particular day on which he was crucified. Three days later, on a date that we can mark on a calendar, that Jesus was raised from the dead and the course of human history was changed forever.

Yet as important as this history is, it is secondary to our current and future life with God. Becoming a child of God isn't just something that happened to us at our baptisms . . . it continues to occur every day of our lives. Our past relationship with God has molded us into the people we are, and yet it is only in the future—in paradise—that we will completely and wholly become the people God created us to be.

This sacred truth isn't limited to New Year's Eve; it is valid for every single day of our lives. But perhaps on this day, the one that marks our culture's recognition of the passing of another year, we can look at what has been and say, "Yes, that is all a part of me," while we also look ahead and say, "Imagine what is waiting."

You crown the year with your bounty; your wagon tracks overflow with richness. (Psalm 65:11)